DATE DUE

AP 29 99		
OC 16 01		
RENEW		
N00 1 00		
MR 23 02		
NV 1 02		
FE 13 03		
OC 8 03		
MY 11 06		

DEMCO 38-296

THE FARRAKHAN FACTOR

The FARRAKHAN FACTOR

African-American Writers on Leadership, Nationhood, and Minister Louis Farrakhan

Edited by AMY ALEXANDER

Grove Press   New York

Published simultaneously in Canada

Printed in the United States of America

FIRST EDITION

Library of Congress Cataloging-in-Publication Data

The Farrakhan factor : African-American writers on leadership, nationhood, and minister Louis Farrakhan / edited by Amy Alexander.

p. cm.

Includes bibliographical references.

ISBN 0-8021-1623-X

1. Farrakhan, Louis.   2. Black Muslims—Biography.   3. Afro-Americans—Biography.   4. Black Muslims—Politics and government.

I. Alexander, Amy.

BP223.Z8L57336 1997

297.8'7—dc21

[B]   97-28272

CIP

Design by Laura Hammond Hough

Grove Press

841 Broadway

New York, NY 10003

98 99 00 01 10 9 8 7 6 5 4 3 2 1

To Joseph P. Williams, Jr.,

for his love and innate leadership

Contents

Acknowledgments

This book came together with the help and support of many. Foremost, I thank the contributors. Where others feared to tread, you walked with uncommon grace and honesty. I am especially thankful for the wisdom, professionalism, and warm friendship of Jim Moscr, executive editor at Grove Press. As always, my mother, Hazel N. Fermon, provided unconditional love and guidance, as did my brother, Eric Fermon; my sister, Gladys Fermon; and all the members of my extended family. You bless my life each day. Lori Perkins and Peter Rubie of Lori Perkins Associates, parents of the idea for this collection, found during its complicated development the exquisite balance between attentiveness and hovering. Thank you.

Other friends, mentors, and a few kind individuals who know me only as a voice on the telephone provided brainstorming and names of possible contributors. I am indebted to them: Betty Medsger, Robin D.G. Kelley, Sheryl McCarthy and Len Hollie, Constance Buchanan, Florence Ladd and Bill Harris, Tananarive Due, Gayle Pemberton, Nancy Ancrum, Farai Chideya, Michele Wallace, Gwendolyn Lister, Margo Jefferson, Annmarie Dodd, Roy Larson,

Beryl Vitch, Bill Boyd and Lisa Getter, Stanley Crouch, David Bank, Itabari Njeri, Jenny Lo, Erna Smith, and Henry Louis Gates, Jr. Others provided expert legwork and technical assistance, including laughter and long conversations during my bleakest hours. For them I am deeply grateful: Tamara Kerrill, Mary Schmich, Richard Newman, Tamara Ingram-Augustin, Liz Doup, Joanne Kendall, Anthony Duignan-Cabrera, Lois Henry, Amy Hundley, Naomi Davis-Rawls, Irene Monroe, Patricia Andrews, Jae Roosevelt, Pete and Colleen Higgins, Trish Power, Chip Johnson, and Maria Elena Camposeco. Many thanks to the remarkable Phoebe Flowers, whose keen insight, efficient typing, and wry humor helped me survive the calamitous early stages of this book. Thanks also to Haki Madhubuti, who for years has been laying the groundwork for a book such as this.

INTRODUCTION

Our Brother, the Other: Farrakhan and a Vigil for New Black Leadership

Amy Alexander

AMY ALEXANDER *is a writer in Cambridge, Massachusetts. A former minority affairs reporter at* The Miami Herald, *she is now a contributing writer at* The Boston Globe.

This is how one woman I know, a former member of the Black Panther Party, responded when I asked her to write for this book: "I don't have anything to say about Louis Farrakhan. The man is a demagogue. He is the worst thing that could happen to black people at this time."

We are in a Cambridge restaurant on a warm June night, and I am table hopping. A few months earlier, in a hallway at the Afro-American Studies Department at Harvard, I had introduced myself to this woman. At that time, she displayed easygoing dignity in the face of my fawning. Her remarkable thirty-year journey had taken her from the street-based vanguard of 1960s Black Nationalism to a writing fellowship at the nation's premiere African-American think tank, and I admired her strength. Now, on this summer night, I

1

calculated the risk in approaching her with this question over red wine and appetizers. That is how this woman came to slide, *sotto voce,* into a long list of reasons she would not like to write about Louis Farrakhan and black American leadership.

Leaning in, I heard from her a five-minute soliloquy involving the minister's sharp eye for controversy, his shady business practices, the megalomaniacal nature of his rhetoric. She mentioned the FBI. She raised questions about the minister's "true purpose." It seemed to me that she had plenty to say about Louis Farrakhan.

But, considering what I knew of her personal history, of government surveillance and infiltration, of abandoned Marxist ideals, of street actions and tear gas and jail cells and betrayals; considering what I imagined to be her thwarted hopes for new black leadership, I doubted that I would get her to express her thoughts on Farrakhan in this book. Her rebuff, direct and good natured, was shaped by the formidable combination of history and circumstance.

As it turned out, that woman was the first of several black American writers and scholars who passed on the chance to air, in this collection, their thoughts on Louis Farrakhan and black leadership. I learned, ultimately, that the minister inspires among many black Americans a level of ambivalence and confusion that is not too different from that which exists in much of the white community. The challenge, then, was before me: To gather a collection that accurately reflects the wide, varied range of African-American opinion on Louis Farrakhan and the state of black American leadership today. I suspected that God, Allah, and Lady Luck would have to be on my side if I was to meet that challenge.

In attempting to shape this collection, I was comforted by one belief: We all agree that Louis Farrakhan has arrived in the late 1990s larger than life, a burnished totem on which many Americans, black and white, hang the best and worst of their cultural myths and leadership dreams. For us, loving him or hating him is not really the issue: The minister is forcing black Americans to reexamine our definition of leadership.

It is a daunting task, this examination of leadership, for with its undertaking we must inevitably dissect our own values and mores, turn inward the critical lenses of scholarship, experience, and emotion. It is worth the effort, I believe, and worth the pain that introspection can bring.

More important, black Americans have learned by now, in this media-drenched final hour of the twentieth century, that if we don't stake out solutions to these confounding questions, someone else will. The former Black Panther I spoke with sounded a lot like hundreds and thousands of African-Americans who disdain the minister. To them, the less said about Louis Farrakhan in public, the better. The downside of that strategy, though, is that our silence is often mistaken for acquiescence. Looking at that vast, chattering, infotainment-besotted universe where most Americans reside, away from the isolated terrain of scholarly journals and literary salons, one might conclude that black Americans are not given to entertaining philosophical questions of leadership. Meanwhile, we groan in private when mainstream media covers a "black story," moan at the line-up of African-American academics and usual suspects who serve as our surrogates on the national stage. "They are so out of touch," we tell each other, all the while holding close our own opinions of Louis Farrakhan and the yawning void atop our leadership structure.

In truth, many black Americans—including those who like myself are middle-class, educated, and Christian—do ponder the leadership construct, however fleetingly, however myopically. Our hopes for effective leadership, at least the tentative hopes of my post–Civil Rights Era contemporaries, stop and start around Louis Farrakhan like so much feedback at a hip-hop concert. For us Farrakhan warrants a good amount of skepticism and a greater amount of respect.

Obviously, Farrakhan is a new wrinkle in what we've come to expect in a black leader. He is not Huey P. Newton, or Martin Luther King, Jr., or Julian Bond. He is an alluring conundrum, a kettle of fish not to be handled lightly or heavily by hungry throngs. At the same time, for many of us, the leap from skepticism to cynicism is short, where the minister is concerned. Nevertheless, many of us—especially the fledgling intellectuals and artists, the Next Generation of Black Thinkers whose numbers are burgeoning on college campuses and street corners as I write this—would love to fall behind a brother with so much obvious fire, a powerful black man who says he loves us more than himself.

Yet something doesn't feel right—and not just with Minister Farrakhan. We have a hard time cottoning to the notion of black leadership, as we've come to know it. Indeed, if we can presume to use the term *leader* in this context at this time in history, why should we expect Louis Farrakhan to lead us? If we accept Marcus Garvey's definition of leadership as that which requires everything— blood, pain, and death—would not such a leader require the complicity of the masses, our vigilant and commited involvement, to succeed?

Or, even if we adhere to a definition of leadership from outside the African-American canon, for example Max Weber's observation that a leader earns authority solely by proving his strength in life, we still face the question of why we require a leader, or where, precisely, we are to be led. Moreover, what do we, as individuals, do in our daily lives, the twenty-four-seven of our shared existence, to improve the condition of our American community?

Answering these questions requires, among other things, a willingness to examine one's own definition of what it means to be American. We also must consider whether black Americans, more so than white or Native Americans, for example, really need an individual to mold us into a productive place in this nation. Is this what all Americans require to become healthy citizens?

Most black Americans can admit that history has showed us time and again the futility of expecting a single individual—whether Frederick Douglass or Sojourner Truth or Adam Clayton Powell, Jr.—to draw closed for us the psychic and tangible gap that exists between blacks and whites in America. On the other hand, too many of us do not know our history.

Are we unwise to expect a "leader" to remove from us the mantle of Other that we carry in our own nation? Perhaps what we need is an Ecclesiastical Everyman to mend our soul fissure, a visionary who can repair the widening alienation that rends and splits us, our relations with white America notwithstanding. It is probably a safe bet that whoever leaps next to the front of the line will find behind him not willing or even timid followers. Our next Great Black Hope will turn to find foot soldiers weary of being led, even as they fail to organize themselves.

More important, perhaps black Americans will be wary of anyone who seeks to lead—even a charismatic, quasi-religious figure such as Louis Farrakhan. In the short space of my lifetime, it seems that many black Americans have moved with alarming speed from skepticism to cynicism about our leaders.

While it is true that many Americans of all races and socioeconomic stratifications have become more cynical about politics, religion, government, the media, and other former cultural sacred cows than they were fifty years ago, this development is late coming to much of black America. And it is now acute.

Since the 1940s, a church-going African-American candidate (usually male) was likely to succeed in regional politics thanks to a segregated, southern-born voting population whose civic identity was rooted firmly in the sanctuary. From there, the sacred union of the Black Church and Black Political Power was made, an uncontested formula that brought men like Jesse Jackson and Adam Clayton Powell, Jr., to national political prominence. If those pioneers were not always above moral reproach, you could not successfully argue that they didn't know their Bible.

Now, some of us smile politely and shake the papery hands of the church-proud political relics. They are quaint, and we perceive them as hard working but hopelessly ineffective at dealing with modern issues like drug abuse, gun play, and the deadly ennui that hangs over many of us. Everyone has an opinion about the litany of statistics that have come to define "the black condition" in America:

One in three black men between the ages of twenty and twenty-nine is in the criminal justice system; hundreds of thousands of black men cannot vote because they are locked up; single women head 46 percent of all African-American households; 45 percent of all black women earn about $7.50 per hour; and on and on. The same middle-class angst that afflicts many Americans comes to blacks as an especially bittersweet reward: How much should we celebrate the fruits of our hard work while so many of us founder? All the while, no one appears capable of locating our spiritual center, of touching and revitalizing the precious life that resides there. And too many of us seem to lack the skills, wherewithal, or good sense to find and rejuvenate that core for ourselves.

I know that black Americans do not all vote alike (or shop alike or raise their children alike or learn alike). But our diversity should not preclude our sharing goals and a working list of options for achieving those goals. We are not vigilant about the concerns that fueled our grandparents, including improving the practical and spiritual condition of our children and using efficiently the available tools of our democratic society (voting, education, and ownership) to press us forward. Meanwhile, the Freedom Train and the Great Northern Migration Special no longer serve our contemporary plantations, and too many of us are abandoned outside the gates of Black Suburban Estates. Farrakhan speaks to those black Americans who have missed the Middle-Class Express.

And while some argue that we must forge alliances with the looming New Majority in urban America—Latinos and Asians—the minister reaches out to those who hear of fledgling "black-brown" alliances and despair of being left behind yet again.

Farrakhan seems to know that for every black American who has bootstrapped her way out of the ghetto—thanks in part to Martin Luther King, Jr., and Malcolm X—there exist a hundred more who will wind up done in by drugs and crime on some unforgiving urban pavement. It hardly seems to matter that Farrakhan cannot possibly reach down and restore so much unfulfilled promise: He says he wants to save us, and those words are a tonic. For many of us born after the assassinations of the Civil Rights Era, the lurid death of Huey P. Newton on a gritty west Oakland street in 1989 was heavy with meaning. We know that now, instead of sweaty, rifle-toting rednecks to take out our champions, we have our very own killers to do the job. Can Farrakhan really neutralize those killers? Take the guns from our hands and replace them with history texts and class schedules? Can he possibly restore our belief in ourselves?

Strange, how we live each day with the tragic residue of history and still manage to overlook the most useful lessons of our past. In the 1960s, our moral ground was clearly defined. At the risk of romanticizing matters, I do believe that we knew inherently then that we were worthy Americans. And, while not wholly united even during the height of the Civil Rights Movement, we at least seemed to agree that we were human beings, worthy kindred who helped pull this nation into its impressive state brick by brick, state by state.

If our brothers in Greensboro could get beaten down at lunch counters over their right to sit and eat there, then surely we could suffer being tear-gassed at San Francisco State University in the fight for ethnic studies programs. Now, at the twilight of this millennium, I wonder if African America has somehow allowed its ambitions to stray from the larger picture, the ever-lengthening trajectory of our American story.

We do need role models, whether they take the shape of politicians, school teachers, artists, or religious figures. We have the means to celebrate uncounted "regular folk" who each day live clean, productive, fulfilled lives. We know that Abraham Lincoln had his models, that Toni Morrison might not exist without Phillis Wheatley. But in the swirl of our daily lives, where do we look for our guiding lights?

Media deserves some of the blame for our disconnection, for as an increasingly omnipresent part of our American experience, it is ravenous for stories of the Successful Black Spokesman and the Dangerous Other. We know how easy it is for extremely complicated experiences to get ground down and encapsulated in nifty little log-lines like Negligent Nannies, or Psycho Roommates, or Famous Black Football Players Who Beat Their Wives. Black Americans should know themselves better than the flimsy images we see on the screen or printed page, yet our focus is off.

Every day, we make the mistake of reaching around our humble role models in search of the next Black Leader.

We lack common ground upon which to sift through our differences (which are mostly superficial anyway, as any black American who abandoned the Republican Party in the early 1960s and reconverted in the 1990s can tell you).

Not very long ago, we seemed willing to acknowledge the supremacy of our shared humanity, a deceptively simple admission that provided enough momentum to keep us moving forward reasonably en masse. Now, we don't need a leader to tell us we shall overcome. We need a referee to keep us moving upfield.

These days, among some of my peers, Jesse Jackson's watchwords "Keep hope alive" inspires as much humorous scorn as "We shall overcome" inspired pride and action forty years ago. This is not a favorable development. It is beyond cynicism, heading fast for pathological self-defeat. Just short of total powerlessness, far afield of having truly Made It, we no longer rally as readily as we once did. Instead of looking back in order to learn from our mistakes, and move forward improved by that knowledge, we seem to see only how we've been let down—by the System, by our Elders, by bullet-ridden rap heroes.

At the same time, sentimentality is viewed through a skewed prism, dismissed as naivete and Old School foolishness. While we fiddled with the language of nationhood, grew preoccupied with identity politics and generation wars, Martin Luther King, Jr., and

Malcolm X became icons of our failed dreams instead of martyrs to a cause in which we still believe.

Let's pretend that the centuries-old model holds true: Black Americans want and need an individual leader to guide us into a successful place in America, a triple threat who can hit, field, and pitch. First, our bench is shallow. And so far in this post–Civil Rights season, only one player aside from Jesse Jackson has shown the kind of flash we typically associate with promise, for better or worse. But how does this player, Louis Farrakhan, size up alongside those black men and women who have worn the mantle of black leadership for the past four hundred years in America? Where does he factor into the impressive cast of black Americans in our long, rich, history of leadership? Does it make sense, in this quest to define new leadership, for us to look to those figures for inspiration, to pinch off a little bit of W.E. B. DuBois's sparkling intellect here, a dash of Malcolm X's boldness there?

I wonder. Will my children sit in tiny wooden chairs in classrooms adorned with four-color reproductions of Frederick Douglass, Martin Luther King, Jr.—and Louis Farrakhan? And if they gaze upon images of the light-skinned brother with the bow tie and tightly curled hair, what narrative will accompany those images?

Surely the minister deserves our attention, if for no other reason than he articulates loudly and regularly much of the frustration felt by black Americans in the 1990s. Farrakhan speaks the unspeakable and does it with obvious relish. But how much should we invest in him?

After rap star Biggie Smalls was killed in the spring of 1997, dozens of mourners turned up in a spontaneous vigil in front of the performer's Bedford-Stuyvesant home. The teenagers and young-adult blacks who gathered to mourn Biggie, the local fans who lighted candles and incense in his memory, spoke of promise unfulfilled and of hopes dashed. (Similarly, after Huey Newton was gunned down in west Oakland, neighborhood folk turned out to reflect on the dead former revolutionary. Back in 1989, as a journalist dispatched to the scene, I listened to the handful of men and women who had set up a vigil of flowers and candles near Huey's killing ground. Those mourners were older than the youth who turned out for Biggie's vigil in 1997, but the sentiment was the same. Another case of promise snuffed out prematurely.) What would we say of Farrakhan, and of ourselves, were we to line up at his sidewalk vigil? It helps to consider the times in which we live.

Throughout 1990s America, politicians and racial provocateurs have haggled over whether affirmative action policies are unfair to white Americans (most black Americans, especially those of us struggling to find jobs in the new Global High-Technology Economy, rightfully hoot at this red herring). The Supreme Court, the same institution that once interpreted the letter of the law in support of white supremacy but eventually reassessed its charge in favor of human rights, turned a hostile eye toward blacks and members of America's growing economic underclass. The 1991 appointment of Clarence Thomas to the Court, contentious and emotionally wrenching for many black Americans, set the tone for a decade-long debate.

The generational rifts exposed by Thomas's appointment, the gender and class divides highlighted by his ascension, widened before us unabated. Now, white politicians play the black community like a late season Exacta, quickly and without sophistication, while black politicians seem hamstrung by a lethal combination of middle-class frigidity and arrested intellectual development.

Who are our alternatives? Some of our spanking-new political turks say weightily that "the black community is not a monolith," as if voting Republican in the 1990s makes one a priceless chip off the old African-American block. (Consider the straight-backed Oklahoma Republican Congressman Julius Caesar Watts and the well-fed offspring of Jesse Jackson and Martin Luther King, Jr. These young adults show little indication that they are willing to step far outside their own Black Suburban Estates to undertake the hard work of improving the conditions of masses of African-Americans.

We see these privileged babyfaces as comfy and familiar, the pedigreed examples of the church-based black leadership model. They are also not likely to spark us to action.)

Our Democratic, southern-born president says he wants to begin a "dialogue" on race relations in America and seems oblivious to the havoc that the deep cuts in public assistance he approved will wreak for millions of blacks and other low-income Americans. The NAACP gives a top award to boxing promoter Don King, while the nation's premiere black golfing champion tells talk show titan Oprah Winfrey he considers himself not black at all but "Cablinasian."

From the mists of this mire, Farrakhan appears like a sudden light, spectral and entreating. For all his shape-shifting, he seems somehow more concrete, more real, than most other high-profile black Americans.

To many of us, the minister's words are soothing in their directness: You must not depend on the White Man to do right by you, Farrakhan says. You must learn your history, practice self-discipline, stop eating pork, and refrain from dipping into the cesspool of American popular culture. Yet is Farrakhan's outspokenness all that we require to reconnect us to this nation?

For all his verbal excoriations of America's white power structure, odds are not good that Farrakhan will finesse his way through the halls of that power and gain for us, whether by legislation or intimidation or some other means, our slice of the American Dream.

The minister's separatist rhetoric is less evident these days, and with good reason. The idea of giving up our ground in the United States—however shaky or small—is impractical and unappealing to most African-Americans.

We've seen the era of Black Militancy; been there and done the era of Moral Imperative. Why should Farrakhan be more successful than Martin or Malcolm before him? The media-driven fear of Farrakhan aside, we have a sneaking suspicion that the Minister will amount to little more than a guilty-pleasure diversion in the long run.

Consider, for example, the life of one black American woman. Am I made cynical by my times, too jaded to believe in the time-honored model of black leadership? Yes and no.

In 1971, my family moved from public housing projects to a neat neighborhood of single-family houses on San Francisco's racially mixed west side. For us, social activism took the shape of egalitarian cool, the practice of being integrationist without fear of, or malice toward, white people. As second-generation westerners, my family was geographically if not spiritually removed from the Deep South and the horror wrought by the Civil Rights Movement there. In the decades after my birth in San Francisco in 1963, we were black and proud and expected by the adults in our lives to view Martin Luther King, Jr., as the epitome of morally sound black leadership. The names of Malcolm X and the members of the Black Panthers were rarely mentioned in my home.

In my youth, we found positive examples all around us: schoolteachers (usually women, oftimes black women), church folk (white and black, in the Methodist church of our neighborhood); and the coworkers with whom my parents sometimes socialized (blacks and whites, men and women).

By the early 1970s, I had not seen up close a black Muslim or a Nation of Islam temple. Muhammad Ali was a member of the Nation of Islam, but we thought of him foremost as a supreme athlete and hilariously egotistic entertainer. When my mother told us Ali's birth name was Cassius Clay, we laughed with delight. And the name Kareem Abdul-Jabbar was somehow more palatable to us than the name Lew Alcindor.

The political and religious reasons those two sports figures arrived at their respective name changes were incidental. Yet, when my family moved to the Ingleside from the projects, I was intrigued by the presence of a Nation of Islam temple in my new neighborhood. The classmates I took up with seemed blasé about the Muslims. Alternative lifestyles and nonconventional religious orders did not automatically inspire suspicion among us. (Also, Muhammad Ali belonged to the Nation of Islam, so how scary could it be?)

From local media and the homegrown grapevine, I knew about the Black Panthers, the Symbianese Liberation Army, and the People's Temple. Even amid that collection of fringe groups, the Nation of Islam seemed to me mysterious and isolated, an inscrutable group of bow-tie–wearing men and shrouded women who kept to themselves and didn't seem interested much in "regular" black folk. The modest Nation of Islam temple, blocks away from the new elementary school I attended, became a source of mild curiosity for me. Unlike other fringe groups, the Nation of Islam had set up shop on my modest slice of San Francisco. Who were these people? And why did they seem so rigid? A watery mural depicting Elijah Muhammad covered the building. Located on a busy commercial strip in a predominantly black section of my neighborhood, the building also showed a mural of crescent moons and yellow stars.

A restaurant-bakery occupied the temple's storefront and boasted crude hand-painted signs that advertised bean pies and fresh fish. Sometimes, through an open side door, I could make out a large meeting hall with a stage and rows of carefully stacked folding chairs.

Some of my new classmates whispered about the goings-on in the temple. "They don't let the women have jobs," my friend Elizabeth White told me. She had lived longer than I in that neighborhood and had watched as the temple took shape. "And check this out," Elizabeth said. "All the girls gotta wear scarves over their heads, long gowns, and walk ten paces behind the men."

We watched them silently, we Christians, not knowing quite what to make of their orderly, insulated presence. We wondered about their experience. Was it true they hated all white people? If they adhered to Islam, did that mean they spoke Arabic? Did their leader, the serene-looking elder called Elijah Muhammad, really kill Malcolm X?

In my youth, the Nation of Islam existed at the edges of my consciousness, warranting little more than respectful curiosity.

In a blink of twenty-five years, all that has changed. Today, we know little more about the inner workings of the Nation of Islam than I did as a schoolgirl. But over the years, our collective curiosity has increased out of all proportion to any concrete understanding of Farrakhan and his organization. Fear seems to drive some of our interest, and the old repulsion-attraction equation, which one could psychoanalyze ceaselessly without resolution. (Many black Americans fear Farrakhan's outspokenness at times, which is not the same as being afraid of him.)

Once again it comes down to an individual's reference points. And in the context of my lifetime—in which a madman in a Guyanese jungle whipped up a lethal Kool-Aid cocktail for nine hundred people, and a wild-eyed stargazer convinced thirty-nine people to kill themselves in the hopes of joining a spaceship hidden behind a streaking comet—I find the idea of Farrakhan as Dangerous Black Leader a ridiculous proposition. Black Americans listen to the minister's critics carrying on about his supposed resemblance to Hitler and scoff. We have seen the face of Death, and it does not look anything like Louis Farrakhan.

At the same time, Farrakhan's ability to muster hundreds of thousands of black men in Washington, D.C., in 1995 says more about our neediness than it does about his leadership ability. The most steadfastly bourgeois among us knows that we needn't fear or follow Minister Farrakhan. And the most disconnected among us don't believe the minister can connect us, anyway. Either way, there is no sense of urgency. We decry a dearth of "true leaders" and seem stymied when it comes to growing one ourselves. Paradoxically, the fact that the minister inspires such a high degree of fear and loathing among white Americans is tantalizing.

What is it about Minister Farrakhan, we wonder, that makes the Man so afraid? Didn't white Americans learn from Marcus Garvey and Malcolm X that scary-sounding speeches do not automatically lead thousands of black folk to rampaging and pillaging? Indeed, the largest civil disturbances of my lifetime have arrived after black folk decided to respond, however destructively, to the actions of white people. Further, why should we take responsibility for white America's fears?

No, we can listen to Farrakhan's rhetoric. We watch the Million Man March and wish the best for those brothers who line up, hand in hand, and lower their heads in prayer. But there is much to deter us from truly falling behind Minister Farrakhan, our growing cynicism and the larger question of whether we should fall behind *anyone*, aside. Between the numerology and the crescent moons, the failed business enterprises, the funky doctrines of Ezekiel's Wheel, and Yakub the Evil Scientist, Farrakhan is no more skilled at drawing us into a truly productive group-think than is the classroom cutup.

We adore him for his ability to relieve tension in the room, for his chivalrous willingness to skewer the stiff-necked teacher. We laugh at his punchlines and amen when his spitball finds its target. We also sympathize with him because we know he'll be repeating that subject again, long after we've moved on.

Black Americans don't often make headlines for taking Farrakhan with a grain of salt (unless they are being denounced by white pundits for not publicly denouncing the minister). But our silence does not signify our whole-hog acquiescence to the minister's doctrines. He is a necessary thing, the manifestation of our barely suppressed anger. As I see him, Minister Farrakhan is the easily identifiable Other, a familiar and handy repository for all that we cannot vocalize.

I accept Farrakhan as he is and, unlike some of his white detractors, do not view his Otherness as a source of fear. His most potent weapon to date has been his rhetoric, and until the act of spewing unpleasant verbiage becomes illegal in America, the minister can spew until the cows come home.

He pulls the center to the left and the right, forcing black Americans to dive and swerve and get moving toward defining our leadership ground. As our brother—and Farrakhan is our brother in the sense of our shared genealogical roots—he also represents that secret place within our psyche to which we can retreat when the hour is late and we are bone tired and up to here with struggling on.

So, we should listen to each other, and speak forthrightly and with gathering momentum about our shared future and Farrakhan's place within our great pantheon of black leaders. The voices in this collection represent a starting point in our quest to redefine black leadership. It is my hope that this book provides a framework by which we can begin to examine, in a measured dialogue free of rancor and hysteria, our expectations and our needs. Our hopes for our American future. Farrakhan, the unmistakable cynosure of our times, is an excellent touchstone for that conversation.

In the end, I struck out with the revolutionary emeritus but crossed homeplate just the same. Inevitably, the controversy that surrounds Louis Farrakhan played a role in shaping this collection.

Some prospective contributors, without saying so explicitly, saw no percentage to be gained with their black constituents by publicly sharing their disdain for the minister. But my peculiar trinity—God, Allah, and Lady Luck—came through. And after uncounted telephone conversations and meetings in cyberspace, our panel is assembled. What follows are the words of writers who, I am hopeful, best reflect the wide range of black American opinion on Louis Farrakhan and the leadership conundrum.

In attempting to cover as much real-world ground as possible, this collection approaches the question of Farrakhan's place among black leaders from several perspectives, including the economic viability of the minister's Nation of Islam enterprises; the history of the Nation and other Black Nationalist groups; personal narratives; and the legal, social, and religious underpinnings of Farrakhan's rise to prominence.

In a modern classic of the journalistic profile, we will also hear from the minister himself. Published originally by *The New Yorker* magazine, this interview perfectly sets the stage for our discussion.

Any fair-minded assessment of Louis Farrakhan's place in the black leadership structure must be informed by the minister's life, and by his own words. From there, we can begin to determine whether his actions match his words, and whether his actions suit our needs.

The contributors include academics, community activists, poets, journalists, and historians from all across America. Their personal and professional experiences make for a diverse gathering.

It is my hope that within this collection black Americans can find the tools to begin rebuilding our definition of leadership, establish a model that is born independently of white America's views. And in the process, if we are honest and careful, perhaps we can summon a newly vigilant spirit, a guiding light imbued with the best strengths of those who have come before us.

The Charmer

Henry Louis Gates, Jr.

HENRY LOUIS GATES, JR., *is the W.E.B. DuBois Professor of Humanities and chairman of the Afro-American Studies Department at Harvard University. He is author of several books, including* Colored People. *A staff writer at* The New Yorker, *he is also coeditor of the* Norton Anthology of African-American Literature.

The drive to Louis Farrakhan's house, on South Woodlawn Avenue, took me through the heart of black Chicago—past campaign billboards for a hot city-council race, past signs for Harold the Fried Chicken King and Tony's Vienna Beef Hotdogs. Much of the area is flecked with housing projects and abandoned lots, but when you turn the corner at Woodlawn and Forty-ninth Street, things abruptly look different. You can see why the late Elijah Muhammad, who led the Nation of Islam—the Black Muslims—for almost four decades, built his house in this little pocket of opulence. It's a street of large brick houses, enshrining the vision of black-bourgeois respectability, and even grandeur, that has always been at the nostalgic heart of the Nation of Islam's creed. The neighborhood, known as South Kenwood, is integrated and professional. In 1985, Farrakhan bought Elijah Muhammad's house—a yellow brick neo-Mediterranean structure—and he has lived there ever since; the creed and the neighborhood remain intact.

It was a warm spring morning the week after Easter, and everything was peaceful, quiet, orderly, which somehow made matters all the more unsettling. I wasn't expecting the Death Star, exactly, but I wouldn't have been surprised to see a formidable security detail: the Fruit of Islam patrolling the roof and gates with automatic weapons; perhaps a few attack dogs roaming the grounds. In fact, the only security measure in evidence was a rather elegant wrought-iron fence. After I spent a minute or so fumbling around, trying to find a hinge, a baby-faced young man with close-cropped hair and gleaming black combat boots came over and flicked the gate open. Together, we walked up a short, curved driveway, past two marble lions flanking the front door, and into the house that Elijah Muhammad built.

People in the Nation of Islam refer to the house as the Palace, and it does have an undeniable, vaguely Orientalist splendor. There is a large center hall, two stories high, filled with well-tended tropical plants, some reaching up between ten and twenty feet. Sunlight floods in from a huge dome of leaded glass; at its center, Arabic characters spell out "Allahu Akbar," or "God Is Great." To the right is a large and vibrant triptych: The Nation's founder, Wallace D. Fard; his prophet, Elijah Muhammad (with a set of gold keys in his hands); and Elijah's successor as the head of the Nation, a very youthful-looking Louis Farrakhan. The walls are spanking white, the floors are tiled in white and gray marble. A C-shaped sofa is upholstered in white fabric and covered with clear vinyl—the same stuff my mother put on to protect *her* good furniture, back in Piedmont, West Virginia.

Farrakhan's wife, Khadijah, came down to check on me, and to make sure everything was tidy now that company had arrived.

Khadijah Farrakhan has a soft brown face and a warm smile. I had a bad cold that day, and she offered me some advice on how to unblock my ears, which still hadn't recovered from the flight to Chicago. "Open your mouth wide, and shift your jaw from side to side," she said, helpfully demonstrating the motion. We stood facing each other, our mouths contorted like those of a pair of groupers.

That is about when America's great black Satan himself came gliding into the room. Farrakhan was resplendent in a three-button suit of chocolate-brown silk, a brown-and-beige bow tie, and a matching pocket square. Only then did I notice that my own trousers did not match my suit jacket. Moments later, I referred to his wife as "Mrs. Muhammad," and there was a glint of amusement in his eyes. The truth is, I was having a bad case of nerves that morning. For good reason. After I criticized Farrakhan in print three years before, a few of his more impetuous followers had shared with me their fervent hope for my death. Now that I was face to face with Farrakhan, I did feel, in fact, pretty deathly. "I'm a wounded warrior," I admitted.

Farrakhan, relaxed and gracious, made sure I was supplied with hot tea and honey. "Get the battlefield ready," he said, laughing. For the rest of a long day, we sat together at his big dining-room table, and it became clear that Farrakhan is a man of enormous intelligence, curiosity, and charm. He can also be deeply strange. It all depends on the moment and the subject. When he talks about the need for personal responsibility or of his fondness for Johnny Mathis and Frank Sinatra, he sounds as jovial and bourgeois as Bill Cosby; when he is warning of the wicked machinations of Jewish financiers, he seems as odd and obsessed as Pat Robertson.

Not long after we began talking, Farrakhan told me about an epiphany he had recently about the waning of white cultural supremacy. Farrakhan takes moments of revelation very seriously; one of his most profound occurred, he has said, while he was aboard a giant spacecraft. This particular revelation, less marvelously, took place at a Lionel Ritchie concert. There Farrakhan saw a beautiful young blond woman and her little daughter, who both clearly idolized this black performer. And when Ritchie told the mostly white crowd to raise their hands in the air, almost everyone joined in. Farrakhan saw this as something not only amazing but telling.

"I see something happening in America," he said. "You go into white folks' homes, you see Michael Jackson on the wall, you see Michael Jordan on the wall, you see Hank Aaron on the wall. Their children are being influenced by black faces. And I say to myself, 'Where is this leading?' And what I see is that white supremacy is being challenged in so many subtle and overt ways, and gradually children are losing that thing about being superior."

The myths of black superiority are also going by the wayside. Someone might believe that a white cannot play the horn, he said, "then Kenny G blows that all away." (Joe Lovano, maybe, but Kenny G?) It used to be that white people listened to the blues but could never sing it. Now, though, "white people are experiencing that out of which the blues came," he said. "White people are suffering. Now you drive your streets and you see a white person with stringy hair sitting by the side of the road plucking his guitar, like we used to do in the South. Now *they're* into that." What people must do is "outgrow the narrowness of their own nationalistic feelings," Farrakhan declared. "When we outgrow the color thing, outgrow the race and the ethnic thing, outgrow the religious thing to see the oneness of God and the oneness of humanity, then we can begin to approach our divinity."

I scratched my head: we'd gone from Kenny G to God in a matter of seconds; "the blue-eyed devils"—Elijah Muhammad's favorite designation for white folk—are learning the blues, and we're mightily impressed.

It turns out that there is in Farrakhan's discourse a strain that sounds awfully like liberal universalism; there is also, of course, its brutal opposite. The two tendencies, in all their forms, are constantly in tension. Pundits like to imagine that Farrakhan is a kind of radio program: the incendiary Louis Farrakhan Show. In fact, Farrakhan is more like a radio station: what you hear depends on when you tune in. His talk ranges from far-fetched conspiracy theories to Dan Quayle–like calls for family values. Farrakhan really does believe that a cabal of Jews secretly controls the world; he also suspects, I learned later in our conversation, that one of his own grandparents was a Portuguese Jew. Apologists and detractors alike feel free to decide which represents the "real" Farrakhan. The result may score debating points, but it has little to do with the man who lives at South Woodlawn and Forty-ninth Street.

Much is made of Farrakhan's capacity to strike fear into the hearts of white liberals. And it does seem that for many of them Farrakhan represents their worst nightmare: the Nat Turner figure, crying out for racial vengeance. As Adolph Reed, Jr., writes of Farrakhan, "he has become uniquely notorious because his inflammatory nationalist persona has helped to center public discussion of Afro-American politics on the only issue (except affirmative action, of course) about which most whites ever show much concern: What do blacks think of whites?"

A subject that receives far less attention is the fear that Farrakhan inspires in blacks. The truth is that blacks—across the economic and ideological spectrum—often feel astonishingly vulnerable to charges of inauthenticity, of disloyalty to the race. I know that I do, despite my vigorous efforts to deconstruct that vocabulary of reproach. Farrakhan's sway over blacks—the answering chord his rhetoric finds—attests to the enduring strength of our own feelings of guilt, our own anxieties of having been false to our people, of having sinned against our innermost identity. He denounces the fallen in our midst, invokes the wrath of heaven against us: and his outlandish vitriol occasions both terror and a curious exhilaration.

Farrakhan is a distinctive figure with a distinctive message, but it is a message that has a context and a history. In the summer of 1930, a door-to-door salesman appeared in the Detroit ghetto selling raincoats and silks. In those days, he was known as Wallace D. Fard; later, in the literature of the Nation of Islam, his name would be given an Arabic form—Farrad Muhammad. Some say that Fard was a white man, and others believe he was an Arab; Farrakhan has said that Fard's mother was "from the Caucasus."

Fard told his customers in the early thirties that he carried silks of the same kind that Africans were still using. He seemed to know a great deal about Africa, and soon he was holding meetings about African history at the homes of various customers. For black people at that time, this was news they could use. He had, for instance, all sorts of dietary tips: he pointed out foods that were bad for black people, explaining that the people of their native land never touched them and were always in good health. Before long, Fard moved toward religious expostulations. If the diet that your African ancestors followed was best for you, so was their religion. As time went by, the numbers of people who wanted to attend Fard's meetings grew to the point that his followers rented a hall and called it the Temple of Islam. And so, while inner-city Detroit struggled through the Great Depression, a new religion was born.

Fard taught that although the world was still dominated by "the blue-eyed devils," they were only temporary interlopers. Fard himself had been sent to awaken the consciousness of the Black Nation, the earth's "Original Man." Those who sought to join Fard could send him their current surnames—their "slave names," that is—and receive their true Islamic surnames by return mail. In time, Fard began to refer to himself as the Supreme Ruler of the Universe. And then, in June of 1934, he mysteriously vanished, never to be seen again.

After the vanishing, Fard's fiery chief minister, Elijah Muhammad (né Poole), declared Fard to have been an incarnation of Allah, thus elevating himself to the status of Prophet, or Messenger—Muhammad's title in the Koran. Fard's birthday, February 26th, became a holiday, Savior's Day, and the organizational—and doctrinal—basis for the Nation of Islam was established.

"I must create a system, or be enslav'd by another man's," William Blake wrote in "Jerusalem." In that spirit, Elijah Muhammad's creed offered a unique creation myth, Leviticus-like strictures on diet and behavior, and a strong component of prophecy. In the world according to Elijah Muhammad, blacks were descended from the tribe of Shabazz, which "came with the earth" when an explosion separated the earth and the moon sixty-six trillion years ago. White people, by contrast, came into existence less than seven thousand years ago, the result of the genetic experiments of a wicked scientist named Yakub. Whites were drained not only of color but also of humanity: "The human beast—the serpent, the dragon, the devil, and Satan—all mean one and the same; the people or race known as the white or Caucasian race, sometimes called the European race." Black Muslim theology features no afterlife; what it offers is the promise that the reign of the blue-eyed devils is nearing its end. One could be sure of this because of a particularly splendid element of Elijah's cosmogony: the whole of history was written ahead of time, by twenty-four black scientists, under the supervision of a twenty-fifth.

Not all doctrine pertained to such lofty matters. Elijah Muhammad also published several books on "how to eat to live." Tobacco and alcohol were forbidden, and so were corn bread and pork. Small navy beans were permissible; lima and pinto beans were not. The Messenger instituted for members a regimen of two or more temple meetings a week. Men would be expected to do some proselytizing—or "fishing for the dead," as it was known. A woman's behavior was strictly circumscribed: she was not to let herself be alone in a room with any man who wasn't her husband; her dress had to be modest.

The idiosyncrasies of the Nation of Islam should not blind one to Elijah Muhammad's organizational genius. Fard was not the only black Messiah to have achieved prominence in the thirties, or the most influential, but his was the only legacy that has thrived. Similarly, the esoteric details of Black Muslim doctrine should not obscure the real sense of absence that Elijah Muhammad addressed. Louis Farrakhan told me that the Nation of Islam might be understood as a kind of Reformation movement within the black church—a church that had grown all too accommodating to American racism. It's true that, despite the prominence of such groups as the Southern Christian Leadership Conference during the civil-rights movement, most black churches were extremely conservative when it came to race matters. Dexter Avenue Baptist Church achieved legendary status because of the leadership of Martin Luther King, Jr., and yet the same church had fired King's predecessor, Vernon Johns, for protesting racism with too much zeal. Muhammad's fierce militancy and his inversion of reigning notions of racial inferiority should be seen in relation to the failures of the black churches— especially when it came to providing a moral language in which to address the political sins of state-sponsored racial inequality.

Louis Farrakhan, for his part, remains firmly tethered to the tradition of Christian homiletics. I asked him something that my father wanted to know: How did a good Episcopalian boy like Farrakhan, born Louis Eugene Walcott, end up leaving the true church?

Farrakhan laughed, and said I should tell my father that he never really left. "I thought I did," he said, "but my love is there, my roots are the church." And that's true: references to the Koran in his speeches are perfunctory, with passages from the Old and New Testaments taking pride of place.

"We were from St. Cyprian's"—an Episcopal church in the Roxbury section of Boston, where he grew up—"and I was in the choir," he went on to tell me. He still refers to Nathan Wright, the minister when he was growing up, as "Father Wright." Roxbury retains its hold on him in other ways, too. He spent his formative years in a bustling working-class neighborhood, which was populated by immigrants from the West Indies and boasted flourishing black-owned businesses and a thriving musical scene. It has been suggested that this experience of a tight-knit, prosperous, all-black community may undergird Farrakhan's conservative social views.

Born in 1933, Gene, as he was known, was the younger of two sons of Mae Clark, who was from Barbados. Gene was named after his father, a very light-skinned man from Jamaica; he was a philanderer, whom the family seldom saw—an exceptional circumstance in what was largely a community of intact families. Nathan Wright tells me the mother was "a little old-fashioned and a disciplinarian," even "a bit too strict." Mae Clark stressed education and paid for private music lessons for both her sons. Gene played the violin.

"When I was a young boy, hardly anybody in my all-black school could not read," Farrakhan recalled. "By the time I left the eighth grade, I knew every country on this earth, every capital. I knew their lakes and rivers, I knew what those countries produced for wealth." An honor student in high school, Gene studied, among other subjects, Latin and German, calculus and medieval history. He was also a star on the track team.

A couple of decades later, an accomplished scholar, musician, and athlete like Gene Walcott would have been given the financial aid to go to one elite university or another. In fact, in his high-school yearbook Walcott wrote that he wanted to attend the Juilliard School of Music. Instead, in 1950 he went off to a teachers college for blacks in Winston-Salem, North Carolina, on an athletic scholarship. It was there, in the South, that he first experienced the full impact of racism. Once, stopping over in Washington on the way down, Farrakhan decided to take in a movie, only to be told that tickets were not sold to Negroes. "A very close friend of mine had just been killed in Korea, and I walked down the street with a twenty-dollar bill in one hand, my wallet in the other, and at that point I was very, very angry with America," he said. "I started writing a calypso song called 'Why America Is No Democracy.'"

Within a few years, Gene Walcott had dropped out of college and taken up a career as a calypso singer, styling himself the Charmer. Among those charmed, he would recount years later, were many women: "I wouldn't go to bed with them. They wanted to give me money. . . . I told them, 'You're out of your damn mind.' They said, 'I think you're a faggot.' And I said, 'I *know* what I am. *You'll* never find out.'"

At about the same time as the Charmer was making a name for himself in Boston, Malcolm X was making the rounds as a Black Muslim preacher. "A friend of mine tried to get me to go to the temple," Farrakhan told me. "He said, 'You know, Gene, the white man is the devil.' And I looked at him and said, "If I go home to-night and my wife is in bed with a black man, *she* has committed adultery. And if I pick up a gun and kill them, *I* have committed murder. Where's the devil in that?' He couldn't give me an answer. So I went on about my business—I wasn't about to join the Muslims." Still, Farrakhan described himself as having grown disillusioned with the Episcopal Church: "I couldn't understand why Jesus would preach so much love and why there was so much hate demonstrated by white Christians against black Christians."

In 1955, Walcott was playing the Blue Angel night club in Chicago, and he ran into some old friends who had got involved with the Nation of Islam. Walcott agreed to go to hear Elijah Muhammad preach at the mosque, and when he did, he liked what he heard. That night, he went back to his hotel and started copying out the standard form letter to register as a Muslim:

> Dear Saviour Allah, Our Deliverer:
> I have attended the Teachings of Islam, two or three times, as taught by one of your ministers, I believe in it. I bear witness that there is no God but Thee. And, that Muhammad is Thy Servant and Apostle. I desire to reclaim my Own. Please give me my Original name. My slave name is as follows. . . .

"I wouldn't call it a conversion experience, because I wasn't thoroughly convinced," Farrakhan said. In any case, he never received a reply. Then, just a few months later, when he heard

Malcolm X preach, back on the East Coast, sympathy turned into something like conviction. "I'd never heard any man talk like that," Farrakhan went on, brightening now. "*Then* I was convinced that this was where I wanted to be."

While Farrakhan was telling his story, one of his daughters—a cheerful young woman in a sari-like dress—came by with a real-estate brochure. She wanted to show her father a picture of a three-story brownstone that she and her husband were hoping to buy; Farrakhan expressed his approval. By that point, I'd already met his son Nasir, a handsome, self-possessed young man who was interested in filmmaking, and another daughter who, Farrakhan boasted, was attending law school. Farrakhan plainly was a man who was enormously proud of his children and seemed to enjoy a relaxed and affectionate relationship with them. A bit later, we were visited by a pregnant granddaughter, in her early twenties, who tapped her belly and beamed. "I'm going to be a great-grandfather again," Farrakhan said, in the tone of a happy patriarch.

Farrakhan may have grown up without a father himself, but he speaks often of his mother and her brothers. Indeed, his early interest in the Black Muslims was only a new twist on an established family tradition. Most of Farrakhan's relatives were already followers of the most widely influential black nationalist of the century—Marcus Garvey, whose Universal Negro Improvement Association achieved fame and notoriety in the early twenties. Even so, the reaction of Gene's mother to his decision to join the Muslims was less than effusive. "She was a very reserved, strong woman," Farrakhan said, "and she said, 'It's very interesting.' She didn't say nay or yea."

Before long, her son emerged as Minister Louis X, of the Boston Temple. He had been trained well by Malcolm in public speaking, and he also brought his own particular gifts to the task. He recorded a song entitled "A White Man's Heaven Is a Black Man's Hell," which was a hit in Black Muslim circles, and he swiftly established himself as one of the most promising members of the ministry. He wrote—and performed in—a play entitled "Orgena" ("A Negro" spelled backward), a satire about assimilated blacks. He also wrote "The Trial," in which a black prosecutor (usually played by Louis) tries the White Man for his myriad sins, and at the conclusion a black jury finds the defendant guilty and sentences him to death. Audiences responded with clamorous ovations.

But the Black Muslims would soon be appearing on a far larger stage, for Elijah Muhammad was discovering that even ostensibly hostile exposure in the mass media could serve him well. In the summer of 1959, Mike Wallace and Louis Lomax produced a television documentary on the Black Muslims, a group that then numbered less than thirty thousand. The Nation seemed to arouse alarm in white audiences, but that alarm only deepened its appeal to its natural constituency. The religious scholar C. Eric Lincoln, who in 1961 conducted a landmark study of the Nation of Islam, points out that weeks after the documentary appeared, Muhammad's following doubled in size.

Malcolm X was the public, charismatic face of the Nation of Islam in those years, while Louis, eight years his junior, proved his best student. Close as they were, however, there were occasional flareups between them, especially as a rift between Malcolm and Elijah was gradually making itself felt. C. Eric Lincoln recalls a signal incident in the early sixties: "Alex Haley and Louie and I were all seated with Malcolm in a Muslim restaurant down in Harlem, and Lou, who is very irreverent and outspoken, suddenly said to Malcolm, 'Malcolm, why don't you stop all this "Mister Muhammad" shit and go out and lead your *own* movement? Man, you could—' And before he could get the words out of his mouth, Malcolm had shot up like an onion in the rain. His face was contorted, he was so angry. And he was *reaching* for Lou, and Alex Haley stepped between them. Malcolm said, 'Lou, we've been friends a long time. But don't you ever say that to me!'"

In 1964, however, Malcolm finally did break with the Nation of Islam, telling newspapers that he had been disillusioned by discovering that Elijah Muhammad had fathered children with his young secretaries. (Since the facts of Muhammad's philandering had long been an open secret among the Muslim elite, Malcolm's claim to have been shocked by such revelations struck his brethren as spurious and vengeful, aimed solely at causing embarrassment.) And Louis proved himself staunchly loyal to the Nation of Islam, denouncing in thunderous tones the Judas in its midst.

In a column that appeared in December of that year in *Muhammad Speaks,* the Nation of Islam's weekly newspaper, Louis wrote some now notorious words: "The die is set, and Malcolm shall not escape. . . . Such a man as Malcolm is worthy of death." Malcolm was assassinated in Harlem on February 21, 1965. Farrakhan has been dogged by speculation that he was somehow involved in the killing. One of the men convicted of the murder said that, once Malcolm had been denounced as a traitor, he simply understood it to be his duty to take him out. In recent years, Farrakhan has admitted his responsibility in helping to create the poisonous atmosphere in which the killing took place; still, he denies any more direct involvement.

Just as Fard's disappearance had propelled Elijah Muhammad into preeminence, Farrakhan was now left to fill the void left by Malcolm. By the end of the year, Farrakhan had assumed Malcolm's old position as minister of the Harlem Mosque No. 7 and as Elijah Muhammad's national representative. Yet for some the aura of regicide would never fade. Eldridge Cleaver, who considers the assassination of Malcolm one of the crimes of the century against black people, speaks about the succession bitterly: "It was the old show-business adage: 'The show must go on.' And so, with Malcolm not being present, where was the best clone they could find? Farrakhan gravitated to the top of the heap as the slimeball, scheming, renegade bandwagoner that he is. He was able to get the position because, unlike any of the others around him, he was able to sing Malcolm's song."

.

In recent years, Malcolm has been retrieved by the mainstream as a palatable culture hero, whose path to enlightenment can be contrasted with Farrakhan's blinkered vision. The civil-rights activist Julian Bond says, "Malcolm grew. Farrakhan never did." It's hard to speak conclusively about Malcolm, since he was assassinated so soon after he announced his univeralist creed, but the fact remains that, his conversion to Sunni Islam aside, he never really relinquished black nationalism. Like Malcolm, Farrakhan says that we must learn to move beyond color and transcend all the divisions of humanity; like Malcolm, he asks the black community to develop its own self-reliance in the meantime. So the supposed contrast between the two men can seem more convenient than convincing.

It's equally difficult to recapture a sense of the enmity that existed between black radicals and the civil-rights mainstream in the sixties. Malcolm and Martin Luther King (whom Malcolm used to refer to as the Reverend Dr. Chicken Wing) have in some measure been melded through martyrdom. But the Muslims' rhetoric was far from conciliatory. "I was a Muslim then," Farrakhan said to me. "I wasn't for integration—I was a separatist. I thought Dr. King wasn't going in the right direction." But he also spoke of these tensions as part of a historical pattern. "In all the years of our progress in our century, there have always been these two poles. The masses are hearing the arguments like a tennis match, and all the time there is a level of consciousness coming up." This was also true during the civil-rights era, when Malcolm X and the nationalists were squaring off against Dr. King and the integrationists.

"The argument was healthy," Farrakhan went on. "You can see it now, when you are getting old and about to die. We've tried socialism, some have tried communism, we've tried nationalism, we've tried Americanism, we've tried integration. But in all these experiments we've become wiser, and what I see today is that there is and was good in every step that we made, and now what we need is not a thesis and an antithesis—what we need is a synthesis of the best ideas of this hundred years of struggle. And that's why in my maturity or my process of maturing I fell in love with Dr. King."

In the sixties and seventies, the Nation of Islam also began to attract followers for its level of discipline, its political savvy, and its emphasis on self-help. The eminent African-American novelist Leon Forrest served as managing editor of *Muhammad Speaks* in the early seventies, when many of its editors and writers were, like him, non-Muslims. He recalls that Elijah Muhammad was so politically agile that he ordered the paper not to write anything bad about Richard Nixon, hoping to profit from Nixon's proposal to set up enterprise zones in the inner city. That model of economic self-reliance was altogether consonant with the preachings of the Messenger. "The base of Elijah's movement and personality was steeped in a real deep conservatism," Forrest says. "Any number of whites who knew I worked for the Nation of Islam would say, 'You know, I really admire the Muslims.' And it was because it represents all the old American values of thrift and hard work, discipline, respect for the family and the women. Keep to yourself. Build small businesses. All the old American values, really. And then Elijah put in a little radical stuff here and there. But when you think about all the in-your-face, ready-to-duke-it-out vision people have of the Muslims, how many white people did they kill?"

As Elijah Muhammad's health declined, in the early seventies, many people believed that he was grooming Farrakhan to be his successor. And yet when Muhammad lay dying, in 1975, he designated not Farrakhan but, rather, his own son, Wallace Deen Muhammad. It was a bizarre choice. Wallace—or Warith, as he then renamed himself—had sided with Malcolm X against his father in the sixties, and had even been excommunicated for several years. He had also been taking very seriously his studies of Sunni Islam, and the teachings of his father had struck him as essentially heretical. Now that he was at last at the helm of his father's movement, he renounced the doctrines of Yakub, of racial demonology, of the divinity of

Fard, even of his own father's status as prophet. He also set about divesting himself of Nation properties; soon an estate thought to be worth as much as a hundred million dollars had gone the way of the original Black Muslim doctrine.

By 1977, Louis Farrakhan had had enough. He announced that he was breaking with Warith's organization in order to reestablish the Nation of Islam according to the original tenets of the Messenger. Carrying on the tradition of *Muhammad Speaks,* Farrakhan started up *The Final Call,* in which Elijah Muhammad's credo would be faithfully reproduced in every issue. Farrakhan also revived the creation myth of Yakub.

As a literary critic, I've long been impressed by Elijah Muhammad as a man who invented his own mythology. I asked Farrakhan whether he really believed the story of Yakub—or was it better understood as a metaphor?

"It is not, in our judgment, metaphorical," Farrakhan replied stolidly. "The reason it seems like an invention—and I know you meant that in the best sense—is that it was not heard before. And, rather than credit it as a revelation, intellectually we give it a name that allows us to deal with it. Personally, I believe that Yakub is not a mythical figure—he is a very real scientist."

Nevertheless, Farrakhan does seem to have quietly downgraded Elijah Muhammad's cherished demonology. Muhammad was asked, a few years before his death, whether he would really label *all* white people "blue-eyed devils." His reply was "Whether they are actually blue-eyed or not, if they are actually one of the members of that race they are devils." But now Farrakhan said, "If you saw a picture of Master Farrad Muhammad"—that is, Wallace Fard, the founder—"he looked like a white man." He went on to say that many of his own relatives, including his father and his grandfather, were fair-skinned, so how could he hate people because of the color of their skin?

While the burden of slavery and history and societal structure cannot be ignored, he argued, black men and women must accept responsibility, "more so than in any other time in our history," for their failures. "It's so easy to put it on the white man," he said. "As long as we can beat up on white people and make the world think that everything that went wrong in the world is due to them and we had nothing to do with this, then we rob ourselves of the impetus, the motivation, and the inspiration for personal change and for accepting personal responsibility. I say to black audiences today, 'There was a time when you could blame the white man and there was a time you could say the white man is a devil, but, with the way we're raising hell today and the way we're inflicting evil and pain on each other, you can't say that anymore.'"

In the late seventies and early eighties, Farrakhan was busy trying to shore up the ranks of the Nation of Islam, both economically and ideologically, but the nation at large was barely aware of his existence. Then came 1984, Jesse Jackson's campaign for the presidency, and Farrakhan's decision to break with Elijah Muhammad's principled abstention from politics.

Inspired by Jackson's campaign, Farrakhan registered to vote and volunteered the Nation's Fruit of Islam to provide security for Jackson. According to Farrakhan, Jackson's bid alarmed Jews, who distrusted his attitude toward Israel, and sought to derail the campaign by using Farrakhan's extremist rhetoric against Jackson. The wildly menacing statements, the apocalyptic imagery of race warfare, and all the other staples of Black Muslim oratory played well at Mosque Maryam, in Chicago, but were less warmly received on network television. Farrakhan complained that Jews controlled the media, and then raised his voice even more when he was attacked as a "black Hitler." Around the same time, Jackson got himself in trouble when a black reporter quoted him referring to New York City as "Hymietown." Farrakhan thereupon made things worse for Jackson by urging the black community to ostracize the reporter and adding that one day traitors like him would be killed. Then came the press conference at which, in reply to a question about the Hitler comparison, Farrakhan said that any man who is talked about forty years after his death is a great man but that Hitler was wickedly great. (It's clear, in context, that Farrakhan meant "great" in the same spirit in which *Time* named Hitler Man of the Year for 1938.)

"The next day, in the Chicago *Sun-Times,* in the New York *Post:* 'JACKSON PAL HAILS HITLER,'" Farrakhan recalled. "I took umbrage at being compared with Hitler. I haven't even been arrested for spitting on the sidewalk or doing anything violent to anyone. And now you're going to call me a Hitler, like I'm planning to do something evil to Jewish people?"

Four months later, Farrakhan made a radio broadcast during which he talked about Israelis' "using God's name to shield your dirty religion." Now he said, "Fine. I said that. They said I said 'gutter,' but it was 'dirty.' I had no reference whatsoever in my mind to Judaism. However, anybody who distilled that could say, and rightly so, that I was talking about Judaism. So the headline the next day was 'FARRAKHAN CALLS JUDAISM A GUTTER RELIGION.'"

It is true that the two things nearly everybody knows about Farrakhan—that he extolled Hitler as a great man and deplored Judaism as a "gutter religion"—are, strictly speaking, false. That point may not speak well of the accuracy of some of our leading media, but it hardly absolves him of the larger charge of anti-Semitism. And, for all his talk of reconciliation, Farrakhan refuses to budge. "It doesn't make any difference what I say, how I explain myself," he said. "I have never got away from 'Judaism is a gutter religion,' 'Hitler is a great man.'" He shrugged. "I'm a *man*—I'm not afraid of white folk. And so if they got the nerve to say that about me I got nerve enough to defend myself and to drop an accusation on them that I believe to be true. So the fight was on—me and the Jews." He spread his arms, holding up two clenched fists, like a pugilist.

If the public consternation over the Black Muslims in the late nineteen-fifties magnified Elijah Muhammad's influence, the controversy in the wake of the Jackson campaign performed a similar service for Farrakhan. David Jackson, of the Chicago *Tribune,* notes that Farrakhan's 1983 Christmas address attracted a small handful of listeners on folding chairs, whereas today he routinely commands audiences of ten thousand and more. The commentator Roger Wilkins says of Farrakhan's Jewish critics, "I'm not saying they're wrong to strike back—I'm never going to tell the guy whom somebody slams in the stomach, 'Well, here's what you must do now.' But, once they struck back, he became a national figure. These attacks don't hurt him in his base; they enhance him, because he has told his people that though he is not anti-Semitic, there's this free-floating Zionist plot that is directed at him. So when the Anti-Defamation League attacks him, all he has to do is turn to his people and say 'See?' Then, of course, one of the messages is 'They are attacking me because I am supporting you and your interests.'"

Louis Farrakhan will say, up and down, that he reveres the Jewish people. Listen to him: "Personally, I don't know what this argument has served. Jewish people are the world leaders, in my opinion. They are some of the most brilliant people on this planet. The Jews are some of the greatest scientists, the greatest thinkers, the greatest writers, the greatest theologians, the greatest in music, the greatest in business. And people hate them sometimes because of envy, and because the Jews succeed in spite of the hatred of their Gentile brethren, or anybody else's hatred. I admire that, as God is my witness."

Farrakhan has a theological explanation for Jewish preeminence. His theory is that the Jews have had many prophets in their midst and so have been the greatest recipients of divine revelation, and that this elevated wisdom has translated itself into achievement of all kinds. "When you have a people who receive revelation," he says, "they can do very good things or they can become very base, evil, and use the revelation for wicked purposes."

For many years, Farrakhan has been saying that there is a small group of Jews who meet (variously) in a Park Avenue apartment or in Hollywood to plan the course of the nation. I had to ask, "Do you think that there's a cabal—that there's a central planning group within the Jewish community?"

"I do believe that," Farrakhan replied. "I believe that there are very, very wise Jews who plan good and there are very wise Jews who plan evil." He added, "I am not hateful. I am deeply respectful of the Jewish people, man. I know they are great, but I also know that there are some scoundrels among them. And those scoundrels have to be condemned by them. And if they don't condemn the scoundrels—well, that's all right. I will."

I began to focus on Farrakhan's reddish ocher complexion and his silky, wavy hair—what we called "Jesus moss" when I was growing up. "Do you know anything about your white ancestry?" I asked him.

Farrakhan explained that his father was very light-skinned and had straight hair, and that his mother had told him his father's parentage was, in fact, white Portuguese. Then he said, "I'm going to tell you something. You really want to know what I think? I think they were members of the Jewish community." This sounds like a fantastical joke, but it is highly probable, given what we know about migration to the West Indies. Orlando Patterson, a historical sociologist at Harvard, who has made a study of merchant populations in the islands, confirms that nearly all people of Iberian descent in Jamaica and Barbados, even today, are of Sephardic Jewish ancestry.

"I believe that in my blood, and not in a bad way," Farrakhan said. "Because when I was a little boy, I used to love listening to the Jewish cantors in Boston. They had a program, and every week I would listen. I was struck by the cantor, and I've always loved the way they sing or recite the Torah." Farrakhan is always happy to elaborate on his admiration for Jewish musicians. "When my mom put that violin in my hand and I fell in love with that instrument, I never was thinking Jew, Gentile, anything like that," he said. "But all my heroes were Jewish. The greatest was Jascha Heifetz, and I loved him then and I love him now. I was driving my car when it came over the news that Vladimir Horowitz, the pianist, had passed. I pulled my car over to the side of the road, and I said a prayer for his soul." He went on, "If in my lineage there are Jews, I would hope that in the end, before my life is over, I not only will have rendered a service to my own beloved community of black people but will also have rendered a service to the Jewish community." What he seemed to have in mind was not what most people would consider a service: he was evidently referring to the notorious book *The Secret Relationship Between Blacks and Jews*, published by the Nation of Islam, the implicit assumption of which is that a Jewish predilection for evil is visible throughout the centuries.

"You read *The Secret Relationship Between Blacks and Jews*," Farrakhan said.

"And critiqued it," I put in.

"And critiqued it," he said, nodding. "I didn't order anybody to research this. They wanted to defend me, so they went to research it. We are making the point that the Jewish people were involved in slavery, and 75 percent of the Jews owned slaves." He gave me a level look. "You have a relationship with Jews of scholarship and brilliance, whom you can admire and have a lovely friendship with," he said. "I know there are Jews like that, and I could have a wonderful friendship with them. I'm hoping and I believe that in the future it will develop. Sometimes, Dr. Gates, when you are new in the neighborhood, you get in a fight and you bloody the guy's nose, and he bloodies your nose, and before you know it you end up being the best of friends. But you're not friends without mutual respect."

Farrakhan took a deep breath and continued, "But my point is I don't like our relationship with Jews. I think it's a weak relationship. I think it's a paternalistic relationship. I don't like a relationship where they are the agent or the manager and we are the talent alone. We bring a lot to the table, but we get so little from the table. The IRS puts the principal in jail and the accountant gets away with the money. This is wrong. There is so much injustice here."

What is one to make of all this? Farrakhan isn't feigning admiration for Jews as a distraction from his hate-mongering. Rather, his love and his loathing flow from the same ideas. There's a sense in which Farrakhan doesn't want his followers to battle Jews, but, rather, wants them to *be* Jews. Yet when he describes Jews as "world leaders," it is a double-edged compliment. There is no sense in being gladdened when he extolls Jewish wisdom and troubled only when he warns of Jewish evil: both sentiments are sincere, and both are aspects of a single unhealthy obsession.

In speeches he has made over the past several years, Farrakhan stresses the fact that he is condemning only some Jews—the scoundrelly ones. But the question begged is one of relevance: What makes a scoundrel's ethnicity or religion of central concern to Farrakhan or his audiences? Farrakhan protests that he didn't say all Jews, he said *some* Jews, but the protest misses the point. Partitive anti-Semitism remains anti-Semitism.

Consider, even, the figure that Farrakhan often returns to: that 75 percent of the Jews in the South owned slaves. He returns to it because, he says, no one has refuted it. It is a fact—the result of an 1830 survey—and not something just concocted. But facts, as Ronald Reagan once said, are stupid things. The historian Harold Brackman points out that in 1830 only a third of America's Jews lived in the South. Those southern Jews tended to be middle-class urban dwellers, with small numbers of domestic servants; by contrast, Jewish representation among the plantation owners who held most of the slaves was miniscule. Furthermore, in 1830 black slave owners outnumbered Jewish slave owners by fifteen to one.

But the real question is why the results of this 1830 survey should be of such concern to a constituency that you might think had more pressing matters to contend with: mounting poverty, crime, AIDS. Farrakhan arouses the indignation of inner-city audiences when he speaks of an exploitative relationship between Jewish agents and black talent. You may cringe, but when you scan his flock you see that there's something bleakly comic about it, too. They're struggling to make ends meet. Agents? Accountants? What is Louis Farrakhan talking about? And why?

"Whenever our interests seemed diametrically opposed," Farrakhan told me, "Jews followed what they felt was in their best interest." And he cited Jewish opposition to Jackson's candidacy, and Jewish opposition to affirmative action. But, since most whites opposed Jackson and most whites are hostile to affirmative action, one might think that the more interesting fact is that Jews are disproportionately represented among those whites who did support Jackson, and who favor measures like affirmative action. Blacks, Farrakhan has said, must pursue their self-interest. But hurling invective at liberal allies doesn't sound like prudent self-interest to me. Even if Farrakhan's discourse on the Jews can't be reduced purely to a matter of fear and loathing, it doesn't bespeak sweet reason, either.

The truly paranoid heart of Farrakhan's worldview has been revealed in recent speeches in which he has talked about a centuries-old conspiracy of international bankers—with names like Rothschild and Warburg—who have captured control over the central banks in many countries, and who incite wars to increase the indebtedness of others and maximize their own wealth. The Federal Reserve, the IRS, the FBI, and the Anti-Defamation League were all founded in 1913, Farrakhan says (actually, the IRS was founded in 1862 and the FBI in 1908, but never mind), and then he poses the favorite rhetorical question of all paranoid historians: "Is that a coincidence?"

What do you do with a religious demagogue who promulgates the theory that Jewish financiers have manipulated world events for centuries? Well, if you're a Republican contender for the presidency, and the demagogue's name is Pat Robertson, you genuflect. It turns out that Farrakhan's conspiracy theory of Jewish cabals is essentially identical to Robertson's. "Rest assured, there is a behind-the-scenes Establishment in this nation, as in every other," Robertson writes in *The New World Order,* his best-selling book. "It has enormous power. It has controlled the economic and foreign policy objectives of the United States for the past seventy years, whether the man sitting in the White House is a Democrat or a Republican, a liberal or a conservative, a moderate or an extremist." Robertson goes on to inveigh against the tentacular Rothschilds and Warburgs. Michael Lind, who has analyzed Robertson's conspiracy theories at length, suggests that not since the days of Father Coughlin has the grassroots right been as overtly anti-Semitic as it is now.

And Farrakhan? He, too, believes all this conspiracy stuff and thinks he's just telling it like it is. He must realize that such talk goes down well with inner-city audiences hungry for secret histories that explain how things went wrong. He turns mainstream criticism to his advantage, winning ovations by representing himself as the persecuted truth-teller. But turnabout isn't always fair play: and the fact that Farrakhan is a black American only makes his deafness to historical context all the more dismaying. Within his own lifetime, one of every three Jews on the face of the earth died at the hands of a regime suffused by the same language about nefarious Jewish influence. Ultimately, Farrakhan's anti-Semitism has the characteristics of a psychological obsession, and once in a while he shows signs of recognizing this. "I would prefer that this whole conflict would go away, in truth," he said to me. His voice sounded husky and a little tired. "But it's like I'm locked now in a struggle. It's like both of us got a hold on each other, and each of us is filled with electricity. I can't let them go, and they can't let me go."

Farrakhan's peculiar mixture of insight and delusion would be a matter of mainly academic interest if it weren't for his enormous populist appeal among black Americans—an appeal that was clearly demonstrated in 1995's Million Man March. That occasion has been widely seen as an illustration both of Farrakhan's strengths and of his weaknesses. "If only somebody else had convened it," the liberal minded are prone to say. But nobody else—not Colin Powell, not Jesse Jackson—could have.

Some of the most heartfelt tributes to the event's success are also the most grudging. There's little doubt, after all, that the Farrakhan phenomenon owes much to a vacuum of radical black leadership. (Jesse Jackson has emerged over the past decade as the leading spokesman of the American left, I submit, rather than of black America.) "We have the worst leadership in the black community since slavery," Eldridge Cleaver maintains. "Farrakhan saw that vacuum, saw nothing motivating the people, no vision being projected to the people, and he came up with the defining event for a generation of people, this Million Man March."

Timing had a lot to do with the event's success, of course. As Roger Wilkins likes to say, Newt Gingrich was one of the main organizers of the march. "If the white middle class feels it's losing ground, the black working class and unskilled working class are being slaughtered—hit by a blitzkrieg that no one notices," Wilkins points out. "And their plight is not on anyone's agenda anymore. Farrakhan supplies an answer, and an emotional discharge."

Farrakhan's people have won some real credibility in the black community. "It's as if Malcolm was having a march on Washington," Robert Moses, the civil-rights activist and education reformer, says. And Wilkins says, "Nobody else can go into the prisons and save souls to the degree that they have. Nobody else is able to put as many neat and clean young people on the streets of the inner city as they are. You think about the fellows who are selling their papers as opposed to those fellows you see standing around the liquor stores. Their men have this enviable sense of discipline, orderliness, and human purpose." (The Nation of Islam continues to have very conservative sexual politics, and Farrakhan is vehemently anti-abortion, but he has also inveighed against domestic violence, and—

in a sharp break from tradition—even named a woman to be a nation of Islam minister.) Hugh Price, the president of the National Urban League, calls the march "the largest family-values rally in the history of the United States." Indeed, another sign of its success was the number of mainstream civil-rights leaders who were present. Whatever their discomfort with Farrakhan's extremist rhetoric, they calculated that their absence might well imperil their legitimacy with the black public.

Attendance or nonattendance was a delicate decision. General Colin Powell was prominent among those blacks who decided that they could not afford to appear. When I asked Farrakhan if he would consider supporting a future Powell presidential bid, he said, "I don't want to support anybody because he's black—I think I have outgrown the need to support somebody because of the color of his skin. What is in the best interest of our people is really in the best interest of the country. So if General Powell had an agenda that is good for the totality of our people—the American people first— and in that package is something that can lift our people, he's got our support."

Farrakhan's level of support among black Americans is vigorously debated. If you gauge his followers by the number who regularly attend mosques affiliated with the Nation of Islam and eschew lima beans and corn bread, they are not very numerous. Estimates range from twenty thousand to ten times that. On the other hand, if you go by the number of people who consider him a legitimate voice of black protest, the ranks are much larger. (In a recent poll, more than half the blacks surveyed reported a favorable impression of him.) The march was inspired by the Muslims but not populated by them. Farrakhan knows that the men who came to the march were not his religious followers. They tended to be middle class and college educated and Christian. Farrakhan is convinced that those men came "to a march called by a man who is considered radical, extremist, anti-Semitic, anti-white" because of a yearning "to connect with the masses."

Not everyone, to be sure, was quite so deeply impressed. "This was an opportunity for the black middle class to feel this symbolic connection, but what were the solutions that were proposed, except atonement?" Angela Davis asks. Julian Bond says bluntly, "You know, that Negro didn't even vote until 1984. He's the leader in the sense that he can gather people to him, but they don't go anyplace when they leave him." And Jesse Jackson, who addressed the marchers, now views the march as fatally flawed by its failure to reach out to Capitol Hill. "The 1963 March on Washington was connected to public policy—public accommodations," he says, and notes that the result was the signing into law of the Civil Rights Act the following year. By contrast, he argues, the Million Man March had "essentially a religious theme—atonement—disconnected from public policy," so it brought no political dividends in its aftermath. "On the very next day—the very next day, *the very next day*—there was the welfare bill," he said, referring to the House and Senate conferences to work out a final draft of a bill excusing the federal government from a degree of responsibility toward the poor. "The next day was the vote on the unfair sentence guidelines. The next day was the Medicare bill," another hostile measure. "The big debates in Congress took place between that Wednesday and Thursday. And so those who were taking away our rights and attacking us did not see any connection between the gathering and public policy." The lesson he draws is straightforward: "The march was essentially disconnected from our political leadership. Any mass action must be connected to the public-policy leaders."

Some critics express a sense that the mass mobilization may itself be a relic of a bygone era. It was an arena where Farrakhan was able to stake a claim for mass black leadership, in part because of the near-sacralization of the 1963 precursor; but its continued political viability has not been demonstrated. Indeed, the growing fragmentation of black leadership—the irrelevance of the old-fashioned notion of a "head nigger in charge"—is one sign that an elite now exists in black America that does enjoy an unmediated relation to power. Privately, many black leaders say that Farrakhan's moment has passed. Such remarks inevitably carry an air of wishful thinking. White liberal allies sometimes worry that pressure is required to keep black leaders from being "soft on Farrakhan": in reality, no love is lost among those who would compete for the hearts and souls of black America. At the helm of the mainstream black-advocacy groups are men and women who may say conciliatory things about the Nation of Islam, but their jaws are tense and their smiles are tight. They reassure themselves that Farrakhan is bound to remain a marginal phenomenon because of his extremism. Yet the organic leaders of the disenfranchised are seldom moderate in tone; and since, from all indications, the underclass is continuing to expand, Farrakhan's natural power base will only increase.

In the months following the march, Farrakhan dropped out of public view, and he spoke of having suffered from depression, in part because he was still being misrepresented by the press. This response highlights Farrakhan's paradoxical relation to the wider public—that of a pariah who wants to be embraced. "Both Malcolm and Farrakhan had a very tough ideology but at the same time wanted a degree of public acceptance in the white community," Ron Walters, a political scientist and an adviser to Jackson, says. "To me, that's a tremendous contradiction. I don't know whether it's a personality thing or just what happens to you when you reach a certain level of prominence—that you do want a sort of universal acceptance."

Such acceptance has been elusive so far. A few weeks before the Million Man March, Farrakhan gave an interview to make it clear that when he referred to Jewish "bloodsuckers" he didn't mean Jews in particular—he meant all nonblack shopkeepers in the inner city, some of them Jewish but these days more often Koreans or Arabs. He must have found it galling when many newspapers wrested his remarks out of context, leaving the impression that he had merely repeated the original accusation: Farrakhan calls Jews bloodsuckers. Farrakhan's image also suffered when, in early 1995, the Chicago *Tribune* published an investigative series, by David Jackson and William Gaines, revealing financial disarray among Nation-owned businesses. Farrakhan's calls for economic self-sufficiency, it appeared, were not matched by his organization's performance.

Farrakhan hurt himself yet again, with his so-called World Friendship Tour, in January and February of 1996. He claims that his decision to make that trip to third world capitals was a matter of divine inspiration, but it isn't hard to imagine human motivations as well. Public figures who feel that they have been badly used by the local papers often find that solace awaits them in admiring throngs overseas: call it the Jerry Lewis syndrome. Besides, how better to shore up your position as the leader of black America than by being received as such by foreign potentates?

The domestic fallout, however, has lingered. Even many of those who supported Farrakhan were chagrined to find him holding friendly meetings with some of the world's worst dictators: Nigeria's Sani Abacha, Libya's Muammar Gadhafi, Zaire's Mobutu, and Sudan's Omar al-Bashir. Ron Walters observes, "He gave all those people who wanted an opportunity not to have to deal with him the golden reason. The tremendous political capital of the march had been dissipated." Black nationalists were among those who were the most horrified. Molefi Kete Asante, the Afrocentric scholar, says, "What Farrakhan did, in my judgment, was to take the legitimacy of the march and put it in his back pocket, and march around to these terrible governments, as if somehow he were the leader of a million black people. That upset me."

It is a sore subject with Farrakhan. Sure, he met with dictators, he said to me, but when you are dealing with atonement, sin, and reconciliation, you don't travel to the blameless. "It's all right for Jesse to sit down with George Wallace in Alabama and for them to pray together—and there's applause," he went on. "But I can't go sit down with my brother who is a sinner? Nixon died a hero, but I cannot forgive a black man?" There was a surge of anger in his voice. "That's the damnable thing that I hate about this whole damned thing," he said. "If I go to a black man to retrieve him, all of a sudden I'm cavorting with a damned dictator, but Jesus could sit down with the sinners and you give him honor and credit. And Reagan can sit down with Gorbachev, and he gets honor and credit. He sits with the evil empire, but I can't sit with my own brother. To hell with you for that. That's why I am not a politician."

"Has the tour compromised the achievement of the march?" I asked him.

He sounded subdued when he said, "If I lost momentum, I believe it's only temporary."

Farrakhan lays much stress on the imagery of dialogue and concili-ation these days. Certainly the Farrakhan I met was a model of civility and courtesy. I was reminded of Eric Lincoln's account of the last couple of visits he paid to Farrakhan at his home: "Louie insisted on getting down on his hands and knees on the floor to take my shoes off. You know, I'm overweight, and it's a difficult task to get shoes and socks off. And so Louis said, 'I will do that.' And I said, "No, no." And Louis said, 'No, I want to do it.' He took my shoes off and rubbed my feet to get the blood circulating."

If the Farrakhan phenomenon remains disquieting, the man himself seems oddly, jarringly vulnerable. I met someone who was eager, even hungry, for conversation; someone of great intelligence who seemed intellectually lonely. In fiery speeches before packed auditoriums, Farrakhan speaks of plots against his life and does so in alarmingly messianic tones. ("I don't care nothing about my life," he told his audience on Savior's Day in 1995, his voice breaking. "It's *your* life that I want to save!") To me he spoke of his mortality in a quieter mode. He spoke movingly of watching the funeral of Yitzhak Rabin—about the tragedy of a wise and tempered elder statesman assassinated by a callow extremist. He spoke about having a growing appreciation for compromise, about coming to see the value in the positions of his ideological antagonists within the civil-rights tradition. And he told me about a fight of his own, against prostate cancer, over the past several years.

"At first, it was frightening to me—how could I have cancer? I've eaten well, I've tried to live clean. Then I fasted and I prayed and I went into the desert, and after a month I went and had an MRI and one of those rectal ultrasounds, and all they could find was a little scar." He paused, and added quietly, "But then it came back." He looks in splendid health: he is sixty-three, and his skin remains soft and almost unlined. He recently made a health-and-exercise video, which shows him going through an arduous regimen of weight training. And he *is* remarkably fit. He has undergone seed-implantation radiation therapy for his cancer and remains optimistic about the results. "I've never had to take a pain pill, and I hope and pray that God will bless me ultimately to overcome it. At least, all accounts up to date, the PSA"—the blood-screening test for prostate cancer—"has been normal. And so I'm going on with my life, but warning all of us that this is such a hell of a killer of our people. And when you reach your early forties, many of us won't like somebody poking around in our rectum, but we have to encourage our young men and our middle-aged brothers, and the population as a whole, to do that for themselves, because all we have is our health."

We all know that the world isn't divided between saints and sinners. And yet the private Farrakhan's very humanness—those traits of kindness, concern, humor—makes his paranoia all the more disconcerting. He rails against the way the mainstream has demonized him, and yet he refuses to renounce the anti-Semitic conspiracy theories that have made him anathema: to him, it would be like denying the law of gravity. And so he is trapped, immobilized by his contradictory desires. His ongoing calls for dialogue are seemingly heartfelt; he genuinely wants a seat at the table, craves the legitimation of power. Yet he will not engage in the compromises and concessions that true dialogue requires. He cannot afford to. This is a man whose political identity is constituted by antagonism to the self-image of America. To moderate his stance of unyielding opposition would be to destroy the edifice he has spent his life constructing. Moreover, Farrakhan knows that there are people around him whose militancy puts his to shame. Some of them are former lieutenants of his in the Nation of Islam, such as Khalid Muhammad, whom Farrakhan suspended after judging him to have been *too* intemperate in his public pronouncements. Others have established an independent base of support, such as Silas Muhammad, another Elijah loyalist who split with the organization, and whose sect is now based in Atlanta. For leaders whose appeal is based on intransigence, outrage, and wrath, there is always the danger of being outflanked by those even more intransigent, more outrageous, more wrathful. This, in part, is why Farrakhan could not truly atone even at his own day of atonement.

In the end, however, it isn't Farrakhan but Farrakhan's following that demands explanation. We might start by admitting the moral authority that black nationalism commands even among those blacks who ostensibly disapprove of it. In the village where I grew up, there was a Holiness Church, where people spoke in tongues and fell down in religious ecstasy. It was not my church; my family and I shunned the Pentecostal fervor. And yet, on some level, we believed it to be the real thing, realer than our own, more temperate Episcopal services. It was the place to go if you really needed something—if you got desperately sick, say—because the Holy Ghost lived there. (There are Reform Jews who admit to a similar attitude toward their Hasidic brethren.) In this same vein, the assimilated black American, who lives in Scarsdale and drives a Lexus, responds to Farrakhan and Farrakhanism as a presence at once threatening and exhilarating, dismaying and cathartic. Though blackness isn't exactly a religion, it has become invested with a quasi-religious structure. Black nationalism is a tradition extending at least back to Martin R. Delany, in the nineteenth century. Cross it with the black messianic tradition—which spawned the legendary ties of Father Divine, Daddy Grace, and Prophet Jones—and you have the Nation of Islam.

Hard as it is to take stock of the organization's membership, it's harder to take stock of Farrakhan's place in the mind of black America. For his dominion is, in a sense, a dominion of metaphor, which is to say that it is at once factitious and factual. The political theorist Benedict Anderson has defined nations as "imagined communities," and the black nation is even more imaginary than most. We know that thirty-six million sepia Americans do not a collective make, but in our minds we sometimes insist upon it.

The Million Man March had all the hallmarks of a watershed event, yet a march is not a movement. I asked Farrakhan at one point what the country would look like if, by magic, he could turn his hopes into reality. The answer he gave me was long and meandering, but it centered on things like "revamping the educational system" to make it less Eurocentric—proposals of the sort debated by the New York State Board of Regents, rather than something that was radically transformative in any obvious way.

That was, in a sense, the most dismaying response I'd heard all day. Farrakhan is a man of visions. Just weeks before the march, he told congregants in a Washington, D.C., church about the "Mother Wheel"—a heavily-armed spaceship the size of a city, which will rain destruction upon white America but save those who embrace the Nation of Islam. ("Ezekiel saw the wheel, way up in the middle of the air," in the words of the old spiritual.) What gave me pause was the realization that such visions coexist in Farrakhan's mind with a real poverty of—well, vision, which is to say a broader conception of the human future.

Farrakhan is a man of unhealthy fixations, but the reciprocal fixation on Farrakhan that you find in the so-called mainstream is a sign of our own impoverished political culture. Thirteen decades have passed since Emancipation, and half of our black men between twenty-four and thirty-five are without full-time employment. One black man graduates from college for every hundred who go to jail. Almost half of black children live in poverty. People say that Farrakhan is now the leading voice of black rage in America. One day, America will realize it got off easy.

Minister Louis Farrakhan and the Continuing Evolution of the Nation of Islam

Ernest Allen, Jr.

ERNEST ALLEN, JR., *is an associate professor in the W.E.B. DuBois Department of Afro-American Studies at the University of Massachusetts at Amherst. This essay, an examination of the origin and evolution of the Nation of Islam in America, is adapted from a work that appeared in* Black Scholar, the Journal of Black Studies and Research, *Fall–Winter 1996. Mr. Allen is at work on a book about Islamic influences in the Black-American community during* The Great Depression.

One of the more profound cultural and political phenomena of the late twentieth century has been the religious conversion of approximately one million African Americans to Islam.[1] Encroaching upon a domain over which Christianity held virtual sway for one and a half centuries, this recent turn of events owes most of its influence to an organization known as the Nation of Islam (NOI).[2] The NOI—both the original group and its offshoots—offers an intriguing example of a religious-oriented nationalist movement that, over a period of six decades, has come to embrace traditional Islam in halting and contradictory ways. At times this embrace has been direct and deliberate; at other times more indirect and pragmatic, in order that central aims might be more effectively pursued. Minor organizational discontinuities aside, the NOI has proved to be the largest and longest-lived institutionalized nationalist movement among blacks in the United States, far outstripping the widespread appeal and influence of Marcus Garvey's Universal Negro Improvement Association, which flourished during World War I and the immediate postwar years.

With the passing of its supreme leader, Elijah Muhammad, in early 1975, the Nation of Islam reached a divide. Propelled by Mr. Muhammad's son, Wallace, the NOI quickly underwent fundamental changes in structure and belief, as well as in name. From a large sect preaching nominal Islam, the group rapidly evolved into a Sunni Islamic community with substantive ties to a larger international community of religious adherents. In October 1976 the NOI became the World Community of al-Islam in the West (WCIW); in its final incarnation, lasting from May 1980 through May 1985, the organization was known as the American Muslim Mission (AMM), after which time it disbanded. Today the work of Wallace Muhammad—who now goes by the name of Warith Deen Mohammed—is primarily evangelical, his constituency composed basically of African American Muslims who regularly attend some two hundred plus *masjids* throughout the United States. Within Islamic circles at home and abroad, Imam Mohammed's voice carries considerable influence; within the secular world he rarely has been heard from in recent years, save for occasional interviews in the press. Politically conservative and entrepreneurially inclined, Imam Mohammed's secular views correspond with the most reserved elements of the black middle class, its business-oriented strata in particular. The political outlooks of his followers, however, appear to follow diverse paths.

Were that the only story to tell, it would be a remarkable one, indeed. African Americans now constitute the largest single "ethnic bloc" within a religious community composed of millions of Muslims, both immigrant and native born, residing in the United States. However, in 1978 the picture was further complicated by the splintering off of a new formation from the ranks of the transformed NOI—then known as the WCIW. Distressed with the sweeping changes in doctrine and organizational structure as well as the loss of economic empire amassed under the old group, Minister Louis Farrakhan led thousands of dissatisfied followers into a newly constituted Nation of Islam.

Nor was Farrakhan the only defector. By far the most capable and charismatic leader to emerge during the NOI-WCIW-AMM transition period, he nonetheless has distant rivals among others dissatisfied with the course set by Warith Deen Mohammed. These include Silis Muhammad, who along with Abu Koss subsequently established the Lost-Found Nation of Islam (LFNOI), based in Atlanta; Brother Solomon (a.k.a. Royall X Jenkins) and his spokesperson, former NOI secretary Abass Rassoull, whose organization at Camp Springs, Maryland, is known as the United Nation of Islam (UNOI); and John Muhammad, younger brother of Elijah, who, while maintaining a distance from Farrakhan's organization, has retained the NOI name for his Detroit temple.[3] The Five Percenters, an earlier but structurally amorphous spinoff formed in Harlem, New York City, in 1964, continue to exert influence not only upon inner-city youth, but upon college students as well—especially through the medium of rap music.[4] None of these groups have significantly contested Farrakhan's leadership.[5]

Since its break, Louis Farrakhan's NOI has succeeded in expanding its membership, reclaiming a portion of the economic holdings of the pre-1975 group and amassing new enterprises as well. Retaining core elements of the old doctrine while selectively appropriating additional elements of traditional Islam, the perennially militant NOI —like its predecessor—finds principal support among economically dispossessed African Americans, the number of which appears to increase with each passing day. Doctrinally, the LFNOI devotes considerable energies to scriptural prophecy, not least of which is the supposition that Brother Solomon of the LFNOI is identical to King Solomon of the Bible, whereas the UNOI's overriding concern lies in its reparations claims upon the U.S. government.[6] While the Lost-Found Nation of Islam, the United Nation of Islam, and the Detroit-based Nation of Islam also draw upon the "economically challenged," the latter two groups, especially, take pride in preserving venerable NOI orthodoxy against any doctrinal or ritualistic changes, apostasies for which they occasionally chastise Minister Farrakhan. Initially critical of Farrakhan, the LFNOI, for its part, has sought a rapprochement with the NOI leader, with no reported success thus far.[7]

Without question, the principal "competition" for members on the African American Islamic front now rests between the constituencies represented by Warith Deen Mohammed and Louis Farrakhan. The primary difference between the two, however, lies in the realm of religious orthodoxy, social-class constituency, corresponding degree of militancy, and organizational centralization. The followers of both tend to associate their economic successes—and how could they not?—with the righteousness of their respective spiritual trajectories. And both groups tend toward political conservatism.

The Nationalist Legacy of the Universal Negro Improvement Association

African American nationalist tendencies in the twentieth century have been shaped largely by the Universal Negro Improvement Association, a Jamaican-based organization transferred to the United States in 1917 by Marcus Garvey.[8] The Garvey movement, as it came to be called, demanded the liberation of the African continent from colonial rule, promoted the racial pride of people of African descent, and sought to establish economic ties between African peoples of the mother continent, the West Indies, and the United States. For complex reasons, Garvey by 1921 had linked the quest for black self-determination on the African continent to a vigorous attack upon African American claims to civil and political liberties within the United States.[9] This dubious strategy lay at the core of controversies surrounding the Garvey movement in the 1920s, resurfaced with neo-Garveyite groups and the original Nation of Islam in the 1950s, and seems to have been put to rest only recently by Minister Farrakhan's endorsement of Jesse Jackson's presidential campaign in 1984. The NOI's later cooperation with right-wing whites was prefigured in Garvey's infamous meeting with Edward Young Clarke, imperial kleagle of the Ku Klux Klan, in 1922; in his subsequent affiliations with arch-racists John Powell of the Anglo-Saxon Clubs of America and Earnest Sevier Cox of the White American Society; as well as in the cooperation of neo-Garveyite groups such as the Peace Movement of Ethiopia with Mississippi Senator Theodore Bilbo's antiblack, African repatriation scheme in 1939. Parallels assuredly can be found in the invited appearance of American Nazi Party head George Lincoln Rockwell at the NOI Savior's Day observance in 1962, and, sometime later, the explicit agreement reached between the NOI and the Ku Klux Klan providing for the nonharassment of NOI members in the South by racist whites. In the mid-1980s Louis Farrakhan himself received public endorsements from a number of white extremist organizations, including the White American Political Association and the Posse Comitatus, which he chose (publicly, at least) to ignore. But members of the association, including its leader, Tom Metzger, reportedly accepted an invitation to attend a September 1985 rally sponsored by the NOI, to which they donated $100. Farrakhan, moreover, has received fulsome praise from Britain's National Front, and in 1990 NOI spokesman Dr. Abdul Alim Muhammad reportedly addressed a conference of Lyndon Larouche supporters.[10]

Ahmadism, Freemasonry, and Moorish Science

While Garveyism has continued to serve as a model of political and economic self-determination for the NOI as well as other African

American nationalist groups, examples of heterodox Islam seem to have arrived from three principal sources: the Ahmadiyyah Muslim sect, the African American Masonic offshoot known as the Ancient Egyptian Arabic Order of Nobles of the Mystic Shrine of North and South America (AEAONMS), and the Moorish Science Temple of America (MSTA).[11] Exported to the United States by Indian missionary Mufti Muhammad Sadiq in 1920, Ahmadiyyah Islam proved traditional in virtually every way—save for the declared prophethood of its founder, Gulam Ahmad. The Ahmadi appeal fell most heavily on African American urban dwellers, and the imaginations of aspiring black religious leaders of all fringes were no doubt stoked by its heterodox claims for an Islamic prophethood succeeding that of Prophet Muhammad. The NOI's uninterrupted employ of Maulana Muhammad Ali's English-language translation of the Holy Qur'an, as well as his numerous books and pamphlets devoted to Islam, suggests an important Ahmadi influence, as does Elijah Muhammad's employ of the pseudonym Gulam Bogans in the early 1940s.[12]

The AEAONMS, on the other hand, was founded by 33° Prince Hall Masons in June 1893 at the Columbia Exposition in Chicago.[13] For their rituals and texts, Black Shriners drew upon materials quietly expropriated from their white segregationist counterparts, whose own organization was known as the Ancient Arabic Order of the Nobles of the Mystic Shrine for North America. This original Shrine was established as a Masonic social organization in New York City in 1871 but in its irreverent legend lay claim to having been founded by "Kalif Alee" (Caliph 'Ali ibn Abi Tabib), cousin and son-in-law of the Prophet Muhammad. As a result of Shriner influence—especially given the ignorance of traditional Islamic practices in the United States—Islam and Freemasonry occasionally came to be identified as one.[14] This tendency was especially true in organizations such as the Moorish Science Temple and the Nation of Islam.[15]

Imprinted with Garveyite, Masonic, and, most likely, Ahmadi influences as well, the Moorish Science Temple was responsible for ushering in the premier African American version of an Islamic-oriented nationalism. Reportedly founded in Newark, New Jersey, in 1913 by North Carolina native Timothy Drew—better known by his Shrine-inspired name of Noble Drew Ali—the original organization seems to have been linked to an earlier formation known as the Canaanite Temple.[16] Details of the MSTA's early years, not to mention those of its founder, remain mired in profuse legend, but by 1925 the organization had firmly established itself on Chicago's South Side. Many of the MSTA's key ideas were absorbed by the fledgling NOI: the fictive notion of an "Asiatic" origin of African Americans; the adoption of "Moorish" dress, including fezes worn by men;[17] a healthy confusion of Islam with Freemasonry; the claim that Islam was the original religion of blacks prior to their having been enslaved;[18] and a religious nationalism nominally infused with Islamic points of reference. In the entrepreneurial realm the influence of Garveyism was equally manifest in the activities of the MSTA and the NOI: for example, a suite of "Moorish" health products, echoes of which would be seen in Minister Farrakhan's own beleaguered line of P.O.W.E.R. cosmetics, and in the desire for land. Striving toward economic self-sufficiency at a most rudimentary level, the NOI established farms in Michigan, Alabama, and Georgia, paralleling the earlier existence of MSTA agricultural enterprises in Prince George County, Virginia; Long Island, New York; Woodstock, Connecticut; and the Berkshires of western Massachusetts.[19]

The Early Nation of Islam: 1930–1946

Established by one W. D. Fard (pronounced Fa-ROD) in Detroit in mid-1930, the Nation of Islam extolled a doctrine that was Islamic only in name. NOI beliefs regarding the anthropomorphic nature of God, the nonexistence of the hereafter, and polygenesis were sufficiently distant from not only the teachings of the Qur'an and the Hadith or Sunna, but mainstream Christianity as well.[20] Forged in the midst of the Great Depression, Master Fard's incipient religious views sought to address two problematic areas of African American working-class life. On the one hand lay the task of reinforcing a sense of personal dignity; on the other, promoting individual material welfare. For Fard, the elevation of black dignity and self-respect depended on the cultivation of a special African American relationship with God, as well as a selective challenging of prepotent views bearing on the origins of humanity and the beginnings of civilization. But the key to Master Fard's thought lay in the imaginative way in which he responded to *specific* arguments of pseudo-scientific racism, biblical cosmogony, and racialist historiography—all within the context of late nineteenth-century upheavals in American Protestantism.[21]

On one level he embraced the scientific viewpoint—or perhaps more accurately, its coattails—wholeheartedly. In the name of science Fard denied the existence of spirit, be it manifested as life in the hereafter or in the more exalted form of what he called the "mystery God" of Christianity. He attacked prevailing Christian teachings that offered the prospect of a good life only after physical death—a future bliss shimmering in stark contrast to the material misery in which African Americans actually found themselves during the depression. One's heaven and one's hell, Fard submitted, were right here on this earth.

Within Fard's worldview, divinity and humanity became as one. This fusion of matter and spirit offered a thorough reconstituting of the African American relationship to God, where "the Blackman" vaulted beyond the status even of God's chosen few to become the Creator incarnate: "The Holy Qur'an or Bible is made by the original people who is Allah, the Supreme Being or (Black man) of Asia." (Here one finds echoes of Moorish Science theology.) As the

Blackman acquired divinity, on the other hand, that same quality was simultaneously distilled into a privileged human form. In contrast to the "spook God" of Christianity, the divine savior of black folk was said to be a living, breathing, anthropomorphic entity in the person of W. D. Fard. Now, on different occasions, it is true, Fard had referred to himself as a prophet and the Son of Man, of whom "rain, hail, snow, and earthquakes" were incontestable manifestations. The Son of Man, he declared, was the "true" and "only" God. Sharing the deific pantheon, moreover, were twenty-three scientists who also played a crucial but enigmatic role in the functioning of the cosmos. But not until after the prophet's disappearance in 1934 would an ensuing religious faction headed by Elijah Muhammad openly claim that Fard himself was Allah, the supreme God, to whom was subordinated the commonplace godliness of the rank-and-file Blackman. No more the worse for its indeterminacy than the idea of the Christian Trinity, this dualistic notion of the divine would remain a pillar of NOI belief.[22]

W. D. Fard (again following Moorish Science lead) opted to promote the fictive identity of African Americans as civilized "Asiatic blacks," thus avoiding confusion with what he deemed to be the "uncivilized" ones of the African variety.[23] "Why does the devil call our people Africans?" asked Master Fard in *Lost Found Moslem Lesson No. 1.* "Answer: To make the people of North America believe that the people on that continent are the only people they have and are all savage." To the contrary, remarked the NOI's *Student Enrollment* catechism, "The Original Man is the Asiatic Blackman, The Maker, The Owner, the cream of the planet earth, God of the Universe." Fard also elevated black Americans to the position of "original people" of the planet, the Lost Tribe of Shabazz. The corollary of the assertion that "all black men are Gods" and of primeval origin was that white folk, the personification of Satan on earth, were said to have been created thousands of years later through a grafting process perfected by an evil black scientist named Yakub.

What also passed for science within NOI circles often was transmitted in the form of mathematically oriented puzzles, the solutions to which did not ordinarily translate into anticipated, arithmetic terms: "After learning Mathematics, which is Islam, and Islam is Mathematics, [it] stands true, you can always prove it at no limit of time," the NOI founder once claimed.[24] "Then you must learn to use it and secure some benefit while you are living—that is, luxury, money, good homes, friendship in all walks of life."[25] Although he was genuinely concerned with the material progress of his followers, there is no evidence that Master Fard advanced an overarching program of economic entrepreneurialism—unlike later developments within the NOI. On the other hand, his instilling of pride and self-respect among his flock (leading to their greater employability), coupled with his recommendations regarding the practice of frugal life styles and proper eating habits, did lead toward notable improvements in their material existence.[26]

Ultimately, the teachings of Master Fard would be received by his followers as knowledge gleaned from Islamic scripture, notwithstanding the doctrinal incongruities between the two or the lack of any mention of the Prophet Muhammad in NOI catechisms. Compared to the extended body of arguments elaborated by Elijah Muhammad beginning in the latter 1950s, Fard's theological legacy was both fragmented and thin—albeit enduring.[27] Following the latter's departure from the scene in mid-1934, after which the organization spun into decline, it was left to Muhammad to evolve a full-blown theology for the group—now variously known as the Allah Temple of Islam (ATOI) or the Holy Temple of Islam—based upon the rudimentary lessons left by his teacher.[28] But the ATOI's institutional reawakening would have to await Messenger Muhammad's release from prison in 1946, after nearly four years of incarceration.[29] Following his discharge, Muhammad made successful efforts to transform the Allah Temple from a small, inward-looking group to a major mass organization.[30]

In Transition: 1946–1958

Recently arrived southern migrants comprised the NOI/Allah Temple's bedrock constituency from the Great Depression through the early 1950s. The NOI had reached a height of some eight thousand members under W. D. Fard's leadership, but by the early 1950s the ATOI's main temple in Chicago claimed fewer than three hundred adherents.[31] However, the arrival of Malcolm X in 1952 following a six-year prison term was to transform everything. By his own account, Minister Malcolm was largely responsible for expanding the membership from approximately four hundred to forty thousand persons, and the number of temples in U.S. cities from four to well over a hundred.[32] While it is indubitably true that Malcolm X, at this stage, was hardly capable of developing the organization on his own, it seems equally clear that without the energetic assistance of his bright, young, and articulate new minister, Mr. Muhammad would have been hard pressed to expand his group beyond the status of a storefront religious operation.[33] Under the latter's overarching leadership there occurred a steady growth of ATOI-affiliated economic enterprises on a scale eventually extending far beyond Garvey's entrepreneurial legacy. By 1956 the Chicago headquarters boasted a temple, grade school, restaurant, bakery, grocery store, and apartment building. Chicken and beef sold in the grocery store were raised on the ATOI's 140-acre farm at White Cloud, Michigan. Additional businesses were in place by 1958, including an auto repair and paint shop, a laundry, a cleaning plant, and dress and haberdashery establishments.[34]

The Allah Temple's attraction to economic entrepreneurialism lay in a desire for not only economic self-sufficiency, but also the isolation of its followers "from the wicked people and impure life as much as possible."[35] But a decade later organizational growth had inspired overtures to the outer world as well as a return to the original group name. Each Wednesday and Friday the public was invited to nightly forums; marking a major turning point, the Nation of Islam's first truly public convention was held in 1957.[36] Beginning in June 1956 and continuing through August 1959, when the paper changed ownership, articles written by Mr. Muhammad appeared in a weekly column published in the nationally distributed African American newspaper, the *Pittsburgh Courier*. Thereafter, other newspapers, including *Muhammad Speaks* (founded by Malcolm X in May 1960), picked up the slack in the propagation of the NOI word.

The NOI's rapid growth, marked by a modest influence of traditional Islam, coincided with a now enlarged vision of the organization's domestic as well as international roles. Domestically, the NOI held claim to a more "dignified" way for black Americans to secure justice than that proposed by existing civil rights organizations, and asserted the superiority of (nominal) Islam over Christianity as the religion of choice. On the international plane the NOI sought to become the recognized leader of *all* Muslims on the North American continent. Ironically, the NOI's accelerated expansion occurred at a time when substantial civil rights gains by blacks were beginning to be effected in the American South. But the brutal backlash directed against black demonstrators and their supporters, set against the unchanging, marginalized social status of millions of unskilled and semi-skilled black workers, north as well as south, soon led to a questioning of the process by which civil rights leaders were pursuing the goal of black equality. Exploiting these various contradictions, the Nation of Islam counterposed the goal of "separation" to the one of "integration" espoused by mainstream civil rights groups; upheld the superiority of self-defense measures over the tactics of passive resistance;[37] and, as a counter to the prevailing American and Christian identities of black Americans, continued to lay claim to "Asiatic" and Islamic ones. The NOI doctrine of economic and political self-sufficiency was increasingly touted as the "alternative" to African American demands for civil rights— demands that NOI leaders unfairly but effectively characterized as "begging." As with Marcus Garvey (with parallels to Booker T. Washington before him), fundamental citizenship demands were bartered against quests for an African American political and economic autonomy that would never arrive.[38]

Meanwhile, Elijah Muhammad's intense period of Qur'anic study seems to have bolstered an expansive self-confidence on another front. In early 1959 the newly established public relations department of the NOI issued biographical sketches describing him as "The Messenger of Allah" and "Spiritual leader of the Moslems in the United States."[39] Within the tiny, North American Islamic community, the most vociferous challenge to such claims came from the Ahmadis, who possessed little clout in the larger Islamic world, and who domestically, by this time, had been out-organized by the NOI.[40] Belying his domestic critics, in late 1959 Mr. Muhammad undertook a successful visit to Mecca and the Middle East, an indication of the degree to which pragmatic elements within the Arab world were prepared to embrace the rise of Islam, however unorthodox, in the United States.[41]

Doctrinally speaking, the NOI's growth in membership and economic clout during the latter fifties was paralleled by increasing references to the Qur'an in the public writings and speeches of Elijah Muhammad. After advertising for an Arabic instructor for the NOI's grade school, known as the University of Islam, Muhammad received a response from a Palestinian Muslim by the name of Jamil Diab, who was to spend several years teaching at the institution.[42] Out of the close personal relationship that formed between Diab and Muhammad, the latter was exposed to the more traditional forms of Islam: conversance with the *Fatiha* (opening chapter of the Qur'an), *wudu'* (ablution), *salah* (the five daily prayers), as well as a greater respect for the Prophet Muhammad.[43] This new orientation was reflected in the weekly articles that Elijah Muhammad wrote for the *Pittsburgh Courier* at the time.[44] But the Messenger's *omra*, or small *hajj*, to Mecca would lead to a decisive change in direction, according to W. Deen Mohammed. During the 1930s Master Fard apparently had misled his followers into believing that the streets of Mecca were paved with gold, and that once qualified to visit the Holy City the believer would be offered a dazzling choice of mansions in which to reside. What Elijah Muhammad discovered in pre-OPEC Mecca, however, was little more than a rude awakening: unpaved roads; unadorned stone edifices, none taller than three stories; and an economy built upon the bazaar trade of peregrinators. Visits to other cities of the Middle East by this quintessentially American tourist did little to disabuse him of such impressions of rudimentary economic life. Although full of praise for leaders such as Egypt's Gamal Abdel Nasser and others, he no longer regarded the Arab material world as a fit example for black Americans, who assuredly would have to "do for self."

Secularization and Leftward Leanings: 1958–1964

From 1958 to 1964 the NOI entered a more secular phase as well, dominated by concerns with worldly matters and revolutionary political discourse. To be sure, the NOI had placed emphasis on material success since the time of W. D. Fard, when heaven and hell were judged to be "right here on earth!" But the expanding scale of operations was something else again. Although the social backgrounds of new ministers recruited by Malcolm X from the mid-1950s onward had begun to reflect a greater degree of formal education (with some even having college training), the same could not be said for the rank and file—at least immediately.[45] Lacking an educated constituency, the rapid growth of the organization's economic enterprises resulted in pressures to recruit outside technical and managerial staffs. Due to ongoing tensions with immigrant Arab Muslims who often disagreed with Mr. Muhammad's heterodox Islamic doctrine, the most acceptable and readily available source of personnel, it turned out, would be found within the black middle class. In March 1958 Mr. Muhammad publicly appealed to black intellectuals to join NOI efforts to develop African American self-sufficiency. His call for a "united front" of black men four months later made clear his ambitions to become a secular as well as a religious leader of black America.[46] Although Muhammad's larger aims seem to have gone unrealized, eventually African Americans representing ideological views ranging from hard-shelled nationalist to old left were tapped for various NOI positions. Christine Johnson took charge of running the Chicago-based University of Islam and preparing its curricular materials; Dick Durham, John Woodford, and Leon Forrest at various times held the top editorial posts at the weekly newspaper *Muhammad Speaks;* former SNCC leader Diane Nash Bevel became the newspaper's librarian; and journalists Charles P. Howard, Joe Walker, Charles Simmons, and numerous others played prominent roles as correspondents.[47] Although such individuals were salaried employees, not converts, over time the organization did manage to attract a larger percentage of "middle-class" blacks into its actual membership.[48]

The physical layout of *Muhammad Speaks* itself followed the successful format established in the *Pittsburgh Courier* and other similar black publications: one article (or, as in *Muhammad Speaks,* the centerfold) set aside for the weekly scriptural teachings of Elijah Muhammad, the remaining sections devoted primarily to secular news items and regular commentary bearing on women's interests, health, and international events. As the paper steered to the left under its exemplary editorship, Messenger Muhammad's apocalyptic and occasionally rambling articles on the center pages, surrounded by news stories devoted to anticolonial struggles, workers' strikes, antiwar demonstrations, and the plight of political prisoners, appeared incongruous at best. Nonetheless, the formula proved successful: far broader in scope than any black mainstream publication, *Muhammad Speaks* remained a source of hard-core news, introspective commentary, and spiritual sustenance for hundreds of thousands of devoted readers for over a decade.

Codified in newspaper layouts, the doctrinal division between secular and sacred was more significantly reflected in the respective public roles of Malcolm X and Elijah Muhammad from the late 1950s onward. Whereas Elijah Muhammad's writings and speeches occasionally touched upon secular themes, most thoughts that he cultivated for public consumption tended to be expressed in spiritual—generally apocalyptic—terms. And where the earliest public discourses of Malcolm X revolved largely around spiritual issues, by the 1960s the subject of religion, in his public teachings at least, was mentioned mostly in passing: "You aren't oppressed because you're a Baptist or a Methodist," Malcolm chided his African American audiences, "you're oppressed because you're black." Increasingly moved by the socialist revolutions successfully undertaken in China and Cuba, as well as the ongoing anti–imperialist struggles taking place in other parts of the "nonwhite" developing world, Malcolm X sought to cast the African American struggle for human rights in a more encompassing, revolutionary light. Thus while Messenger Muhammad's religious precepts remained invariant, Minister Malcolm's secular call for the political transformation of the United States was pushed to the outer limits. Despite the private sanction given this direction by Muhammad, Malcolm's revolutionary, rhetorical flourishes lacked institutional conviction, and it was left to the Black Panther Party to carry his "premature" call for armed struggle on U.S. soil to a disastrous end.

Officially departing the NOI in March 1964, Malcolm X perpetuated the NOI's spiritual-secular dichotomy by establishing autonomous, short-lived religious and secular organizations—the Muslim Mosque Incorporated (MMI) and the Organization of Afro-American Unity (OAAU), respectively.[49] By subsequently seeking to join the civil rights movement in a meaningful way, he also sought to break with the NOI's practice of "talking tough, but never doing anything."[50] Malcolm's assassination in February 1965 seems to have led to a significant falling off of NOI recruitment until the latter part of the decade, when the organization made a substantial comeback. (This revitalization, it should be noted, arrived at a time when civil rights and black power organizations were in terminal decline.)

Economic Development and Bourgeoisification:
1964–1975

At the NOI's third annual convention in 1959 Elijah Muhammad
announced a $20 million project to construct a mosque, school, and
hospital on six city blocks—an endeavor that was never realized.[51]
But building upon earlier acquisitions, by the early 1970s the NOI
had managed to accrue some $14.5 million in Chicago property,
including a string of small bakeries and cleaners, some forty-odd
rental units, a controlling interest in the Guaranty Bank and Trust
Co., a newspaper with annual profits of $3 million, and a super-
market that cleared $325,000 on sales of $1.7 million. The group
also ran a $22 million fish import business and held title to twenty
thousand acres of farm land in Michigan, Alabama, and Georgia—
some $6.2 million worth.[52]

Although overall organizational assets were often reported to
be as high as $70 or $80 million, those figures were much too gen-
erous, according to Wallace Muhammad, who estimated the NOI's
net worth in 1976 to be around $46 million.[53] On the debit side,
for example, there had existed three years earlier some $9.4 million
in long-term debt; losses accruing from the farm operations alone
came to almost $700,000 yearly; and millions of dollars in back taxes
were owed the Internal Revenue Service. Other problems cited
concerned subminimum-wage salaries for employees as well as lapses
in Social Security payments to the federal government. Due to a
severe lack of cash flow, an absence of technical and managerial skills,
and a downturn in the U.S. economy, at its early 1970s peak the
NOI's financial empire already lay in jeopardy. In a frantic effort to
obtain cash, the organization turned to Arab countries and, reportedly, to crime. A $3 million loan—used for the purchase of a Greek
orthodox church subsequently transformed into a mosque—was
obtained from Libya in 1973, but reported efforts to secure funds
from other Arab nations, in exchange for the NOI's relaxing of its

racial policies and the embrace of a more traditional Islam, ended in failure. Libya later refused a second loan request.[54]

The NOI's expanding economic crisis coincided with a deterioration in Elijah Muhammad's health and the effective control of NOI money affairs by a coterie of Chicago-based individuals known affectionately as the royal family: Fruit of Islam-head Raymond Sharrieff, Elijah's son-in-law; Hassan Sharrieff, grandson; and sons Herbert Muhammad and Elijah Muhammad, Jr.[55] With the NOI's growing bourgeoisification endorsed by Elijah Muhammad himself, the organization in early 1972 embarked upon a $2 million project involving the construction of five homes on South Woodlawn Avenue to be built for families of NOI officials at organizational expense.[56] While some NOI members felt such gifts to be well deserved, others took note of a widening economic gap between leaders and followers. In earlier years the NOI had prided itself on holding standards higher than those of the Christian church; now outsiders and some insiders as well began to question whether the difference between Muslim ministers and their stereotypical Christian counterparts was rooted in anything more than narrow doctrinal disagreements.

Responding to the corruptive "rise to power" of Mr. Muhammad's heirs apparent, a rebel group of young Muslims, described as "all in their twenties," took matters into their own hands. In October 1971 Raymond Sharrieff was the target of a botched assassination attempt; shortly thereafter, several dissidents were found murdered.[57] The following month, the group initiated a planned tour of NOI temples in some sixteen cities, ostensibly for the purpose of forming a new organization. But in early 1972 the trip ended tragically in Baton Rouge, Louisiana, where the insurgents had held a rally that culminated in the deaths of two white deputy sheriffs and an equal number of NOI adherents. From his Chicago headquarters, Elijah Muhammad denied any knowledge of the incident.[58] But further incidents of bloodshed—for which calculated efforts at destabilization cannot be ruled out as a contributing factor—would continue to mar the NOI's public image.[59] A year later, in Washington, D.C., a group of NOI disciples murdered seven members of a Hanafi Muslim sect, including five children.[60] Four months later Hakim A. Jamal, cousin of the late Malcolm X and an outspoken critic of Elijah Muhammad, was executed in his Roxbury, Massachusetts, home. The following September James Shabazz, minister of the Newark mosque, was assassinated by former NOI members said to belong to an insurgent group known as the New World of Islam, a tragedy that led to the subsequent murder and decapitation of four other African American Muslims in Newark.[61]

The Passing of Elijah: From Nation to World Community

Elijah Muhammad's death in February 1975 set into motion a chain of events that would change the face of Islam in the United States.[62] Taking firm charge of the NOI, Wallace Muhammad instituted theological and structural changes at a dizzying pace. Four months after taking command, he announced a change in policy permitting whites to join the group; around the same time the first female minister was appointed. Harlem Temple No. 7 on 116th Street was renamed after Malcolm X, and a new temple opened in Spanish Harlem in an effort to increase the number of Hispanic members. Legal fees for NOI members accused of crimes were no longer to be automatically paid. The NOI's stringent dress code was relaxed, its security force, the Fruit of Islam, abolished. No longer celebrated, as in the past, as a commemorative religious holiday, Savior's Day in 1976 was made the occasion of the first-year anniversary report; the following year the observance became known as Survival Day. By early 1978 it was reported that every top-ranking administrative post had been changed at least twice, with ministers placed on fixed salaries at $150–300 per week, instead of being able to set their own rate. The ministers—now designated as *imams*—were removed from business operations, and unprofitable enterprises were scrapped.[63] In line with these structural transformations, a most fundamental change occurred within NOI doctrine as well. No longer would the racialized elements of NOI eschatology issue from its gatherings and propaganda organs: the organization's beliefs were becoming fully consonant with those of Sunni Islam. Prophet Muhammad was declared to be seal of the prophets also known as the Final Prophet, the Holy Qur'an the last book. Henceforth the group would observe the Five Pillars of Islam, the *yaum al-jumu'a* (Friday congregational prayers), as well as the practice of traditional *salats*, or prayers, for which seats were ripped out of the former temples in order to provide appropriate space.[64]

The financial turmoil resulting from Elijah Muhammad's having died intestate pitted the claims of some family members against those of the organization. For years, cash had been taken in with no accountability; in many instances Elijah Muhammad's personal holdings proved inseparable from those of the NOI. As a result, some of the properties, including Your Supermarket, the Fish House, Salaam Restaurant, and the Shabazz Bakery, were divided among the family; others went to the organization.[65] In the process the state did its best to withhold as many resources as possible from the NOI.[66] In mid-1986 a Chicago probate court ruled that a $5.7 million Poor Fund Account belonged not to the former Nation of Islam, but to Mr. Muhammad's personal estate. Awarding the amount to his twenty-two documented children,[67] the court ordered the repository for the account, Dai-Ichi Kangyo Bank (formerly First Pacific Bank) of Chicago, to relinquish the funds.[68]

Having inherited an economic morass that was years in the making, Wallace Muhammad announced to his followers in 1976, "You are in debt, debt, debt."[69] With the selling off or leasing of NOI properties, millions of dollars of inherited financial obligations were eventually retired. Stepping down as leader of the WCIW in 1978, Muhammad noted that the organization's "image has been changed from one of financial empire to one of a real religious movement and I hope it remains that way."[70] But the claim was not quite accurate: Although the WCIW had dropped the rhetoric of economic nationalism and involuntarily liquidated many of its properties, the quest for economic empire seems to have burned just as strongly as ever.[71] Early the following year, American Pouch Foods, Inc. (APF), a joint economic venture begun by the WCIW and members of Chicago's Chinese business community, signed an eighteen-month initial contract with the Defense Department to produce "MRE" (meal-ready-to-eat) plastic and foil pouches, replacing the C-rations formerly used by U.S. combat troops. After missing two delivery dates, its $21.3 million contract (the largest ever awarded a minority-controlled firm) was canceled, and APF folded. Despite this setback, by 1986 enterprises under Warith Deen Mohammed's command claimed properties worth $12 million.[72]

In order to cushion the rapid pace of ideological and structural changes occurring within the organization, a series of transitional stages was undertaken by leadership. Beginning in early 1976, as a sop to repressed nationalist undercurrents within the organization, members were referred to as Bilalians, after the devout Abyssinian Muslim, Bilal ibn Rabah, whom the Prophet Muhammad appointed as the first *muezzin,* one who calls the prayer. Thereafter, the *Muhammad Speaks* newspaper became the *Bilalian News.*[73] Later that year the NOI name was changed to the World Community of al-Islam in the West, a move that emphasized the internationalist ties of Muslims over the nationalistic bonds of African Americans, or *ummah* over *'asabiya.*[74] In the spring of 1980 the group renamed itself the American Muslim Mission, an identification retained until its dissolution five years later. At that point formerly affiliated mosques were urged to "associate and collaborate with other Islamic groups of all races and ethnic origins."[75]

With changes in religious orientation came a newfound focus on American patriotism: "The problem is," affirmed Wallace Muhammad in 1978, "we don't identify with America. . . . We haven't been raised to believe that citizens have a voice and power." It was, of course, the centuries-old suppression of the "voice and power" of African Americans that, for many of them, had soured any sense of devotion to the state. But on July 4, 1979, with optimism ringing in the air, thousands of Bilalians marched down Chicago's Michigan Avenue bearing American flags and posters affirming their patriotism: "America Is Hope," "Races Unite!" "Build One Nation!"[76] "How can we better serve this country?" Imam Warith Mohammed was asked in a later interview. "We cannot make much of a contribution to the country as citizens," he replied, "if we ourselves don't have those healthy sensitivities that the citizens have for the future of the country in politics and even in business."[77] Mohammed's "sensitivities" were later reflected in his support for conservative Republican political candidates throughout the 1980s and early 1990s, including his backing of George Bush over Bill Clinton.[78] His highly publicized leading of the U.S. Senate in prayer, in February 1992, has been depicted by some as a decisive, symbolic victory for Islam in the United States, by others as a shameful sellout to the Great Satan. Despite undeniable changes in secular as well as religious orientation, Mohammed remains wedded to earlier NOI precepts of self-sufficiency, economic entrepreneurialism, and political conservatism. Today he has become the most prominent spokesperson for Islam in the United States, but his direct constituency is much smaller. "I represent my supporters who are mostly African American Muslims of one history and one aim—excellence,"[79] Imam Mohammed recently affirmed. Precise figures are still hard to come by, but in 1986, by his own account, that represented some twenty-five to thirty thousand active supporters.[80] The fact of Mohammed's wide-ranging influence has not been lost on Islamic states eager to gain influence over U.S. foreign policy. But he has rejected any lobbying role for himself, along with an unprecedented opportunity to employ the international pressure of Arab states to improve the social conditions of black Americans.

A Ruffling of Ill Winds: The Rebirth of the NOI

In early 1977 Wallace Muhammad claimed that only five or six ministers had departed the organization as a result of his newly implemented policies.[81] Significantly, however, old-guard administrators John Ali, Abass Rassoull, and Raymond Sharrieff had been ousted.[82] Minister Silis Muhammad departed the organization soon after it was opened up to whites, as did Minister Jeremiah Shabazz. Independently of one another, Muslim chapters in Culver City, California, and Dothan, Alabama, began publishing newspapers bearing the name *Muhammad Speaks* after the original organ was renamed *Bilalian News*.[83] Then, beginning in early 1978, the WCIW reportedly suffered a plunge in membership, an event given impetus, no doubt, by the official departure of Abdul Aleem Farrakhan, the name by which Louis Farrakhan was then known. Details are lacking, but it was apparently this deteriorating state of affairs that forced the resignation of Wallace Muhammad as organizational head in the fall of that same year and led to his replacement by a regional council of six imams.[84] By May 1985 the group, after going by the name of the American Muslim Mission for a period of five years, elected to disband, allowing its several hundred masjids to go their own way.

Minister Farrakhan's break with the WCIW became known to the general public in March of 1978, but he had already indicated plans to reestablish the Nation of Islam the previous November, despite having been offered his former position as head of the Harlem mosque several months earlier.[85] When dissatisfied followers of W. Deen Mohammed departed the WCIW, however, they did not do so in order to attach themselves to a reconstituted NOI, for there was no public organization to join, no open proselytizing on Farrakhan's part—a cautionary lesson gleaned, no doubt, from Malcolm X's tragic departure from the parent organization fourteen years earlier. The new movement began subterraneanly, reproducing itself in temporary storefronts and makeshift back rooms. As one observer notes, "Not until 1980 did the Minister start picking up momentum with a national telephone conference call to followers. The first Savior's Day convention in 1981 attracted an estimated 5,000 to 8,000 people. A permanent office wasn't acquired until the Final Call building was purchased in 1982."[86] But the real organizational takeoff had to await Jesse Jackson's presidential campaign in 1984. From that point forward the NOI enjoyed a meteoric rise, which has resulted in the presence today of some 120 mosques in U.S. urban centers and several internationally, as well as the establishment of a multimillion dollar economic empire dependent, in large measure, on public funds.[87] Included in that empire are not-for-profit organizations such as the *Final Call* newspaper, Muhammad University of Islam, and a network of mosques that themselves engage in business, but also profit-making enterprises privately held by members of Minister Farrakhan's inner circle. The latter include companies engaged in soap and cosmetics distribution, pharmaceuticals, media ventures, restaurants, clothing stores, and, most lucratively, apartment-complex security firms tied to government funding.[88]

Old Teachings v. New Realities

It is apparent, in retrospect, that in the late 1970s and early 1980s conditions were far from conducive to a return to an unmodified NOI ideology and practice. At the forefront lay challenges spawned by the triumphs of the civil rights movement as well as the mounting social problems of African countries in the wake of formal decolonization. Second, the collapse of inner-city economic life wrought by the deindustrializing of America had undercut the dreams of traditional entrepreneurial nationalism. Third, fueled by immigrant forces as well as African American conversions, an unprecedented dissemination of traditional Islam throughout the

United States had taken place. And, finally, there existed a double problem bearing upon Farrakhan's own legitimation. One concerned his relation to both the Prophet Muhammad and Elijah Muhammad, as he had initially endorsed the direction taken by the WCIW. The other arose with respect to the moribund civil rights establishment and involved obtaining its blessings for his ability to rally grassroots blacks while remaining aloof from actual civil rights projects. Compared to the earlier climate of corporate liberalism, however, the rise of ultra-right political formations in the eighties posed no clear disadvantages to a reconstituted NOI, which, like its predecessor, embraced a highly conservative social outlook.[89]

Passage and subsequent enforcement of the Civil Rights and Voting Rights acts in 1964 and 1965 transformed the domestic political landscape in numerous ways. The effect upon African American nationalism in particular was to lay to rest a principal source of African American political alienation: the suppression of black voting rights in the South. Many African Americans—particularly those undergoing socialization in subsequent years—would begin to think of themselves as undisputed citizens of the United States. Then too, as time went by, the mounting social difficulties of nominally independent African states—as measured in outbreaks of famines, plagues, and ethnically based political strife—rendered increasingly bleak the utopian vision of an African American "return" to the continent. The overall result could only be a further undermining of traditional African American arguments for domestic territorial autonomy as well as emigrationism.[90] Adjusting to these new realities, Minister Farrakhan declared in 1985:

> God wants us to build a new world order. A new world order based on peace, justice and equality. Where do we start? . . . Physical separation is greatly feared [by whites], and it is not now desired by the masses of black people, but America is not willing to give us eight or ten states, or even one state. Let's be reasonable. . . . What we propose tonight is a solution that is in be-

tween two extremes. If we cannot go back to Africa, and America will not give us a separate territory, then what can we do here and now to redress our own grievances? . . . We propose that we use the blessings that we have received from our sojourn in America to do for ourselves what we have been asking the whites in this nation to do for us.[91]

What "doing for self" meant, in Farrakhan's words, was the "redirecting of our 204 billion dollar purchasing power." But at the close of the twentieth century, such a strategy could only mean a return to the program of economic nationalism advanced by Booker T. Washington a century ago, with its attendant downplaying of civil and political rights. Such an outlook remains problematic even without the NOI's former policy of denouncing these rights, and especially so given today's conditions.[92] For the NOI, the collapse of inner-city economic life in the 1980s revealed a twofold edge: on the one side, a growth in the numbers of disaffected African Americans who would become potential candidates for NOI re-cruitment; on the other, evaporating community resources that a revitalized NOI could no longer draw upon in its attempt to regain and even surpass Elijah Muhammad's former economic empire. Simply put, the time-tested entrepreneurial nationalism of former decades was no longer sufficient. Despite $5 million in start-up capital from Libyan Colonel Muammar Gadhafi, in the 1980s, Farrakhan's P.O.W.E.R. line of Clean & Fresh toiletries remains in a state of economic limbo—not quite moribund but not exactly thriving either.[93] The NOI's fish importation business, Blue Seas, was dissolved in 1982; its successor, Blue Seas Chicago, faced an identical fate ten years later.[94] Faced with uninspiring returns from such ventures, Minister Farrakhan, following the lead of W. Deen Mohammed, began to solicit government contracts—a complete turnabout from earlier NOI practices.[95]

In the late 1930s NOI members had refused Social Security identification numbers, regarding them as "the mark of the beast."

In soliciting funds from the "white folks' government" half a century later, Farrakhan could no longer portray federal and state agencies as undistilled repositories of satanic influence. The new trajectory began with the NOI's successful attempt to rid a Baltimore housing project of drug dealers; thereafter, the NOI sought federal and local monies for similar purposes in Washington, D.C., Los Angeles, Dayton, Pittsburgh, Chicago, and elsewhere.[96] The irony is that the positive cash flow to security firms privately owned by members of the Farrakhan family circle depends on the continued existence of inner-city crime.

Under Elijah Muhammad the NOI developed modest retail and service enterprises centered around its urban mosques, as well as an unprofitable, small-scale agribusiness. But as one commentator has noted, the organization "never entered such lucrative fields as middle-level retailing, wholesaling, manufacturing, insurance, and investment."[97] Recently, following what has been characterized in the press as a three-year plan, the NOI opened a $5 million food-service complex, called Salaam Restaurant, on 79th Street in Chicago—a dramatic, albeit local, achievement in substance as well as symbol.[98] Also planned is the expansion of the NOI's trucking firm, restaurant outlets in four U.S. cities, and a two thousand-seat auditorium.[99] Such ventures are not impractical to attain, but will nonetheless require onerous tithing of devoted followers. Yet there also have been economic moves that seem far more symbolic than substantial. For example, while Farrakhan's partial reclaiming of former NOI land in southwest Georgia in early 1995 clearly indicated his determination to reassemble the NOI's former economic empire, the reality was that, under Elijah Muhammad's direction, the farms had amassed debts of nearly three-quarters of a million dollars per year. Presently, the NOI is said to own two thousand acres of land in Michigan and Georgia, with plans to acquire eight thousand more. But the question remains as to whether the present-day NOI has truly managed the art of running a small-scale agribusiness, or has allowed its economic vision to be clouded by nostalgic yearnings.[100]

Legitimation: Responses to Tradition and Orthodoxy

In electing to return to the old teachings, Farrakhan faced a two-fold problem of legitimation: finding acceptance among the NOI faithful as the Messenger's rightful heir, on the one hand; and on the other, cultivating a sense of ambivalence, if not approval, within traditional Islamic circles regarding his spiritual authenticity. Formidable obstacles blocked Minister Farrakhan's belated bid to insert himself in the direct line of leadership succession to Elijah Muhammad. For three years, after all, the world was made to understand that Wallace Muhammad, son of Elijah, had been chosen by the Messenger of Allah as his successor. And Louis Farrakhan himself had proclaimed, "No ill winds will ruffle this divine nation. No one among us is high enough to tie the shoelaces of Wallace."[101] Since a direct endorsement from Elijah Muhammad was no longer possible, Farrakhan was forced to pursue a more symbolic route to legitimation. By purchasing the Messenger's former homes in Chicago and Phoenix, as well as the NOI's original mosque and school on South Stony Island in Chicago, he placed himself literally at the seat of former power. Second, by gradually reassembling the economic empire of his former teacher, he is showing himself to be the Messenger's equal in secular affairs—a claim that, of course, could never be stated openly without dissolving the mystique of Mr. Muhammad's proffered omniscience.

Fortuitously, the critical endorsement that once seemed impossible eventually came to pass. In the fall of 1989 Minister Farrakhan revealed that while visiting Mexico *four years earlier* he had received a *vision* in which he was transported inside the NOI's Mother Plane (better known as Ezekiel's Wheel of the Old Testament). There, via a loudspeaker, the voice of Elijah Muhammad came to him bearing a cryptic warning regarding U.S. plans to wage war on Libya. But it appears that the more important objective of Farrakhan's thoroughly remarkable press conference on the subject—captured on videotape and widely circulated by the NOI in pamphlet form as well—was to demonstrate an unassailable affirmation of Elijah Muhammad's support for him.[102]

Equal in import to the partial civil rights victories of the 1960s was an amendment to the U.S. Immigration and Nationality Act, effective at the very end of 1965, that sparked the entry of foreign-born Muslims into the United States by the hundreds of thousands. From 1965 to 1986 the number of Muslim immigrants admitted to the United States each year (most of whom hailed from the Middle East, North Africa, and Asia) multiplied by a factor of eight. By the latter year the total number of Muslims living within U.S. borders was estimated at four million.[103] Carried past immigration check-points by an unprecedented wave of adherents, traditional Islam rapidly spread to key U.S. cities, further narrowing the possibilities for the Nation of Islam to pass off its private doctrine as being syn-onymous with Qur'anic wisdom. The pressure on Farrakhan to drop, or at least to modify, basic NOI beliefs became formidable.

One of the most visible breeches of Islamic tradition existed in the form of prayer originally taught by Master Fard. In order to close the ritualistic gap, a West African sheikh was brought in to instruct the faithful in matters of traditional prayer.[104] Regarding the vast difference between its projected doctrine and that of tradi-tional Islam, however, the NOI has resorted to a number of expla-nations, including a cabalist twist affirming the existence of two Qur'ans—the esoteric, manifest version with which all Muslims are familiar, and a more profound, esoteric one whose meaning can be divulged only through numerological analysis of the former.[105] But when all else fails, the organization reverts to Elijah Muhammad's stock explanation: The NOI version of Islam is tailored to African American conditions, while that of Arabs is excessively ethnocen-tric, if not tainted by racism. In contrast to an earlier era, on the other hand, the demonizing of Euro-Americans has been more or less downplayed, bringing the NOI that much closer to the uni-versal ideals portrayed in the Qur'an.[106]

Facing potential isolation due to the growing numbers of traditional Muslims in the United States, Minister Farrakhan has sought alliances with black secular organizations in a way reminiscent of the earlier, fruitless outreaches of Elijah Muhammad. Also, he likely viewed his links to the Congressional Black Caucus as according greater potential access to government contracts. Moreover, given the demonstrated reality of African American citizenship and the apparent lack of political alternatives, participation in electoral politics (an issue that Elijah Muhammad treated equivocally in earlier years but without actually ever endorsing a candidate[107]) would be increasingly difficult for Farrakhan to avoid, especially given the overt political activities of W. Deen Mohammed.[108] The careful groundwork laid in developing these political liaisons was uprooted by public outrage over continuing anti-Jewish remarks made by Minister Farrakhan and one of his associates (now former spokesman), Khalid Abdul Muhammad.[109] Questions remain as to why Farrakhan resorted to anti-Jewish diatribes in the first instance, and why he continues to hold his ground on the issue despite a resultant undermining of his business enterprises and political alliances.

Anti-Semitism and the Clash of Right-Wing Nationalisms

Once again, the history of the UNIA proves instructive. When the political content of Garveyism shifted to the right in mid-1921, its characterization of the chief enemy of black liberation in the United States underwent a transmigration as well—from the dominant classes, government, craft unions, and groups such as the Ku Klux Klan, to *black people themselves.* "Having had the wrong education as a start in his racial career, the Negro has become his own worst enemy," wrote Garvey in 1923, responding to formidable attacks that had mostly to do with his repudiation of civil rights for black

Americans.[110] In this way, the UNIA's African American detractors conveniently served as an external threat contributing to the organization's internal cohesion, as well as a ready scapegoat whenever UNIA plans failed to evolve as anticipated. Moreover, the militant, public condemnations and threats that Garvey unleashed upon such critics not only stoked his mass popularity, but also tended to obscure the conservative political content of his domestic message. Needless to say, his attacks upon civil rights advocates also endeared him to trenchant Negrophobes who, when all was said and done, had no more use for Marcus Garvey than for those whom he publicly chastised.

Identical factors hold true with respect to Minister Farrakhan's effective characterizing of Jews as a principal enemy of African Americans, beginning in mid-1984.[111] It is worth remembering, however, that when criticisms of Jews arose within the old NOI, they tended to do so within specific contexts. One of these was experientially based, centering on the economic exploitation of blacks by Jewish landlords and merchants (usually in cities of the northeastern United States). Another concerned the negative impact of Israel, backed by the economic and military might of the United States, on Middle East Islamic states. And a third was tied up with revelations of Israeli government support for South African apartheid. But Elijah Muhammad's NOI was never overly concerned with the subject of Jews: "We make no distinction between Jews and non-Jews so long as they are all white," Malcolm X once stated. "To do so would be to imply that we like some whites better than others. This would be discrimination, and we do not believe in discrimination."[112] However, what Farrakhan was to learn in the 1980s, perhaps by happenstance, was that his verbal attacks on Jews carried the same political advantages as had Marcus Garvey's diatribes against his black critics in the 1920s, including the support of the ultra-right. Just as Garvey had elicited the support of Negrophobes for his attacks on civil rights advocates, so did Farrakhan gain the approval of powerful right-wing, anti-Semitic forces for his verbal assaults against Jews. For example, shortly after the minister's anti-Jewish campaign took hold in the mid-1980s, the organ of the ultra-right National States Rights Party denounced a recent publicizing by the media of Martin Luther King's pro-Jewish statements of the 1960s: "The future leader of the blacks will not be a King who bows to the Jews," one of its articles concluded, "IT WILL BE A FARRAKHAN WHO HAS THE GUTS TO STAND UP TO THE JEWS!"[113]

Farrakhan's anti-Jewish stance brought additional benefits as well: a generating of publicity disproportionate to the actual instances of such remarks uttered in public, and an appeal to anti-Zionist elements throughout the Arab world. Aside from those instances when his remarks were twisted or edited by the media to make them appear what they were not, Jewish Americans had every reason to be offended by his numerous, confirmed statements bearing an anti-Jewish character.[114] The continued proliferation of anti-Semitic rhetoric has placed principled Jewish organizations in a quandary. Any reluctance on their part to respond to anti-Semitism is to invite its spread; but to overreact, on the other hand—for example, by presumptuously demanding that African American organizations repudiate any connections with Farrakhan—is to risk providing ammunition for Farrakhan's classic anti-Semitic claims of "Jewish domination and control." However, in much the same way that Minister Farrakhan has offered a distorted portrait of Jews as the principal enemy of blacks, right-wing Jewish institutions such as the Anti-Defamation League have themselves dishonestly characterized blacks as the most dangerous single bloc of anti-Semites in the United States.[115] As one perceptive journalist remarked, "One can only speculate on the reasons why so much time and energy are wasted savaging Farrakhan, especially when there are white fascist paramilitary organizations running around the country dedicated to the physical extermination of their many 'enemies,' most prominently American Jews."[116]

Fortunately or otherwise, the issue of "black anti-Semitism" as the main danger to Jewish Americans took a back seat following the bombing of the Oklahoma City federal building by (apparent) members of an ultra-right paramilitary group, only one of many that seem quite prepared to use force to eliminate Jews and African Americans (not to mention government agents of whatever ethno-racial background) from the face of the earth. And, most recently, Farrakhan's approaches to Jews have tended to be vacillatory and equivocal, intermixing anti-Semitic outbursts on one day with violin concerts of atonement on the next. For Farrakhan as for Garvey, the challenge of reconciling competing demands of mass organizational dynamics and primitive capital accumulation appears to be an onerous one.

The Million Man March and Its Aftermath

Constituting one of the most uplifting media events of the twentieth century, the Million Man March held on October 16, 1995, marked the highest point of Minister Louis Farrakhan's tenure over the Nation of Islam.[117] The purpose of this Washington, D.C., pilgrimage, celebrated as a "Holy Day of Atonement and Reconciliation," was, according to Farrakhan, to "reconcile our spiritual inner beings and to redirect our focus to developing our communities, strengthening our families, working to uphold and protect our civil and human rights, and empowering ourselves through the Spirit of God, more effective use of our dollars, and through the power of the vote."[118] As a symbolic gathering, the Million Man March was an unqualified success. But the real measure of its significance would lie in its "follow-up" activities, the presence or absence of which would determine whether the march would be enshrined as a perennial "feel good" symbol, or, more hopefully, function as a catalyst for a genuine grassroots movement capable of fulfilling its stated aims. The answer would rest in the quality of programs and mechanisms that march leaders would put into operation, as well as in their determination to carry them out. Two years following the Million Man March, the balance sheet offers decidedly mixed results.

The organizational vehicles assigned to transforming the energies of the march into coordinated activity at the grassroots level were the some 340 Local Organizing Committees (LOCs) that brought the march into being (and that were reportedly composed of local political, religious, business, and community leaders) and the National African American Leadership Summit (NAALS) chaired by former NAACP head Benjamin Chavis. Organs such as the *Final Call* tend to carry little information on the progress of such groups, and independently tracking their work is a difficult task. However, charges did arise just months following the march that NAALS, although conceived as a collective black leadership forum, was not truly functioning in that spirit.[119] On a more positive note, even mainstream media most hostile to Farrakhan have conceded that the positive spirit generated by the Million Man March has inspired a greater participation of black men in the affairs of their communities. In the Denver black community, for example, the firebombing of homes by youth gangs in the winter of '96 was met by African American public pressure organized by the local march committee, thereby (arguably) contributing to a curtailing of gang activities.[120] To cite yet another positive example, NOI Mosque No. 13 in Springfield, Massachusetts, under the leadership of Minister Yusuf Muhammad, has enrolled a large cross-section of the Springfield black community in its Million Man March Committee, which meets regularly to plan proactive interventions in local affairs.[121]

Judged by the effusive rhetoric of the Million Man March, one would think that the NOI's national leadership might have poured considerable resources into such Local Organizing Committees, identifying those that have been most successful in community outreach projects and publicizing their specific successes as well as organizing techniques. To the contrary, three months following the march, Louis Farrakhan embarked on a World Friendship Tour, which carried him to some twenty countries in Africa and the Middle East. This tour became, in essence, an international evangelical crusade, the aim of which was to "take the spirit of the . . . Million Man March to Africa and establish an international Day of Atonement, Responsibility and Reconciliation."[122] (However, the quixotic content of Minister Farrakhan's World Friendship Tour theme, not to mention his subsequent role as apologist for General Sani Abacha's brutal military regime in Nigeria, should not be allowed to obscure the noteworthy fact that Minister Farrakhan is the first African American since El-Hajj Malik el-Shabazz—Malcolm X—to be received by African and Middle East governments as a de facto head of state.)

In October 1996, at an observance held in front of United Nations headquarters to commemorate the first anniversary of the march, Minister Farrakhan declared that the purpose of the anniversary was to "atone for violence, murder, and war, and to call the kings and rulers of the earth to atonement for violence, murder, and war; and to call the members of the human family, and our Black family, in particular, to the spirit and process of atonement for violence in the world and in our communities and the lust to kill that pervades this society, and pervades the earth."[123] But even if "violence, murder, and war" are not endemic to the human condition, it is clear that Farrakhan's unfocused "soul-saving" crusade is a goal without a foreseeable end. On a more tangible plane, on the other hand, march organizers also convened a National Political Convention—the agenda of which included a call for transforming American politics to a "God-centered system"—on September 27–29, 1996 in St. Louis. But outside sources claimed a gathering of only some four hundred to six hundred delegates, with an additional five thousand persons in attendance at Minister Farrakhan's keynote address. Where Minister Farrakhan may go from here is anyone's guess, but his direction at this time would seem to be other than toward the strengthening of grassroots community organizations, over which the Nation of Islam would have difficulty exerting direct

control, and therefore away from some of the more tangible man-
dates of the Million Man March.[124]

On the positive side of the balance sheet, Louis Farrakhan
often provides an exemplary example of black male leadership. He
articulates the aspirations of large numbers of African Americans
(including our entrepreneurial strata) and speaks out forcefully against
incidents of African American oppression. Generally speaking, his
internationalism presents a salutary aspect of his leadership as well,
a constant reminder that we, as black Americans, must strive to avoid
the trap of parochial thinking and steadfastly conceive of solutions
to our social and political problems in global terms. Finally, whatever may have been the limitations of the Million Man March, it
has provided a catalyst for untold numbers of black men to involve
themselves in their local communities, an achievement that cannot
be gainsaid even by Farrakhan's most trenchant critics.

Viewed overall, however, Minister Farrakhan's liabilities may
far outweigh his positive contributions. He is, in the first instance,
burdened by an appropriation of multiple public leadership roles
and a proffering of agendas too numerous for any one individual or
organization to carry out coherently. He is simultaneously the helms-
man of the Nation of Islam, a significant spiritual and political leader
of black America, an international shuttling diplomat and evange-
list, an American celebrity figure of outstanding rank, and the head
of an entrepreneurial "royal family" dedicated to the amassing of
private wealth. The fulfillment of these roles tends to pull him in
contradictory directions, and the inherent conflicts of interest are
often glaring. Farrakhan's public actions, moreover, have frequently
proved capricious, if not downright irresponsible. That freedom of
speech should be tempered by personal and political responsibility
is a lesson that has not come easily to this leader of tens of thousands. Too often his public posturings seem geared more toward
obtaining a greater "market share" of media attention than toward
forging solutions for African America's unending problems. And
whenever, in such cases, the minister draws inevitable fire either

from government or from well-heeled right-wing organizations, black folk feel nonetheless compelled to publicly defend his actions, however whimsical, thus siphoning away energies that might be used for infinitely more constructive purposes.

With respect to his undisputed oratorical abilities, Minister Farrakhan, compared with the late Malcolm X, as he invariably is, leans more toward exhortation than elucidation, swapping the possibilities of genuine instruction for the pinnacles of inspirational rhetoric. Entertaining bouts of scriptural prophecy, conspiratorial conjecturing, and word play usually overshadow meaningful analysis in Farrakhan's powerful—often vituperative—speeches. His recent infatuation with the theme of atonement seeks to elicit social solutions by means of individual confession rather than through broad structural change. And finally, his employ of equivocal language more often than not masks the lack of clear-cut policy. For example, even today the minister cannot seem to make up his mind as to whether or not the Nation of Islam is a separatist organization. At times he dismisses separatism as a viable option; at other moments he projects it as a fall-back position if African Americans fail to obtain full citizenship rights in the United States. On top of it all, he continues to employ the old NOI's prophetic language of political separation ("Come out of her, my people" [Revelation 18:4], for example, reinterpreting the passage as the need for black people to "come out" of old ways of thinking).[125]

Louis Farrakhan remains the militant voice of the downtrodden and the dispossessed among African Americans. Long-range indications, however, are that African American Muslims as a whole will remain a conservative political force wedded to the vision of economic empire. From this perspective, the upward economic mobility of black Americans is scheduled to arrive in the form of capital accumulation by brute force, large proceeds of which are actually destined for private bank accounts, zakat notwithstanding. One of the long-term, salutary roles of the NOI, both old and new, has been its demonstrated capacity to resurrect the "fallen" of the race and restore them to productive lives. But the unfinished task of providing African American communities with a full measure of political and economic democracy would appear to lie far outside the confines of the "bootstrap" economic policies proposed by Minister Farrakhan. Surely a better fate awaits black Americans than as mere consumers of goods and services proffered beneath the NOI's entrepreneurial tent. Such a strategy cannot even begin to engage the corporate roots of African American economic disenfranchisement. The alternative, one admittedly difficult as well as dangerous, is a *collective* assault upon the structures of institutionalized inequity. If a large-scale, more socially progressive African American Islamic movement is ever to emerge, it is likely to come not from within existing organizations, but rather from a splintering off of new groups against the backdrop of an emerging, broad-based secular movement for social change in the United States.

Notes

1. Carol L. Stone, "Estimate of Muslims Living in America," in *The Muslims of America,* ed. Yvonne Yazbeck Haddad (New York: Oxford University Press, 1991), 27.

2. Earlier influences came, of course, from enslaved African Muslims during the antebellum period; however, between life in the slave quarters and that of twentieth-century African American communities, no demonstrable continuity of Islamic institutions can be found. From 1920 onward a more durable, albeit heterodox source of Islamic teachings was available through the Ahmadiyyah movement. See Allan D. Austin, *African Muslims in Antebellum America: Proud Exiles* (New York: Routledge, forthcoming 1997); Michael A. Gomez, "Muslims in Early America," *Journal of Southern History* 60 (November 1994): 671–710; Clyde-Ahmad Winters, "Afro-American Muslims—From Slavery to Freedom," *Islamic Studies,* 17.4 (1978): 187–205; and Richard B. Turner, "The Ahmadiyya Mission to Blacks in the United States in the 1920s," *Journal of Religious Thought* 44 (Winter–Spring 1988): 50–66.

3. Information for most of these groups is extremely sketchy. The LFNOI, with some twenty mosques located mainly on the eastern seaboard and in the South, was founded in August 1977 and has published its newspaper, *Muhammad Speaks,* since 1984.

Publisher of the weekly newspaper, *Your Muhammad Speaks,* and in existence at least since 1992, the UNOI also claims mosques in Missouri and Connecticut. From the Highland Park enclave of Detroit, Michigan, John Muhammad's organization publishes its own newspaper, *Muhammad Speaks Continues.* H. Khalif Khalifah reports the existence of some ten independent organizations (the aforementioned groups included) bearing the NOI name in one form or another, including a mosque in Cleveland, Ohio, two in Richmond, Virginia, and one in the Bronx, New York City. Details concerning the LFNOI and its ideology have recently become available in Peter Noel, "One Nation?" *Vibe* (February 1996): 73; and Mattias Gardell, *In the Name of Elijah Muhammad: Louis Farrakhan and the Nation of Islam* (Durham, North Carolina: Duke University Press, 1996), 215–23. For further, brief information on the UNOI, see Peter Noel, "The Final Call: Power Struggle in the Nation of Islam," *Village Voice* (February 15, 1994): 23, 29; for John Muhammad's NOI see Aminah Beverly McCloud, *African American Islam* (New York and London: Routledge, 1995), 83–84.

    4. In an event virtually unnoticed outside New York City at the time, in 1964, after departing the NOI, Clarence 13X formed a group of approximately two hundred youths recruited from the streets of Harlem and Brooklyn. Popularizing the NOI's esoteric, internally held doctrines as its own, the Five Percenters, as the loosely knit group came to be called, would have far-reaching effects on black popular culture of the 1980s. See Prince-A-Cuba, "Black Gods of the Inner City," *Gnosis* 25 (Fall 1992): 56–63; Prince-A-Cuba, ed., *Our Mecca Is Harlem: Clarence 13X (Allah) and the Five Percenters* (Hampton, VA: U.B. & U.S. Communications Systems, 1995); Yusuf Nuruddin, "The Five Percenters: A Teenage Nation of Gods and Earths," in *Muslim Communities in North America,* ed. Yvonne Yazbeck Haddad and Jane Idleman Smith (Albany, NY: State University of New York Press, 1994), 109–32; and Ernest Allen, Jr., "Making the Strong Survive: The Contours and Contradictions of 'Message Rap,'" in *Droppin' Science: Critical Essays on Rap Music and HipHop Culture,* ed. William Eric Perkins (Philadelphia: Temple University Press, 1996), 159–91.

    5. And there are those who have chosen to remain, more or less, on the sidelines, opting instead to preserve and propagate the original teachings of Elijah Muhammad in their pristine form: for example, in Chicago, the Committee for the Remembrance of the Honorable Elijah Muhammad (CROE), led by Munir Muhammad; United Brothers and United Sisters Communications Systems, based at Hampton, Virginia, and headed by H. Khalif Khalifah, publisher of the newspaper *Your Black Books Guide,* as well as numerous books and pamphlets; in Atlanta (recently relocated from Cleveland) the group Secretarius MEMPS (Messenger Elijah Muhammad Propagation Society), publisher-distributor of *Message to the Blackman: The Magazine,* audiotaped speeches by Elijah Muhammad, and other works, led by Minister Nasir Makr Hakim; and Sam Shabazz Muhammad's African-American Genealogy Society, located in Compton, California, which has reproduced, in two volumes, many of Elijah Muhammad's c. 1950s newspaper articles.

6. Abass Rassoull, "What Must Be Done . . . After the Coming of God!" *It's Time to Know* (UNOI) 2 (Fall 1994): 14–17; *Reparations Petition for United Nations Assistance Under Resolution 1503 (XLVIII) on Behalf of African-Americans in the United States of America* (Hampton, VA: U.B. & U.S. Communications Systems, 1994). The equating of Brother Solomon and King Solomon is not unlike the practice accorded Elijah Muhammad, who was often held to be the prophet Muhammad of the Qur'an as well as the prophet Elijah of the Bible. Most recently, however, in a leaflet advertising UNOI meetings in Kansas City in July 1995, Brother Solomon claimed the mantle of "Allah."

7. *Your Black Books Guide* 5 (February 1994): 9–10. A January 1994 issue of *Muhammad Speaks* (LFNOI) reportedly carried a public apology from LFNOI head Silis Muhammad to Louis Farrakhan for past criticisms of the latter's policies.

8. Existing literature on the Garvey movement is too vast to cite here. For an overview see E. David Cronon, *Black Moses: The Story of Marcus Garvey and the Universal Negro Improvement Association* (Madison, WI: University of Wisconsin Press, 1955); Robert A. Hill and Barbara Bair, eds., *Marcus Garvey: Life and Lessons* (Berkeley: University of California Press, 1987).

9. See Ernest Allen, Jr., "The New Negro: Explorations in Identity and Social Consciousness, 1910–1922," in *1915: The Cultural Moment,* ed. Adele Heller and Lois Rudnick (New Brunswick, NJ: Rutgers University Press, 1991), 48–68.

10. Marcus Garvey, *Philosophy and Opinions of Marcus Garvey,* 2 vols. in 1, ed. Amy Jacques-Garvey (1923–1925; rpt. New York: Atheneum, 1969), 2:71, 260–61. Cronon, *Black Moses,* 188–90; *The Marcus Garvey and Universal Negro Improvement Association Papers,* edited by Robert A. Hill (Berkeley: University of California Press, 1985), 4:679; Ethel Wolfskill Hedlin, "Earnest Cox and Colonization: A White Racist's Response to Black Repatriation, 1923–1966," unpublished Ph.D. dissertation (Duke University, 1974), 106–107; Theodore G. Bilbo, "An African Home for Our Negroes," *The Living Age* 358 (June 1940): 328, 330; Arna Bontemps and Jack Conroy, *Anyplace But Here* (New York: Hill and Wang, 1966), 208–211; *Malcolm X: The Last Speeches* (New York: Pathfinder Press, 1989), 122–24; Edwin Black, "Farrakhan and the Jews," *Midstream* 32 (June–July 1986): 3–4; *New York Times* (October 3, 1985): 19; *Washington Post* (October 5, 1985): 11; *Time* (October 14, 1985): 41; *Washington Times* (November 11, 1985): 7; Mattias Gardell, "The Sun of Islam Will Rise in the West: Minister Farrakhan and the Nation of Islam in the Latter Days," in *Muslim Communities in North America,* 38–39.

11. However, a debate concerning the appropriateness of Islam did occur within the UNIA in 1922, and Ahmadis made minor inroads into the organization the following year. See Tony Martin, *Race First: The Ideological and Organizational Struggles of Marcus Garvey and the Universal Negro Improvement Association* (Westport, CT: Greenwood Press, 1976), 75–77; *Negro World* (September 2, 1922): 12; (September 8, 1923): 10.

12. The Ali translation contains four explanatory footnotes referencing the anticipated coming of the Messiah, which may explain the NOI's preference for this par-

ticular version of the Qur'an. As Zafar Ishaq Ansari, "Aspects of Black Muslim Theology," *Studia Islamica* 53 (1981): 170 n2, has indicated, the Ahmadi–NOI connection deserves further research. See also Turner, "The Ahmadiyya Mission to Blacks" and, for general insight, Yohanan Friedmann, *Prophecy Continuous: Aspects of Ahmadi Religious Thought and Its Medieval Background* (Berkeley: University of California Press, 1989).

13. Joseph A. Walkes, Jr., *History of the Shrine: Ancient Egyptian Arabic Order, Nobles of the Mystic Shrine, Inc.* (Detroit: AEAONMS, 1993), 15. For information on Prince Hall Masonry, see Charles H. Wesley, *Prince Hall: Life and Legacy* (Washington, DC: United Supreme Council, Southern Jurisdiction, Prince Hall Affiliation, 1977); Loretta J. Williams, *Black Freemasonry and Middle-Class Realities* (Columbia, MO: University of Missouri Press, 1980); Joseph A. Walkes, Jr., *Black Square and Compass: 200 Years of Prince Hall Freemasonry* (1981; rpt. Richmond, VA: Macoy, 1989); William A. Muraskin, *Middle-Class Blacks in a White Society: Prince Hall Freemasonry in America* (Berkeley: University of California Press, 1975). A social history of black Freemasons is still sorely lacking.

14. This identification, which gathered steam in the early nineteenth century, was the product of the imaginations of Orientalists, Freemasons, and secret-society conspiracy buffs in their studies of esoteric Islamic sects; of documented affinities between Bektashi Sufis and Freemasons throughout the Middle East; and, toward the latter part of the century, of the actual membership of numerous grand viziers and other Ottoman functionaries in the Masonic lodges of Anatolian Turkey, Egypt, Syria, Algeria, and Europe.

15. For Elijah Muhammad's views on Freemasonry, see his *The Secrets of Freemasonry* (Cleveland: Secretarius Publications, 1994), 39; Hatim A. Sahib, "The Nation of Islam," unpublished M.A. dissertation (University of Chicago, 1951), 90; Elijah Muhammad, "The Truth," rpt. in Sam Shabazz Muhammad, comp., *The Truth, Book #1* (Compton, CA: African-American Genealogical Society, n.d.), 4; and Elijah Muhammad, *The Theology of Time* (Hampton, VA: U.B. & U.S. Communications Systems, 1992), 282–86.

16. See Peter Lamborn Wilson, "Shoot-Out at the Circle Seven Koran: Noble Drew Ali and the Moorish Science Temple," *Gnosis*, 12 (Summer 1989): 44–49; Peter Lamborn Wilson, *Sacred Drift: Essays on the Margins of Islam* (San Francisco: City Lights Books, 1993), 15–50; Yvonne Yazbeck Haddad and Jane Idleman Smith, *Mission to America: Five Islamic Sectarian Communities in North America* (Gainesville, FL: University Press of Florida, 1993), 79–104; Arthur Huff Fauset, *Black Gods of the Metropolis: Negro Religious Cults in the Urban North* (Philadelphia: University of Pennsylvania Press, 1944), 41–51; Bontemps and Conroy, *Anyplace But Here*, 205–08; McCloud, *African American Islam*, 10–11.

17. E. U. Essien-Udom, *Black Nationalism: A Search for Identity in America* (Chicago: University of Chicago Press, 1962), 77 n37.

18. But in explaining the reason for the transatlantic slave trade in his *English Lesson C1*, W. D. Fard invoked not the argument of a "fall from grace" on the part of Africans—a view held by Noble Drew Ali—but *gullibility* on the part of the enslaved

themselves: deceived by a slave trader in Africa into thinking that they would receive gold, blacks foolishly allowed themselves to be captured.

19. For information on MSTA farms see *Richmond Times-Dispatch* (April 11, 1943) and *Berkshire Eagle* (February 10, 1944).

20. See Ansari, "Aspects of Black Muslim Theology," 137–76, for the best comparative analysis of early NOI theology and traditional Islam. Also useful is Mustafa El-Amin, *The Religion of Islam and the Nation of Islam: What Is the Difference?* (Newark, NJ: El-Amin Productions, 1990).

21. See Henry F. May, *Protestant Churches and Industrial America* (New York: Harper & Brothers, 1949); Paul A. Carter, *The Spiritual Crisis of the Gilded Age* (Dekalb, IL: Northern Illinois University Press, 1971); Winthrop S. Hudson, *Religion in America* (New York: Scribner's, 1965), 291–315 esp.

22. Q & A 4, *Lost Found Moslem Lesson No. 1;* Q & A 1, 8–11, *Lost Found Moslem Lesson No. 2.* Taken into custody by Detroit police in late November, 1932, Mr. Fard reportedly told detectives that Fard was the "supreme being on earth." But the surprise registered by one of his followers after reading this account in the newspaper appears to leave intact the claim that the fractious issue of Fard's divinity surfaced within the NOI only following his departure from the Midwest in 1934. *Detroit Free Press* (November 24, 1932): 2; Erdmann Doane Beynon, "The Voodoo Cult Among Negro Migrants in Detroit," *American Journal of Sociology* 43 (May 1938): 897. The lack of hierarchy implicit in the notion that "all black men are gods" contributed, no doubt, to internal challenges to Noble Drew Ali's leadership in early 1929, as well as to the plethora of Moorish "gods" who claimed suzerainty over the MSTA following Ali's death from tuberculosis that same year. Seeking to solidify the lines of organizational authority following Fard's departure in 1934, when Muhammad declared Fard to be Allah, he made certain to emphasize his own role as Allah's Messenger. See my related discussion of the Five Percent worldview in "Making the Strong Survive," 165, 187 n17.

23. See *The Holy Koran of the Moorish Science Temple of America* (1927), chapter 45, page 1. Such a notion was reinforced, no doubt, by references to "Asiatic blacks" and "African blacks" in the work of Herodotus, as well as by claims of the existence of black civilizations in Asia on the part of nineteenth-century commentators such as Godfrey Higgins. See Frank M. Snowden, Jr., *Blacks in Antiquity: Ethiopians in the Greco-Roman Experience* (Cambridge, MA: Belknap Press, 1970), vi–vii, 104–07; Godfrey Higgins, *Anacalypsis: An Attempt to Draw Aside the Veil of the Saitic Isis or An Inquiry into the Origin of Languages, Nations and Religions,* 2 vols. (1836; rpt. Brooklyn, NY: A&B Books, 1992), 1:51–59.

24. Examples of Fard's puzzles can be found in Bontemps and Conroy, *Anyplace But Here,* 220–21.

25. Prophet W. D. Fard, *This Book Teaches the Lost Found Nation of Islam* (n.p., n.d.), Problem 13.

26. So much so, it seems, that during the economic upswing that took place from the late 1930s through World War II, the small, gainfully employed group that consti-

tuted the Detroit NOI was reportedly far less militant than its Chicago counterpart. See Beynon, "The Voodoo Cult," 905–06.

27. See, for example, Beynon, "The Voodoo Cult," 900–901.

28. See, for example, Elijah Muhammad, *Message to the Blackman in America* (Chicago: Muhammad's Temple No. 2, 1965); *The Fall of America* (Chicago: Muhammad's Temple No. 2, 1973); *Our Saviour Has Arrived* (Chicago: Muhammad's Temple No. 2, 1974); *The Theology of Time* (Hampton, VA: U.B. & U.S. Communications Systems, 1992).

29. In May 1942 Muhammad was arrested in Washington, D.C., for failure to register for the draft. Out on bail, he returned to Chicago, where he was re-arrested the following September on additional violations of the Selective Service and Training Act, including that of sedition. In late November he was convicted and sent to prison on the initial charge; having achieved the goal of his wartime incarceration, authorities then dropped the second set of indictments. Memorandum from Special Agent in Charge, Detroit, to Director, FBI, August 9, 1957, FBI file 105–24822–25; Ernest Allen, Jr., "When Japan Was 'Champion of the Darker Races': Satokata Takahashi and the Flowering of Black Messianic Nationalism," *The Black Scholar* 24 (Winter 1994): 23. All FBI records cited in the present study were secured under the Freedom of Information Act.

30. The most complete source on Muhammad's life and thought is Claude Andrew Clegg, III, *An Original Man: The Life and Times of Elijah Muhammad* (New York: St. Martin's Press, 1997).

31. Beynon, "The Voodoo Cult," 897; Sahib, "The Nation of Islam," 99, 108; *Autobiography of Malcolm X* (New York: Ballantine, 1973), 219.

32. Malcolm X, *Autobiography,* 290; Clifton E. Marsh, *From Black Muslims to Muslims: The Transition from Separatism to Islam, 1930-1980* (Metuchen, NJ: Scarecrow Press, 1984), 72.

33. Throughout the 1950s the respective leadership skills of Malcolm X and Elijah Muhammad fairly complemented one another. But most African Americans remained unaware of Messenger Muhammad's deeper wisdom until Malcolm X had endlessly extolled his leader's virtues in public.

34. *Pittsburgh Courier* (April 14, 1956): 3 (mag. sect.); Report of [agent name deleted], December 27, 1956, FBI file 105–24822–13, p. 30; *Pittsburgh Courier* (February 22, 1958): 8; and (March 15, 1958): 5 (mag. sect.). Malcolm X noted a "sharp climb" in the number of Muslim-owned small businesses by 1961 but did not distinguish between privately and organizationally owned enterprises. Malcolm X, *Autobiography,* 263.

35. Sahib, "The Nation of Islam," 84.

36. However, the second openly advertised convention, in February 1958, was publicized as the ninth, which would date the very first (but apparently closed) convention meeting back to 1950. *Pittsburgh Courier* (March 8, 1958): 4–5 (mag. sect.).

37. Coincidentally, the emphasis on self-defense occurred during a period when armed, anticolonial, anti-imperialist struggles on the continents of Africa, Asia, and Latin America were in the ascendancy, a situation that led many African Americans—above

all, Malcolm X—to blur the notion of armed self-defense with that of violent political revolution.

38. Elijah Muhammad's early writings spoke of a "return" to the East and to "best lands," which originally meant the Nile Valley as well as Mecca; later he called for a physical "return" of black Americans to Africa in the vaguest of terms, allowing that if the U.S. government would not pay for their transport, it should set aside a separate territory in the southern states for black settlement. Neither choice proved viable. But Garvey at least purchased steamships, only one of which may have been suitable for transatlantic travel; there exists no concrete evidence of emigrationist plans on the NOI's part, however. Privately, Elijah Muhammad admitted as such. See Louis E. Lomax, *When the Word Is Given* (Westport, CT: Greenwood, 1963), 79.

39. *Pittsburgh Courier* (January 17, 1959): 8. In a message to the African-Asian Conference meeting in Cairo the previous year, Mr. Muhammad proclaimed himself the "Leader, Teacher and Spiritual Head of the Nation of Islam in the West." *Pittsburgh Courier* (January 18, 1958): 5.

40. Some of these challenges came in the form of *ad hominem* attacks; see, for example, *New Crusader* (August 15, 1959): 1. See also Essien-Udom, *Black Nationalism*, 80 n45, 311–17; and C. Eric Lincoln, *The Black Muslims in America*, rvsd. ed. (Boston: Beacon Press, 1973), 184.

41. Essien-Udom, *Black Nationalism*, 275; Lincoln, *Black Muslims*, 246.

42. Information in this section concerning Diab and Muhammad, as well as the latter's Middle East tour, is based on an account given by Warith Deen Mohammed, "Race Relations in America: An Islamic Perspective," videotaped speech delivered at the University of Massachusetts at Amherst, November 16, 1993. Despite such negative impressions, after returning to the United States, Elijah Muhammad subsequently referred to NOI temples as "mosques." Malcolm X, *Autobiography*, 263.

43. "Adhering to the solar calendar, on the other hand, the NOI continued to observe Ramadan in December (possibly for the purpose of challenging the pervasive influence of Christmas), rather than during the ninth month of the lunar calendar as did traditional Muslims"; the form of prayer taught by Master Fard—a slight cupping of the hands with palms facing upward—was unknown to the international Muslim community; and the practice of *jumah* was not observed. What also remained were Fard's basic teachings concerning the nature of God and Spirit, polygenesis, and a fundamental disregard for the Prophet Muhammad. As a result, Sheikh Diab ultimately and bitterly disassociated himself from the NOI. See Lincoln, *Black Muslims*, 183–84. For a brief description of pre-1978 NOI prayer rituals, see also Lasiné Kaba, "Americans Discover Islam through the Black Muslim Experience," in *Islam in North America: A Sourcebook*, ed. Michael A. Köszegi and J. Gordon Melton (New York: Garland, 1992), 32.

44. These articles were subsequently reproduced in the form of topical fragments in two volumes known as *The Supreme Wisdom*, published in the latter 1950s, and wholly in *Message to the Blackman in America* and other works.

45. Marsh, *From Black Muslims to Muslims*, 73; Malcolm X, *Autobiography*, 249–50.

46. *Pittsburgh Courier* (March 8, 1958): 7; (July 19, 1958): 8. In a repeat of this pattern, in late 1972 Elijah Muhammad requested a meeting of five hundred New York black business and professional leaders to discuss the expansion of NOI activities. Anticipating a genuine dialogue, several participants expressed disappointment at having been lectured to by Mr. Muhammad as if they had no ideas themselves to contribute. *New York Times* (October 2, 1972): 24.

47. For insights into the running of the newspaper, see John Woodford, "Messaging the Blackman," in *Voices from the Underground,* 2 vols., ed. Ken Wachsberger (Tempe, AZ: Mica Press, 1993), 1:81–98; Leon Forrest, *Relocations of the Spirit* (Wakefield, RI and London: Asphodel Press, 1994), 66–116. In the early 1960s assessments of the Nation of Islam by the Communist Party U.S.A.'s black leadership were divided. Based in Chicago, where the party had established a rapport with the NOI, Claude Lightfoot was generally supportive; in New York City, where it had not, James E. Jackson was highly critical. See Claude Lightfoot, "Negro Nationalism and the Black Muslims," *Political Affairs* 41 (July 1962): 3–20; and James E. Jackson, "A Fighting People Forging Unity," *Political Affairs* 42 (August 1963): 41–46.

48. The success of these early recruitment efforts is noted by Malcolm X in his *Autobiography,* 262; see also Marsh, *From Black Muslims to Muslims,* 73. The growing inclination on the part of the NOI to recruit more of its members from the middle class also may have had to do with cultivating a wealthier constituency from whom more substantial revenues could be tithed. In "The Rise of Louis Farrakhan," *The Nation* (January 21, 1991): 54, Adolph Reed, Jr., has noted a connection between the NOI's middle-class recruitment and its drive for economic growth in the early 1970s.

49. For a discussion of the OAAU's significance, see William W. Sales, Jr., *From Civil Rights to Black Liberation: Malcolm X and the Organization of Afro-American Unity* (Boston: South End Press, 1994).

50. Malcolm X, *Autobiography,* 289.

51. *Pittsburgh Courier* (February 28, 1959): 4–5 (mag. sect.).

52. *Chicago Tribune* (March 12, 1995): 16.

53. *Newsweek* (March 15, 1976): 33.

54. *Chicago Tribune* (March 1, 1976): 1; (March 12, 1995): 16; *New York Times* (December 6, 1973): 37; (February 26, 1976): 14; Bruce Michael Gans and Walter L. Lowe, "The Islam Connection," *Playboy Magazine* (May 1980): 130. In a *Muhammad Speaks* interview c. December 1973, and at a press conference as well, Minister Farrakhan steadfastly denied that Muslims had engaged in crime in order to bolster sagging NOI revenues. A reprint of the interview can be found in 7 *Speeches by Minister Louis Farrakhan* (Newport News, VA: Ramza Associates & United Brothers Communications Systems, 1974), 43–64; see also *New York Times* (December 11, 1973): 74. More recently an internal FBI report transmitted surreptitiously to the Anti-Defamation League's domestic intelligence operation claimed—perhaps deceptively—that high-ranking members of the present-day NOI had engaged in white-collar crime for the purpose of improving the group's cash flow. Specifically mentioned were instances of federal tax violations, credit card fraud, and bank loan scams, the last-mentioned being an offense for which

former NOI minister Khalid Abdul Muhammad actually served prison time. Equally troubling was the inference that forty-one members of the New Orleans–branch NOI had offered cash and other items to food-stamp recipients in exchange for their stamps, which would then be redeemed at a substantial profit from local banks. "San Francisco Police Affidavit in Support of Search Warrant for A.D.L. Offices," April 1993. See also Robert I. Friedman, "The Enemy Within," *Village Voice* (May 11, 1993): 27 ff.

55. See Marsh, *From Black Muslims to Muslims,* 74. National Secretary John Ali appears to have played an advisory role with respect to this privileged inner circle. In *When the Word Is Given,* 82, journalist Louis Lomax identifies John [X] Ali as a former FBI agent.

56. *Chicago Tribune* (January 14, 1972): 2, sect. 1D. Perhaps to silence anticipated criticisms of this ostentatious measure, Elijah Muhammad simultaneously announced plans for the construction in Chicago of one hundred single-family, low-income homes financed by the NOI. The latter project does not seem to have materialized, however. *Chicago Tribune* (January 15, 1972): 1.

57. *Chicago Tribune* (January 13, 1972): 2, sect. 1D; (January 14, 1972): 2, sect. 1D.

58. *New Orleans Times-Picayune* (January 11, 1972): 1, 2; (January 12, 1972): 1, 2; (January 13, 1972): 2, 3; *Chicago Tribune* (January 14, 1972): 18; (January 15, 1972): 1; (May 1, 1973): 1, 3; *New York Times* (January 21, 1972): 1, 21; (May 1, 1973): 35; (April 1, 1975): 25. Nine Muslims were eventually found guilty of murder, but the convictions were overturned on a technicality.

59. Nor was the NOI image helped by the fact that African Americans affiliated with Dar Ul Islam, a traditional Islamic organization based in Brooklyn, were involved in a deadly gun battle in early 1974; to the general public, to be black and Muslim was to be a "Black Muslim," or NOI adherent. See *New York Times* (February 6, 1974): 44.

60. Its leader, Hamaas Abdul Khaalis, had recently sent a second series of letters to ministers of NOI mosques urging them to reject the teachings of Elijah Muhammad. *New York Times* (January 19, 1973): 1, 13; (January 31, 1973): 10.

61. *New York Times* (May 3, 1973): 26. Authorities claimed that Shabazz was killed because he taught that Elijah Muhammad was the messenger of Allah, contradicting the dissident group's belief that he was Allah in person. *New York Times* (September 5, 1973): 50; (May 3, 1974): 3.

62. See Zafar Ishaq Ansari, "W. D. Muhammad: The Making of a 'Black Muslim' Leader (1933–1961)," *American Journal of Islamic Social Sciences* 2.2 (1985): 245–62; "C. Eric Lincoln, "The American Muslim Mission in the Context of American Social History," in The Muslim Community in North America, eds. Earle H. Waugh, Baha Abu-Laban, and Regula B. Qureshi (Edmonton: University of Alberta Press, 1983), 215–33." Lawrence H. Mamiya, "From Black Muslim to Bilalian: The Evolution of a Movement," *Journal for the Scientific Study of Religion* 21 (1982): 138–52; and especially Lee, *The Nation of Islam,* 98, 101.

63. *Time* (June 30, 1975): 52; *New York Times* (June 17, 1975): 9; (February 26, 1976): 14; *Chicago Tribune* (March 1, 1976): 1; (February 19, 1976): 1, sect. 2; (March 1, 1976): 1; *New York Times* (March 7, 1978): 18.

64. *Time* (March 14, 1977): 59.

65. *Muslim Journal* (January 10, 1986): 2; (February 11, 1986): 2; (March 21, 1986): 8 (WNE sect.) World News Events, a special section of the *Muslim Journal.*

66. It was also the intention of the Federal Bureau of Investigation to generate "factionalism among the contenders for Elijah Muhammad's leadership or through legal action in probate court on his death." See excerpts from FBI memorandum in *Muslim Journal* (April 4, 1986): 4.

67. Fourteen of the children were conceived outside of his marriage to Clara Muhammad. Devotees continue to represent Mr. Muhammad's acts as having fulfilled a prophetic role and the secretaries with whom he entered into carnal relations as his "wives." Others point out that, under the NOI code of conduct, lesser-ranking members had been suspended from the organization for engaging in similar activities. True, Elijah Muhammad himself called the Bible a "poison book" for its overtly depicting the moral lapses of prophetic figures, but whether he considered the "poison" to be in the doing or in the telling is a matter of conjecture.

68. *Chicago Tribune* (July 11, 1986): 1–2. The fact that the NOI had deposited approximately $20 million in a Japanese bank is of more than passing interest. In the early 1960s Japanese businessman Seiho Tajiri "arranged for a major Japanese food company to provide for the fish sold in the Nation of Islam's shops and restaurants." But Elijah Muhammad's pro-Nippon leanings can be traced back thirty years previous. See Frank McCoy, "Black Business Courts the Japanese Market," *Black Enterprise* (June 1994): 216; and Allen, "When Japan Was Champion," 25, 32.

69. *Newsweek* (March 15, 1976): 33. See also *New York Times* (August 8, 1976): 34.

70. *Chicago Tribune* (September 13, 1978): 1, sect. 3. In later years Muhammad would interpret the *zakat,* or tithe, as a *responsibility* to engage in commerce: "Business is a religious obligation. It is a religious obligation for Muslims." *Muslim Journal* (February 7, 1986): 2.

71. Even as Wallace Muhammad announced the existence of $900,000 in short-term and $4.5 million in long-term debt some two years earlier, the NOI continued to purchase Chicago properties. *Chicago Tribune* (March 1, 1976): 1.

72. *Chicago Tribune* (January 7, 1979): 6; *Black Enterprise* (March 1981): 20; *Muslim Journal* (April 18, 1986): 7; Lincoln, "American Muslim Mission," 229.

73. *New York Times* (February 26, 1976): 14. *Bilalian News* subsequently became the *American Muslim Journal,* and then simply the *Muslim Journal.*

74. *New York Times* (October 19, 1976): 33. For a discussion of *ummah* and *'asabiya* see McCloud, *African American Islam,* 4–5.

75. *Chicago Tribune* (May 3, 1985): 1, 24.

76. *New York Times* (May 25, 1978): 20; James Emerson Whitehurst, "The Mainstreaming of Black Muslims: Healing the Hate," *Christian Century* (February 27, 1980): 229.

77. *Muslim Journal* (February 21, 1986): 2.

78. *New York Times* (May 3, 1993): B7.

79. *Muslim Journal* (March 17, 1995): 15.

80. *Muslim Journal* (April 18, 1986): 6. This number is to be distinguished from weekly attendance figures at "affiliated" mosques during the same period, which has been reported in the hundreds of thousands.

81. *Time* (March 14, 1977): 59.

82. *New York Times* (February 26, 1976): 14.

83. *Chicago Tribune* (January 7, 1979): 6.

84. *Chicago Tribune* (September 13, 1978): 1, sect. 3; *Christianity Today* 23 (October 6, 1978): 45.

85. "BBB Interviews Minister Abdul Farrakhan," *Black Books Bulletin* 6 (Spring 1978): 45, 71; Gardell, "The Sun of Islam Will Rise," 25. See also Mamiya, "Minister Louis Farrakhan and the Final Call," 234–53; and Jabril Muhammad, *This Is the One: The Most Honored Elijah Muhammad, We Need Not Look for Another!* rvsd. ed. (Phoenix, AZ: Book Company, 1993), 154. For background information on Louis Farrakhan see Arthur J. Magida, *Prophet of Rage: A Life of Louis Farrakhan and His Nation* (New York: Basic Books, 1996).

86. Black, "Farrakhan and the Jews," 6. See also Madhubuti's instructive account, "The Farrakhan Factor," regarding Farrakhan's use of Chicago-based nationalists to build his initial following. Haki R. Madhubuti, *Claiming Earth: Race, Rage, Rape, Redemption: Blacks Seeking a Culture of Enlightened Empowerment* (Chicago: Third World Press, 1994), 71–98.

87. *Time* (February 28, 1994): 26.

88. See *Chicago Tribune* (March 12, 1995): 1 ff. Minister Farrakhan's fiery riposte to the *Tribune's* series of sensationalist exposés of his operations failed to dislodge the claim that many NOI-affiliated firms were privately owned.

89. Leon Forrest recalls that when he was first hired as a reporter for *Muhammad Speaks* in 1969, the paper was under instructions from Elijah Muhammad to withhold criticisms of President Richard Nixon's new administration. During the presidential campaign Nixon had promised to create "Enterprise Zones" in black communities if he won the election, and the Nation of Islam apparently entertained dreams of cashing in on them. Forrest, *Relocations of the Spirit*, 91–93.

90. There was by now, of course, the promise (or threat) of an African American domestic homeland advanced by ultra-right-wing paramilitary groups such as Posse Comitatus and Aryan Nation, who evinced a desire to partition the United States into racial enclaves. To be sure, such plans smacked more of a Bantustan or concentration-camp governance than of genuine autonomy; and Farrakhan, despite his apparent ties to such groups, has declined to endorse such plans publicly. See *Washington Times* (November 5, 1985): 7.

91. *Back Where We Belong: Selected Speeches by Minister Louis Farrakhan,* ed. Joseph D. Eure and Richard M. Jerome (Philadelphia: PC International Press, 1989), 154–56. Here Farrakhan confesses publicly what Elijah Muhammad earlier admitted in private.

92. See, for example, Sigmund Shipp, "The Road Not Taken: Alternative Strategies for Black Economic Development in the United States," *Journal of Economic Issues* 30 (March 1996): 79–95. During the Reagan years, black petit bourgeois elements evolved a strategy to replace the traditional "ghetto nationalism" of earlier epochs: corporate interventionism. Farrakhan has not followed their lead. For a dissection of this particular tack, see Earl Picard, "The New Black Economic Development Strategy," *Telos* 60 (Summer 1984): 53–64.

93. *Time* (February 28, 1994): 26.

94. When Farrakhan was still minister of the Harlem mosque in the 1970s, he oversaw operations of the Fish Force, a NOI fish-import business. For an account of the latter's business activities see Playthell Benjamin, "The Attitude Is the Message," *Village Voice* (August 15, 1989): 25, 27.

95. The situation was roughly analogous to that which Marcus Garvey faced in 1922, in the wake of the post–World War I recession. Several years earlier the UNIA had been awash in self-sufficient funds garnered from a black working-class constituency; in the face of massive employment losses occasioned by the recession, Garvey produced a pamphlet entitled "Appeal to the Soul of White America," requesting monies from whites to support his program of African expatriation. Garvey, *Philosophy and Opinions* 2: 1–6.

96. "The Muslims to the Rescue," *Ebony* (August 1989): 136, 138, 140; *Los Angeles Times* (July 2, 1992): B1, 3; (November 2, 1992): B1; (December 27, 1992): B1, 6; *U.S. News & World Report* (September 12, 1994): 40, 42–43; *New York Times* (March 4, 1994): 1, 18; *Chicago Tribune* (March 12, 1995): 1, 16–17; (March 13, 1995): 1, 10. Success has also been forthcoming to the NOI in obtaining government contracts to treat AIDS patients at its Washington, D.C., clinic, but the victory was also marred by controversy. The clinic's director, Dr. Abdul Alim Muhammad, initially claimed that interferon therapies had "cured" significant numbers of people afflicted with AIDS. Following an outcry from the scientific community, he scaled back his claim to the more credible assertion that interferon helped AIDS patients gain weight. There were also complaints from the black gay community, some members of which claimed that turning AIDS medical testing over to the antihomosexual NOI was akin to turning the fabled black scientist Yakub loose in a nursery. *Washington Post* (July 29, 1993): 25; (September 29, 1993): D1, 5; *New York Times* (March 4, 1994): 10; *Final Call* (October 6, 1994): 7; *Chicago Tribune* (March 14, 1995): 1, 10.

97. Benjamin, "The Attitude Is the Message," 25.

98. *New York Times* (March 1, 1995): C1, 10.

99. *Business Week* (March 13, 1995): 40.

100. A more recent report on NOI economic activities paints an even bleaker picture. See *Washington Post,* national weekly edition (September 9–15, 1996): 6–11.

101. Cited in *New York Times* (June 17, 1975): 9.

102. Louis Farrakhan, *The Announcement: A Final Warning to the U.S. Government* (Chicago: FCN, 1989). W. Deen Mohammed, one notes, has never reported experi-

encing a similar vision. However, Abass Rassoull of the UNOI claims to have been recently informed by the Honorable Elijah Muhammad *in person* that "Minister Farrakhan had been properly relieved of the post of sitting in The Messenger's chair on September 30, 1989."

103. *Annual Report of the Immigration and Naturalization Service, 1966* (Washington, DC: U.S. Government Printing Office, 1967); Stone, "Estimate of Muslims," 25–36.

104. Gardell, "The Sun of Islam Will Rise," 32.

105. Ibid., 34.

106. This liberalizing tendency already had begun under Elijah Muhammad around the 1972–1973 period. In its stead arose the demonizing of Jews. See George E. Curry, "Farrakhan, Jesse & Jews," *Emerge* (July–August 1994): 34–35.

107. See, for example, Muhammad, *Message to the Blackman,* 173, 316.

108. For Farrakhan's views on the efficacy of politics, see "Farrakhan: Some Straight Talk and a Few Tears for Malcolm from the Minister," interview by George E. Curry, *Emerge* (August 1990): 34. Reflecting the implicit assumption that blacks are indeed Americans, Farrakhan claimed in a recent work that "over 30 million Americans live in poverty, and 10 million of those are black." Louis Farrakhan, *A Torchlight for America* (Chicago: FCN, 1993), 15. Where Elijah Muhammad had outright denied the existence of an American identity for blacks, Louis Farrakhan now implicitly assumes its existence. The NOI's initial venture into establishment politics occurred with its support of the Jackson presidential campaign in 1984. Six years later, rather than throw its weight behind individual black politicians over whom it exercised no real control, the NOI decided to run its own candidates directly. Entering the Democratic primary race in Maryland's 5th District, Dr. Abdul Alim Muhammad sought to unseat a well-heeled U.S. congressman seeking a fifth term. Outspent in the campaign by ten to one, Muhammad received only 21 percent of the vote, thus once again putting on hold direct NOI participation in electoral politics. Capturing the NOI's attention was the fact that the black population of Prince George's County, the greater portion of which was located within the 5th District, had grown to 50 percent of the total, thus offering the possibility of a successful run for office based upon a direct nationalist appeal. The assumption proved incorrect. During the same period, NOI members Shawn X. Brakeen sought a school board post and George X. Cure a delegate's seat in the District of Columbia. *Washington Post* (August 2, 1990): D2; (September 12, 1990): A21.

109. For perceptive views on the power struggle within the Nation of Islam, see Peter Noel, "To Kill a Brother Minister: Khalid Muhammad Versus the Nation of Islam," *Village Voice* (August 2, 1994): 21 ff.; Noel, "The Final Call," 23 ff.; and Sylvester Munroe, "Khalid Abdul Muhammad," *Emerge* (September 1994): 40–46. Neither author has any trouble identifying Khalid Muhammad's constituency outside the NOI, but his specific base—if any—within the organization remains unclear.

110. Garvey, *Philosophy and Opinions,* 2: 133. That is not to say that many of Garvey's enemies were not also motivated by petty jealousies or strong progovernment bias as well.

111. The saga began after presidential candidate Jesse Jackson was accused of uttering a slur against Jews. See Curry, "Farrakhan, Jesse & Jews," 30.

112. Cited in Lincoln, *Black Muslims,* 176.

113. *Thunderbolt* 309 (n.d., c. 1985): 5.

114. For examples of deliberate distortions of Farrakhan's remarks, see Curry, "Farrakhan, Jesse & Jews," 37, 40.

115. By 1985 a symbiotic relationship of sorts appeared to develop between Farrakhan and his right-wing, nationalist counterparts within the American Jewish community. First, Farrakhan would utter an outrageous remark concerning Jews, for which Jewish organizations would then expend tens of thousands of dollars denouncing him in full-page newspaper ads. This free publicity only further endeared Louis Farrakhan to black communities coast to coast, increased NOI membership, and, for better or for worse, made Farrakhan's name a household word. Such negative publicity also attracted the attention of "checkbook Zionists" (as they are known within the Jewish community), who would then proceed to pour hundreds of thousands of dollars into Jewish protective organizations. These groups would subsequently demand that prominent blacks denounce Minister Farrakhan for his verbal transgressions. Then began the next round of a ritual of which a good many African Americans have grown weary. To paraphrase an ancient African proverb: "When two right-wing zealotries clash, only rational people get trampled."

116. Benjamin, "The Attitude Is the Message," 24.

117. See Ernest Allen, Jr., "Toward a 'More Perfect Union': A Commingling of Constitutional Ideals and Christian Precepts," *Black Scholar* 25 (Fall 1995): 27–34.

118. Louis Farrakhan, "Why a Million Man March?" *Final Call* (August 30, 1995): 19.

119. George E. Curry, "After the Million Man March," *Emerge* (February 1996): 48. An exception to the meager availability of information on the LOCs was the October 22, 1996, *Final Call,* celebrating the first anniversary of the Million Man March.

120. *New York Times* (March 25, 1996): A1, 12.

121. *Springfield Sunday Republican* (June 30, 1966): A1, 13, 18; *The Spirit: Official Newsletter of the Springfield Chapter of the Million Man March Committee* 1 (October 16, 1996).

122. *Final Call* (January 31, 1996): 3.

123. Louis Farrakhan, "Can the U.N. Avert the War of Armageddon?" *Final Call* (November 5, 1996): 21.

124. Divided reactions to march follow-up activities are reflected in interviews conducted by Darrell Dawsey, "In Their Footsteps," *Emerge* (October 1996): 46–49.

125. Allen, "Toward a More Perfect Union," 32–33; Muhammad, *Message to the Blackman,* 88.

Who's Afraid of Louis Farrakhan:
The Media and Race Relations Coverage

Erna Smith

ERNA SMITH *is chairwoman of the Journalism Department at San Francisco State University. She is author of* Transmitting Race: The Los Angeles Riot in Television News, *a 1994 study for the Joan Shorenstein Barone Center for Press, Politics, and Public Policy at the John F. Kennedy School of Government at Harvard.*

The largely white mainstream media seem to have struck an odd alliance with Louis Farrakhan, a man repeatedly portrayed as an anti-Semite, racist, sexist, homophobe, and looney. Sheer volume of news stories on the minister during the 1990s suggests that the media just can't get enough of the Nation of Islam leader. During the past decade, Farrakhan has received more press coverage than any other African-American public figure except Jesse Jackson, who ran for president twice. The irony is this: The more the media portray Farrakhan as a menace to society, the more sympathetic he seems to African-Americans. Indeed, Farrakhan gets more mileage from bad press than any aspiring leader would ever dream of getting from good press—and he knows it.

"Whatever you write about me, I don't give a damn because you have not hurt me" Farrakhan told a gathering of the National Association of Black Journalists in August 1996. "You have helped me."

My interest in news coverage of Louis Farrakhan began in 1994, when I was invited to join three other writer-researchers in a study sponsored by the Ford Foundation for the Unity Convention, a mega-media gathering of the nation's four leading minority journalists' organizations held in Atlanta.

My interest in, and subsequent research of, race relations news coverage also stems from fifteen years spent reporting and editing at daily newspapers. As the principal researcher and writer on African-American issues for the Unity '94 study, I spent the better part of a year neck-deep in news stories that were either submitted or suggested for review by a blue-chip panel of respected African-American journalists. The more coverage I reviewed, the less it seemed to say about Farrakhan, and the more it seemed to say about how mainstream American journalism covers race relations.

Sociologist Herman Gray believes race relations reporting implicitly promotes the virtues of assimilation, capitalism, and individuality. Thus, individuals and groups who might espouse different views or values tend to be portrayed as being bad for race relations. Since black nationalism invariably is interpreted in the popular media as being antiwhite, nationalist organizations and movements, such as the Nation of Islam and the Black Panthers, are uniformly portrayed as being bad for American race relations. Based on my review of coverage spanning a decade, reporting on Farrakhan and the Nation of Islam powerfully demonstrates Gray's point.

The review found that more reporting is devoted to mainstream, e.g., white, reaction to Farrakhan and the Nation of Islam, especially to charges of anti-Semitism, than to the Nation's conservative philosophy of religion, self-respect, family values, and bootstrap capitalism as a cure for the social ills affecting African-Americans.

At the same time, the coverage of Farrakhan and the Nation, however pervasive and incomplete, does not persuade many African-

Americans to join the Nation, or take up arms, or become separatists. Yet, this fact is often overlooked by a mainstream media that does a better job of reporting on whites' attitudes about Farrakhan (and race relations in general) than of reporting on African-American points of view. The result is coverage that fuels fear and trepidation about Farrakhan among whites and creates sympathy for him among blacks.

Farrakhan's media-assisted ascendance to nationally known public figure, in black and white America, partly reflects mainstream media's attraction to what political scientist Adolph Reed dubbed "the myth of the generic black spokesman." Of course, there are other factors: the historic presence and appeal throughout the twentieth century of nationalist movements, such as the Nation of Islam, in urban, black America dating back to Marcus Garvey; a dearth of black leadership figures who speak with authority to the young, urban, and working poor; and the success of the Farrakhan-led Million Man March. The October 1995 march in Washington, D.C., showed America that African-Americans, unlike most media, are capable of separating the message from the messenger.

Pre-march coverage, for example, largely missed this point. In the week before the march, much of the reporting focused on Farrakhan's critics in the Jewish and African-American communities, featuring news reports accompanied by punditry that, in the main, cast the event as either the coronation of the chief "bigot"—Farrakhan as King of Black America—or yet another symbol of the terrible state of race relations in post–Los Angeles–riots, post–O.J. Simpson–verdict America.

That the Million Man March turned out to be a peaceable assembly of hundreds of thousands of black men praying and pledging to be more responsible for themselves, their families, their communities and country got lost in the full-throttle noise about Farrakhan, the Hatemonger. It is a chorus that began more than a decade before and that continues today.

Farrakhan-as-Hatemonger first burst onto the national media's radar screens during Jesse Jackson's 1984 presidential campaign, when he attacked Jews who attacked Jackson for calling them "hymies" during an off-the-record conversation with two African-American reporters. Jackson's reported comments appeared in the *Washington Post* during his upstart presidential campaign. The comments, as reported by the *Post,* prompted threats on Jackson's life by people purporting to represent and defend Jewish-Americans. Incensed with news of these threats, Farrakhan, whose Fruit of Islam provided Jackson's security when the campaign began, came out swinging. "I say to the Jewish people, who may not like our brother: It is not Jesse Jackson you are attacking," said the minister during the height of the controversy. "When you attack him, you are attacking the millions who are lining up with him. You're attacking all of us. . . . Why dislike us? Why attack our champion? Why hurl stones at him? It's our champion. If you harm this brother, what do you think we should do about it?" (*CBS Evening News,* February 24, 1984).

With these remarks, Louis Farrakhan, news icon, was born. A news icon is a dramatic image or event that comes to symbolize a higher truth, a shorthand that speaks to a shared understanding and requires few words. One example is the "agony of defeat" guy in the opening montage for ABC's *Wide World of Sports*—the ski jumper who takes that nasty spill off the runway during an Olympic competition in the 1960s. One look at that image and you immediately understand the depth of personal commitment required in modern sporting competition. A more recent and serious news icon is the videotape of the 1991 Rodney King beating, a grainy, jumpy few minutes of images that have become synonymous with police abuse of power. Images of the King beating turn up in all kinds of coverage that has nothing to do with King, the criminal trial of his assailants, or the civil revolt spawned by their acquittal.

Some broadcast news organizations—especially the pseudo-news, "infotainment" shows like *Inside Edition* and *Hard Copy*—regularly make the leap from relatively unremarkable stories about individual Cops Gone Bad to stories that imply that All Cops Abuse

Power simply by showing the now familiar pictures from the Rodney King beating at the top of the report.

Thus, news icons are images or loaded phrases that allow us to quickly interpret the world outside the one we live in. (They also allow us to reinforce our very human tendency to divide the world into "us" and "them.")

By 1994, Farrakhan had become an infamous and ubiquitous national public figure. That year, *Time* magazine used a scary headline on its cover story on Farrakhan: "Ministry of Rage: Louis Farrakhan spews racist venom at Jews and all of white America. Why do so many blacks say he speaks for them?" Obviously, the report did not contain opinions from all or even most of America's estimated thirty-plus million black citizens. Yet, in reading the coverlines on that issue of *Time,* with its qualifying phrase "so many blacks" lost amid accompanying words like "rage" and "venom," one could conclude not only that Farrakhan speaks for the majority of African-Americans, but that they feel exactly as he does.

In 1994 alone, more than 40 percent of all major network news stories on African-American organizations and leaders focused on Farrakhan, according to a study by communications scholar Andrew Rojecki. Most of those stories evolved from the fallout over the vitriolic speechifying of the Nation's former national aide, Khalid Muhammad.

A global search of four hundred English-language newspaper databases turned up more stories mentioning Farrakhan in 1995 and 1996 than the search engine, which taps out at one thousand stories, could count. The high volume of stories during this time no doubt resulted from coverage of the Million Man March, which was mentioned in about half the stories. More telling—in terms of what Farrakhan has come to symbolize in the national body politic as reflected by mainstream media—is that more than half the stories mentioning Farrakhan also contained the word "Jewish."

Farrakhan's proximity to Jackson in 1984, coupled with his nationalistic rhetoric, made him a logical target of national media coverage. Since then, the image of Farrakhan-as-Chief Bigot has dogged him, despite the minister's many subsequent public statements denouncing anti-Semitism. To be sure, by virtue of the media attention his aspirations for national and international leadership continue to generate, he has become America's No. 1 anti-Semite and racial bogeyman—a modern-day, media-made Nat Turner, a news icon consumed with rage for white folks, in particular Jewish ones.

This point was driven home to me in 1996, when I invited a young Nation of Islam member to a class I co-taught on coverage of black-Jewish relations in the media. The young man's purpose, which my co-teacher and I described to the students well before he came to class, was to explain how the students could purchase copies of the Nation of Islam newspaper, the *Final Call*. This newspaper, along with the Jewish *Forward,* was part of the assigned class readings.

The mere brief presence of this shy, smooth-skinned, milk-chocolate manchild, donned in bow tie and Sunday-best suit, struck a nerve so raw in students of all colors, Jewish and Christian alike, that you could hear the air sucking out of the room.

The students were so stunned by the young Muslim's visit that we devoted the next class meeting to talking about their reactions. Some white students said they had felt scared speechless in his presence. They admitted assuming that the young man hated them because he was a member of the Nation of Islam. They believed he hated them despite the smiling, mild-mannered demeanor he showed while speaking with them. Conversely, some black students said they felt an odd mixture of annoyance and vindication— annoyance at their white classmates' fear of being hated by black people and vindication at seeing the white classmates experience the discomfort of being despised because of the color of their skin.

The common thread in both reactions was popular media. Much of what most students knew—or thought they knew—about the Nation of Islam when the class began was limited to Louis Farrakhan, and a lot of what they knew of him stemmed from their views of his views of Jews, women, and gays and lesbians. Some students knew more than others, but the average student's knowledge of Farrakhan's views was largely based on by-products of his media icon status: the proliferation of television news soundbites, comedy show sketches, and secondhand accounts of both from friends and family.

At the same time, Farrakhan does not strike the raw, racial nerve in whites alone. For different reasons, his nationalist rhetoric also can push emotional buttons in some African-Americans, especially middle-class, professional ones. For example, in his address to the 1996 gathering of the National Association of Black Journalists in Nashville, Farrakhan called the assembled journalists spineless, godless Uncle Toms and said he did so because he loved them. "You're black journalists that work for white institutions. White folk did not hire you to represent what black people are really thinking and you don't really tell them what you think because you are too afraid of [losing] the little cheap gigs that you have," he said.

The news accounts and columns I read of the minister's Nashville speech sent mixed messages about the black journalists' reaction to being dissed by Farrakhan: The stories seemed to castigate the journalists either for being too fawning or for not being furious enough. (The news reports were also short on unaltered text of Farrakhan's words, and in one case, a black journalist who hadn't attended the speech wrote a column denouncing his brethren for inviting Farrakhan to the convention.) My friends who were in that Nashville audience expressed some degree of anger at the speech, not because Farrakhan offended their sense of journalistic integrity, but because he did not acknowledge the efforts of African-American journalists who work hard to cover him fairly. Those journalists also balked at the minister's questioning the depths of their religious feeling.

"He has no idea what kind of hell people have caught to get fair, positive stories about him in the paper," a twenty-eight-year veteran reporter and editor told me. "But it wasn't until he started saying 'Where's God in your life,' that I got up and left. I mean, he questions folks' religion at a convention where they had a gospel brunch and closed with a prayer."

If my friend had stayed, he probably would have agreed with at least one point Farrakhan made later in the speech about the double standard implicit in his media-made status as America's premier hatemonger. "You mean to tell me, with all the hatred, the big-otry, the anti-Semitism that is in this world, Louis Farrakhan is now the chief of all of this?" he asked rhetorically.

Some alien being learning about America for the first time by tuning in CNN might very well conclude that the answer to Farrakhan's question is yes. The visitor might also conclude from our national press that relations between blacks and whites are in shambles because blacks and whites hold differing views of Farrakhan, the Simpson verdict, affirmative action, and other race-related issues. At the same time, the problem is not derived exclusively from the fact that race relations coverage tends to focus on differences. We know that differences exist, between blacks and whites, and men and women, differences of class, religious beliefs, and sexual preferences. But the *reasons* Americans continue to squabble and do battle over those differences—not the presence of those differences—should be the subject of more reporting than it is.

Yet that type of analysis requires time and a commitment to reporting that is more the exception than the rule, especially in the 1990s, as bottom-line pressures increasingly undermine sound news judgment at many major media organizations. (Journalists of color and gay journalists regularly complain that in-depth stories involving race and gender issues are finding less and less space in the nation's daily news product.) What we get are stories driven by polls that reflect racial fears and anxieties, instead of stories interpreting the results and placing them in a context that might help bridge, rather than widen, the gulfs between our different life experiences and expectations.

In reality, my white students' terrified reaction to the young NOI member suggests the power of media to overcome common sense in even the most open of minds. Furthermore, the indifference of many African-Americans to this power suggests the deep level of skepticism with which they regard mainstream news reporting on race relations. Perhaps a big reason for that is that African-Americans sense a double standard at work in the national coverage of Farrakhan and in many race-related stories. No one expects whites, for example, to denounce whites who make racist statements. Yet mainstream journalists either do not see or are powerless to resist the hypocrisy inherent in telephoning African-American political leaders for comments every time Farrakhan and company make statements that whites find offensive. Moreover, support or opposition to Farrakhan has become a litmus test of a black public official's fitness to lead.

Indeed, another interesting result from the national and international newspaper database search was the number of stories it yielded that contained Farrakhan's name but that were, in reality, about the Farrakhan-baiting of African-American political leaders. One pointed example is an April 5, 1997, *New York Times* story chronicling how New York Democratic mayoral candidate Ruth Messinger managed to work the specter of Farrakhan into the campaign. Reverend Al Sharpton, a long-time Farrakhan sympathizer and one of Messinger's opponents in the race, reportedly said during a meeting of local businessmen that he didn't think Farrakhan was an anti-Semite. Sharpton had been responding to a question lobbed to him during the meeting. Messinger learned of the comment and issued a letter—according to the *Times,* via a reporter—denouncing Sharpton for not denouncing Minister Farrakhan.

It was a typically cynical dust-up, one that originated from and fed on Farrakhan's icon status as Chief Bigot. Another extreme example of how Farrakhan has become a figure of political manipulation comes from Representative Cynthia McKinney's 1996 Georgia congressional campaign. McKinney drew headlines in the *New*

York Times and the *Washington Post* after her father made disparaging remarks about her Republican opponent in the race, a Jewish man who had accused McKinney of being soft on Farrakhan. McKinney's character came under more fire from her opponent because of allegedly harsh comments her father made when he believed his daughter was being held to an unfair standard. The Messinger and McKinney examples represent a perverted form of reflected glory and embody the media's double-standard use of Farrakhan as social litmus test for black Americans. They were cynical, cyclical, self-feeding stories that served only to exacerbate tensions between African-Americans and Jewish-Americans.

The dismal coverage of Farrakhan is able to take place only in the larger context of the media's overall failure to accurately cover matters of race. Consider the October 16, 1995, edition of the *Times,* which contained an inside-page graphic naming "prominent" African-Americans who did and did not plan to attend the Million Man March. "Look," the chart seemed to imply, "here's a list of Black Farrakhan Followers, and Black Farrakhan Detractors!" One day earlier in the *Times,* African-American theologian Cornel West, a Harvard professor and leading advocate of black-Jewish dialogue, felt compelled to pen an op-ed column explaining why he was marching. West also used the forum to take a swipe at mainsteam media: "In casting the demonstration as 'Farrakhan's march,' the mainstream media wants to shift the focus from black pain to white anxiety," wrote West.

Although West's observation suggests that mainstream journalists consciously rather than unconsciously missed the point of the Million Man March, the professor hit the nail right on the head regarding the pre-march coverage and race relations reporting in general.

Another *Times* article published during the pre-march period focused on a group of African-American men discussing the march in a Maryland barbershop and captured both black indifference to news portrayals of Farrakhan as a bigot and distrust of mainstream media. As the men in the story saw it, the media focuses more on negative than representative images of African-Americans. The article read, "One customer spit out, 'Who cares?'" while watching an evening news program showing interviews with Gary Franks, a black Republican who denounced the march, and one Catholic priest who attended and another who did not because of Farrakhan's involvement. Demonstrating how mainstream media coverage of race relations spirals in and around itself without resolution, the *Times* reporter also wrote: "The men here see the march as a way to counter what they view as the media's overwhelmingly negative images of blacks, in particular black males." The *Times* story reported on the barbershop patrons' negative reaction to media coverage without seeming to consider its own role in having shaped the patrons' reactions.

But back in 1994, I was struck by the genesis, volume, ever spiraling plot lines, and geographic pattern of coverage devoted to another "negative" black man media-propelled to notoriety: former Nation of Islam spokesman, Khalid Muhammad. The media saga of Muhammad, a nobody to almost everybody outside the Nation of Islam prior to 1994, began somewhat unusually when a particularly mean-spirited speech he delivered at New Jersey's Kean College brought him before the public eye. The speech was an equal opportunity bashing of just about everyone but the Nation of Islam and might not have attracted nationwide attention if the Anti-Defamation League, worried about Farrakhan's impending discussions with the Congressional Black Caucus, had not purchased a full-page ad of speech excerpts in *The New York Times*.

Within days of this ad's appearance—several months after Khallid made the speech—a posse of esteemed East Coast columnists led by the *Times'* Abe Rosenthal gave chase. This re-ignited a cycle of recriminations between blacks and Jews dating back to Jackson's remarks in 1984. It also set off a lot of political grandstanding, culminating in Congress censoring Muhammad, making the theretofore unheard-of minister the first person in U.S. history to be so chastised for making bigoted remarks. This episode represented another chapter of parochial, national news coverage of black-Jewish tensions that turned a single event, and in this instance an essentially East Coast story, into a nationwide trend.

This phenomenon explains, in part, why African and Jewish Americans are the most frequent topics of reporting on interethnic relations. (Never mind that black Americans do not place their relations with Jews high on their political agendas, or that black-Latino relations, or white-Asian relations might be more important in the coming century.) While the *Times* and *The Washington Post* and the major networks reported extensively on the flap over Muhammad, the story didn't have a very long shelf life west of the Rockies. Nonetheless, it did make Muhammad a nationally known figure and helped further attune the ears of journalists to any signs of similar stories in their own backyards.

For example, in the months following the flap over Khalid Muhammad, there were two such stories in San Francisco and Oakland that attracted national media attention—attention they might not have received had the media not seen the incidents as examples of the growing influence of Farrakhan on black America: One post-Khalid incident involved a class of Oakland high school students who offended some moviegoers by laughing during a showing of *Schindler's List,* Steven Spielberg's stirring film about a German businessman who rescued thousands of Jews from Hitler's gas chambers. The other involved a battle on my campus to remove a student union-commissioned mural of Malcolm X that held Stars of David, dollar signs, and the word "bloodsucker." Numerous student protests over any number of sensitive issues are mounted each month at San Francisco State University, yet the mural drew the national press like flies to honey. Would they have been interested in the display (or the small group who protested it initially) were it not for the Farrakhan-Muhammad coverage that preceded it? My point is that news coverage does not occur in a vacuum. It is not, as many journalists might contend, just a random sample of "what's out there," breaking news that can be reported quickly and economically. When the story is about race, the plot lines more often represent funhouse-mirror reflections of our deeply held yet largely subconscious cultural myths and narratives about race. Political scholar Adolph Reed once said that nothing interests white people more about black people than what black people think of them. I think the same could apply to African-Americans about whites, although less by choice than by necessity.

So nothing quite strikes our collective psychic chord like a black man who scares the bejesus out of white folks—like Louis Farrakhan. And perhaps the greatest irony of all is that with the success of the Million Man March, Farrakhan has transcended the power of mainstream media to define and marginalize him in the black community. We've reached the point where it doesn't matter what the national press reports about him.

Furthermore, the competing image of Farrakhan as the tough-talking yet loving and benevolent savior-prophet of Black America contributes to the minister's growing immunity from press criticism, at least among many African-Americans. This carefully cultivated image is the cornerstone of the Nation of Islam's communications organ, the *Final Call.*

A splashy, full-color weekly tabloid, the *Final Call,* formerly *Muhammad Speaks,* features national and international news stories that the Nation of Islam deems of interest to African-Americans, interspersed with columns and commentaries on everything from the latest crisis in the Middle East to nutritional tips. There are no ads except those hawking Farrakhan's ever burgeoning catalogue of video and audio cassettes of his speeches dating back to the mid-1980s.

The videotaped speeches proffered in these ads range from "Making the New Jew," which despite its provocative title is Farrakhan's rambling dissertation on the apostle Paul's (Saul's) conversion to Christianity on the Road to Damascus, to ads for the minister's own fitness and nutritional regimen, featuring snapshots of a sweatsuited Farrakhan lifting weights in the basement of his Chicago Hyde Park home.

Although Farrakhan's smiling, bow-tied image is omnipresent throughout most *Final Call* editions, the newspaper's chief theologian-scribe is really the late Nation of Islam founder, Elijah Muhammad, whose old speeches are faithfully reprinted each week. A Los Angeles sales representative for the paper, which is largely sold on the street, reports that the Nation sells 900,000 copies of the *Final Call* nationwide each month. With those numbers, Farrakhan is not and will never be solely dependent on mainstream media to build his image in the black community.

In his paper "Deadly Embrace: News Constructions of Black-Jewish Antagonism," communications scholar Rojecki describes two recurring myths that permeate mainstream reporting on African-American political leadership: Reed's theory of the generic race spokesman, and the presence of monolithic black public opinion. Rojecki theorizes that these myths embody an underlying assumption that drives news coverage of Farrakhan: that the minister has a significant influence on the values, thoughts, and beliefs of all African-Americans. I disagree only with the word "assumption." Rather, I prefer West's term, "white anxiety," to describe the driving force behind the ongoing inadequate news coverage of Farrakhan and race relations in America. And, echoing West again, I think that until mainstream American journalism gets better at reporting on black pain, it will continue to play the unwitting accomplice to publicizing a man it deems dangerous.

I'm sure I'll be accused of making the same mistakes with this assessment that I attribute to mainstream media's failure to accurately report on race relations—taking things out of context and blowing an issue out of proportion by focusing on one angle (e.g., Farrakhan's status as news icon, thanks to the shortcomings of the mainstream media). At the same time, I couldn't teach journalism if I didn't believe in its enormous social value, didn't recognize the constraints imposed by deadlines, and didn't have enormous respect for the excellent reporting on race, however scant, that is or has been done. Which is why I want to end on a note of hope.

Although I think mainstream journalism does a better job of reacting to than anticipating racial issues and social attitudes, I recognize that journalism always manages to change with the times—even if its rate of change appears glacial. For the class on coverage of black-Jewish relations in 1996, we assigned students to research and review press accounts of, among other watershed events in the history of black-Jewish relations, Freedom Summer in 1964.

In the process of conducting the review, the students came across a number of articles related to riots that took place that summer more than thirty years ago in Harlem and New Jersey. The stories unearthed by students, in the twenty-twenty hindsight of our modern media history, are laugh-out-loud hilarious when read today: "Uprising of Negroes Is Urged by Peking," read a headline on a short *New York Times* story, a fear-mongering piece that was based on unnamed "analysts" in Hong Kong and an editorial published in an "organ of the Chinese Communist party."

Gone are the days when journalists routinely reported official stories about "Commies" or peppered stories of social unrest with the familar catchall term "outside agitators," those *agents provocateurs* who stirred up mischief among otherwise satisfied blacks. Now I look forward to the day when we can laugh at stories that seemed to lay the blame for all that was wrong with race relations in 1990s America on the shoulders of an unorthodox black minister named Louis Farrakhan.

Minister Louis Farrakhan's Economic Rhetoric and Reality

Julianne Malveaux

JULIANNE MALVEAUX *is an economist and writer in Washington, D.C. She is the author of* Sex, Lies and Stereotypes.

In the United States, there are more than 30 million African-American people with collective earnings of about $350 billion. At 12 percent of the population, we have about 8 percent of the income and 3 percent of the wealth in our country. The amount is not our fair share, but it is a hefty sum. Black folks have more money (and perhaps more problems) than the oil-producing nation of Nigeria does, a larger gross domestic product than the countries of Ireland and Portugal. We number more than the population of neighboring Canada. We might even elbow our presence in as one of the G-7 countries if we were a country. But we aren't a country, not even a colony, just 30 million or so people struggling with issues of dual identity in a nation that some perceive as hostile to us.

So it doesn't take a rocket scientist to posit African-American economic solutions. If every one of those 30 million people put a dollar in someplace, there'd be a $30 million economic development fund raring to support more black-owned businesses. Suppose less than 100 percent participation but a slightly larger bite. If 10 million people put in just $5.00, there'd be $50 million to invest. What if those with the largest incomes were the only ones to pony up? Perhaps 100,000 African-American individuals earn incomes of more than $100,000. If just 1 percent of those folks put up a mere $1,000, there would be $100 million to invest. And the multiplication goes on. The fact is that, despite inequity, there is money in the African-American community. The fact is that if someone can tame the economic tiger that has been weaned on capitalism, individualism, and commercialism, she or he would have a ticket to ride it—and a bunch of black folks—into a prosperous economic sunset.

Both the homies in the 'hood and the Ph.D. economists have calculated the impact of the kwanza principle of *ujamaa,* or cooperative economics. But for all the talk, there has been little action. Just one in ten black dollars goes to patronize black-owned businesses, and despite the lofty rhetoric of an African-American economic revolution, the collective worth of the Black Enterprise One Hundred might barely register as part of the Fortune 500. Economic rhetoric is appealing, though, and that explains, as much as anything, Black America's fascination with the Nation of Islam and Minister Louis Farrakhan. When economic analysts talk about the power of the black dollar, about the notion that "the white man's ice is colder" and that some combination of pathology, self-hate, and economic ignorance keeps African Americans yoked to an economic system that slights them, something deep in the African-American psyche responds.

The facts suggest that we have no choice but to respond, given the economic condition of the African-American community. Conservatively stated, many in the African-American community suffer from a pernicious form of economic strangulation. Regardless of age and education, there are income gaps between African Americans and whites, and since African Americans have lower levels of education than whites, those income gaps are often glaring. On a weekly basis, in 1996, full-time African Americans earned $387, three-quarters of the $506 that full-time whites earned. Among full-time workers, African-American women earned on average, $262, African-American men earned $412, white women earned $428, and white men earned $580.[1] There were similar differences in un-employment rates, with the unemployment rate for both white men and white women measuring 4.7 percent in 1996. African-American men had an unemployment rate of 11.1 percent, while black women had an unemployment rate of 10 percent.[2] Every economic indi-cator reflects a significant disparity.

Whites have more income and more access to credit, own more stocks and bonds, and participate more fully in retirement plans. They own more homes and more automobiles, and their homes and cars tend to be worth more than those of African Americans. None of these data are surprising, given the history of African-American involvement in our nation's economic system and given the documented discrimination that has prevented black's full par-ticipation in economic development. A simple recitation of these facts can elicit outrage from African Americans who feel that the barriers that prevent our full participation have not yet been razed.

In some ways the outrage is a historical outrage, an outrage that screams both outward in frustration at racial unfairness and inward because of failed attempts at economic self-determination. History records more than a century of economic nationalism, beginning with the work of nineteenth-century leaders, including Frederick Douglass ("Until we save more than we spend, we are sure to sink and perish"),[3] Booker T. Washington,[4] and Marcus Garvey, who asserted that "economic self-determination was fundamental to the realization of the political objectives of black nationalism."[5]

The Nation of Islam is part of this historical continuum. E.U. Essien-Udom, author of *Black Nationalism,* one of the earliest stud-ies of the Nation of Islam, writes that the Nation of Islam affirms

Garvey and Washington with greater emphasis. "In fact, among Muslims," he writes, "hard work, thrift, and accumulation of wealth have a semireligious sanction."[6] C. Eric Lincoln notes that "economic security was stressed from the first days of the [Muslim] movement."[7] As early as 1937, there was a focus on saving for economic development, eschewing current consumption for future development, pooling resources, supporting that which is black-owned, and, ideally, making a complete withdrawal from the white community.[8] While complete withdrawal was never realized, the Nation of Islam was considered one of the "most potent economic forces" in the African-American community by 1971. Holdings included more than ten thousand acres of farmland; thousands of chickens, cattle, and lambs; tens of thousands of gallons of milk, pounds of apples and watermelon, and other foods.[9]

During the 1960s and early '70s, Nation-owned businesses included barbershops, small restaurants, dry cleaners, clothing stores, and other businesses in cities such as Chicago, Los Angeles, and New York. The Nation of Islam, then, is part of a powerful legacy of economic nationalism. While many of its assets have been sold since its economic pinnacle before the death of the Honorable Elijah Muhammad in 1975, the economic mission has always been a central facet of the Nation's public posture. Its current leader, Minister Louis Farrakhan, has firmly established himself as part of this legacy, preaching economic self-sufficiency, self-determination, and collective work and responsibility. But that is not the entire content of the minister's message. While Minister Farrakhan has been a consistent advocate of black economic empowerment, he is also a complicated and charismatic icon whose messages are moral, racial, international, and sociological. Farrakhan is America's Rubik's Cube. Viewed one way he is a sexist, homophobic, anti-Semite. From another perspective he is a tireless advocate of African-American self-determination. When a row of cubes are turned, the perspective changes, and there is yet another Farrakhan. He has been portrayed as a genteel music lover who reveres pianist Vladimir

Horowitz, as an advocate of Nigeria's repressive Abacha regime, as a cunning, even charming host who works hard to win over his detractors, and as a numerologist who squandered a nation's good-will—engendered early in the 1995 Million Man March—with his ruminations on the number 19.[10]

For as long as Minister Farrakhan has occupied public space, I've had questions about him, and held them, or voiced them gingerly, partly because I've been fascinated by the way that white people respond to the mere mention of his name, the way they attempt to use him as a litmus test as they weigh and measure African Americans. From this perspective, many African Americans have measured their criticism of Louis Farrakhan. Whatever objections we might have, no one wants to be perceived as "pandering" to white people by raising them.[11] Let me share an example. Two years ago, I gave a lecture at a business school about targeted marketing and African Americans. As I wound down, a man in the back of the room animatedly began to wave his hand, ensuring that he would be called on for the first question. I wondered if he had a question about my remarks on inner-city economic concentration, or a comment on my theories on the effectiveness of boycotts.

It turned out that this man had neither heard my lecture nor noticed me except for the color of my skin. "As a black woman," he asked, "what do you think of Louis Farrakhan?" At a time like that one has to choose between bombast and belligerence. Since the hosts were nice and the visit had been pleasant, I thought getting to the point would do. "Are my remarks more accurate if I don't like Farrakhan," I asked, "or more tainted if I do? More importantly, what does Minister Farrakhan have to do with the talk I just gave?"

White fascination with Farrakhan is a function of the attraction and apprehension with which many approach him, the mixed appeal that rivet's the nation's attention in his direction. He is America's Stagger Lee, the man who jumps into white people's faces and says what few others are willing to say. He relentlessly pushes issues of

African-American empowerment, especially economic empowerment. He gives voice to those vague claims that surely black people
ought to be able to do more with what we have. His rhetoric on
black economic empowerment can be perceived as both radical and
conservative. It is radical, in a pluralistic society, to advocate economic separation. At the same time, it is conservative to view capitalism as the path to progress for an oppressed people.

But has the Nation of Islam, under Farrakhan, truly been able
to develop beyond the 1950s record of amassing small businesses?
Has the NOI been able to tame uncharted waters in the sea of black
economic development? Given the rhetoric of the "three-year economic program," which purports to eliminate "unemployment,
poor housing and all the other detriments that plague our communities,"[12] what has been the reality of the Nation's economic program under Minister Farrakhan? Is the rhetoric of self-sufficiency
matched by reality?

It is difficult to assess, precisely, the nature and size of the holdings of the Nation of Islam. Calls and letters to the Nation's Chicago headquarters went unanswered, and requests for information
were flatly denied. News reports of the Nation's economic accom
plishments have been mixed, at best, and are likely to be discounted
as biased by those closest to the NOI. At least on the basis of external appearances, though, no economic renaissance, no special self-
sufficiency, has been the result of any NOI activity.

To be sure, the NOI has assets. According to *Business Week,* it
owned two thousand acres of farmland in Georgia and Michigan
in early 1995 and planned to acquire eight thousand more acres in
the near future,[13] along with at least a dozen tractor trailers that transport produce around the country. It owns a media distribution
network, including the *Final Call* newspaper, and a book and tape
sales business. It outlined plans to open a series of restaurants in four
urban centers in 1995, but after the mixed record of its Chicago
restaurant, which opened with much fanfare in the early 1990s, apparently decided not to expand.

Indeed, a 1995 examination of the assets of the Nation of Islam suggested that the economic viability of the Nation's businesses is questionable. According to the *Chicago Tribune,* IRS liens, defaulted bank loans, and questionable business practices are all part of the NOI record in Chicago. "Nation-affiliated companies are riddled with debt, failure and allegations of fraud," the *Tribune* reported in a week-long series that was based on court documents, corporate records, and interviews with vendors. A soap and beauty products enterprise launched by Farrakhan with much fanfare in 1985, for example, was entangled in production and distribution snafus from the start and by 1993 was almost seized by the Internal Revenue Service.[14] Further, the fluid networks of bean pie shops, agricultural farms, and property holdings seem to intermingle Nation funds indiscriminately with the personal fortunes of the minister and his family members. And, unlike most traditional churches, which publish audited financial reports, the Nation's books are "shrouded in secrecy," the *Tribune* found.

Predictably, the NOI described the *Chicago Tribune* stories as biased products of the white-owned media. The Nation's unwillingness, however, to set the record straight on its financial matters leaves the impression that there is financial chaos in Nation-owned businesses. Still, the NOI has economic pull, as much for its assets as for its "asset potential." No matter what the past has been, there are many who believe that the NOI can help achieve black economic self-sufficiency, on the strength of Mr. Farrakhan's rhetoric and because of the wallets of his audience. Whenever Louis Farrakhan fills up a stadium with ten thousand to sixty thousand African Americans, who pay a $10 to $30 admission charge and more when the hat is passed, he is looking at hundreds of thousands of dollars for an evening's work. How is that asset potential translated into the betterment of the African-American community?

The Million Man March could be considered a case in point. Farrakhan addressed economic issues in his MMM speech, calling for the establishment of a national black economic development fund to eliminate from organizations like the NAACP the need for corporate and nonblack contributions. He also pledged to share a percentage of march proceeds with the financially strapped District of Columbia. March attendees were asked to pay a $10 registration fee, and there was a collection at the march to which each man present was asked to contribute at least a dollar. In addition, those vendors who sold food, T-shirts, and other wares were charged vending fees. The potential to collect revenue was present at the march, and the willingness to give was also there. Six months after the march, though, Minister Farrakhan reported a deficit in excess of $66,000. The economic development fund, the contribution to the District of Columbia, and other promises were unrealized.

It seems to me there is an arithmetic problem. When the United States Park Service reported march attendance of 400,000, organizers were quick to suggest that there were perhaps three times as many marchers, 1.2 million. Air photographs suggested that as many as 800,000, and perhaps 1.1 million were at the march at its peak. If each of those present contributed a dollar, there should have been between $800,000 and $1.1 million collected at a minimum. Anecdotal accounts of men passing $10, $20, and $50 into buckets raise questions about the accuracy of march accounting and the possibility of financial skulduggery. This possibility was never fully explored because Minister Farrakhan was generating more incendiary headlines only months after the march.

Having drawn the world's attention on his plans for the African-American men who heeded his clarion call, he switched gears and embarked on a World Friendship Tour that featured pit stops in the capitals of some of the world's most outrageous dictators. In Libya, Nigeria, Zaire, and the Sudan, Farrakhan met with despots who repulsed world human rights leaders, dissipating the moral authority he gained during the Million Man March and raising questions about his international agenda. Indeed, weeks after his return from the Friendship Tour, Minister Farrakhan announced that Libya might "give" or invest a billion dollars for African-

American uses. The potential gift was the subject of much press ire, but it was never fully placed in the context of Farrakhan's economic development vision.

The revenue questions raised during the march are also applicable where other mass events are concerned. If these events are a financial success, then where is the money? If they are a failure, was the attendance as large as reported? What role do these events play in the furtherance of black economic development, or are they simply opportunities for the presentation of rhetoric? Is there economic reality? This question has as much to do with the success or failure of mass events as it does with the efficacy of the small business strategy for African Americans.

Currently, a smaller proportion of African Americans than of other populations own small businesses, and it is no stretch to say that the African-American entrepreneurial spirit could use further development. At the same time, regardless of race, the facts establish business failure as more common than business success, so that those who attempt entrepreneurship will often find it a challenging experience. Further, the NOI notion of economic insulation is impossible given the level of integration that exists in the contemporary United States. The Million Man March offers an illustration. While the march itself may have lost money, hoteliers in the District of Columbia were net gainers because of the influx of march participants. Since the only hotel owned by African Americans had closed in early 1995, the revenues that came from occupancy did not enhance the African-American community.

Should these economic failures be laid at the feet of Minister Farrakhan? Perhaps not. A movement that has the development of small business at its base is not likely to change the track record of small business failure. The rhetoric of self-sufficiency is not likely to alter ingrained patterns of economic interdependence. And it is nearly impossible to sell freedom and economic development by admission to coliseum events.

There is another facet to this issue. The focus on economic self-sufficiency and the development of small businesses ignore the current technological and regulatory climate and the fact that structural issues must be as fully emphasized as economic issues. Even if the proportion of black entrepreneurs equaled that of entrepreneurs in the overall population (which it does not), issues of industrial organization and unionization are important. A singular focus on business development may well ignore other economic needs of the masses.

Louis Farrakhan can't be blamed for that. The deindustrialization of America has brought with it the worship of petty capitalism and the opportunities that it brings for small entrepreneurs. To the extent that twenty-first-century economic opportunities will be driven by the development of this petty capitalism, it is important that African Americans participate in it. Still, Minister Farrakhan has prided himself on his boldness, his ability to sit at the cutting edge and set a direction for African Americans. He is part of a significant continuum of exhortation about self-sufficiency in the economic development realm. But he has not matched his rhetoric with bold action in the economic arena, nor has he offered an analysis that takes twenty-first-century trends into consideration. The economic failure of the Million Man March is one of many broken economic promises that the minister has offered the African-American community. It raises questions about the viability of his mission, economic and otherwise.

Notes

1. U.S. Department of Labor, Bureau of Labor Statistics, *Employment and Earnings,* vol. 44, no. 1 (January 1997), p. 204.

2. U.S. Department of Labor, *Employment and Earnings,* pp. 161–63.

3. Frederick Douglass, *Life and Times of Frederick Douglass, Written by Himself* (1882), as cited in E. U. Essien-Udom, *Black Nationalism: A Search for Identity in America* (Chicago: University of Chicago Press, 1962), 163.

4. Booker T. Washington, *Up From Slavery,* as cited in Essien-Udom, *Black Nationalism,* 163.

5. Essien-Udom, *Black Nationalism,* 163.

6. Ibid., 164.

7. C. Eric Lincoln, *The Black Muslims in America,* 3rd ed. (Trenton, N.J.: Africa World Press, 1994), 85.

8. Ibid., 86–87.

9. Ibid., 89.

10. Henry Louis Gates, Jr., "Farrakhan Up Close," *The New Yorker* (April 29–May 6, 1996): 116.

11. Julianne Malveaux, *Sex, Lies and Stereotypes: Perspectives of a Mad Economist* (Pines One Publishing, Los Angeles, CA 1994), "No Means No," 322, and other columns.

12. *Final Call* (February 11, 1997): 27.

13. Ron Stodghill, "Farrakhan's Three-Year Plan," *Business Week* (March 13, 1995): 40.

14. David Jackson, "Allegations of Fraud Trail Farrakhan Aide," *Chicago Tribune* (March 12, 1995): 10.

Louis Farrakhan, Ethnitopia, and the Politics of Race Translation

Michael Eric Dyson

MICHAEL ERIC DYSON *is Visiting Distinguished Professor of African-American Studies at Columbia University. He is the author of several books, including* Making Malcolm: The Myth and Meaning of Malcolm X, *which was named a Notable Book of 1994 by* The New York Times *and* The Philadelphia Inquirer, *and the bestselling* Race Rules: Navigating the Color Line, *from which this essay is adapted.*

The recent rise to mainstream prominence of Minister Louis Farrakhan and the emergence of Colin Powell as a cultural hero have encouraged blacks to revisit an old dilemma: whether to bond with or separate from white America in the search for racial justice. In truth, Farrakhan and Powell are symbols of the divided mind of black America. Those of us who are integrationists want our cake of mainstream values. But many of us want to buy it from a black baker and eat it in a black restaurant in the black section of town. Others of us want our racial separatism. But we often want it in mixed company: a black dorm at a white university, a black history month in a predominantly white country, and a black house in a white suburb. The lure of separatism lingers because integration failed to provide the just society many blacks had hoped would arrive after the civil rights struggles of the sixties. But the failure of separatism is even greater. It has not delivered the *ethnitopia* it promises. That fact is often forgotten when black folk get angry at the slow pace of racial progress.

In a powerful fashion, Farrakhan's and Powell's West Indian cultural heritage has influenced their respective perceptions of the goals and functions of African-American leadership and the role race plays in black America. Their career paths certainly prove that Powell and Farrakhan think quite differently about race. In Powell's case, the glistening surface of his moderate views and military heroism reflects our deepest desires to *transcend* race. Farrakhan's attempted leap from the fringes to the front line of black life captures the disappointment with mainstream black leadership. It captures as well the desire to *translate* race into the dialect of black experience. But when it comes to rehabilitating black culture, Powell's transcendence of race and Farrakhan's translation of race may be, in some ways, flip sides of the same coin. For instance, both agree that self-help is key to black redemption. They both also want to restore conservative cultural values in black families and in American society.

This is partly due to their common West Indian roots. Farrakhan and Powell were reared by parents who valued hard work. Their parents also prized Caribbean beliefs about blacks working among themselves to create a stronger society. In Powell's case, that vision extends from his black family to embrace the entire nation. Powell believes that blacks should fully participate in American democracy. That belief is rooted in his desire to see the brilliant diversity of a predominantly black Caribbean culture come alive, not only for black Americans, but for the entire United States.

Farrakhan's beliefs about black self-determination are rooted in fellow West Indian Marcus Garvey's separatist doctrines. Farrakhan's desire to create a black ethnitopia is rooted in Garvey's notion of black self–help and racial solidarity. Farrakhan is also attracted to Garvey's vision of black Americans finding their true destiny in solidarity with Africans around the globe, free from the shackles of white supremacy. It is not surprising that Powell and Farrakhan argue for radically different paths to racial salvation. What is intriguing is that they may have more than calypso and color in common. Powell is, perhaps, more rooted in black culture than his public image lets on. Farrakhan may be more closely tied to mainstream America than he or his followers care to confess. The transcendence and the translation of race, while certainly discrete, converge at crucial points.

The transcendence of race remains a powerful dream to many whites because it suppresses the bitter memory of race. It would also relieve whites of the hard work that must be done in the present to make things right. Powell's patriotism and conservative values might have taken him a long way with many whites and blacks, but his version of race transcendence also turned off many blacks. The polls taken during the period Powell was considering a presidential run showed he had greater pull among whites than among blacks. Farrakhan's recent rise to black mainstream prominence must be viewed against that backdrop. In crucial ways, Farrakhan is the blackened version of Powell's conservative cultural beliefs and social values, a different translation of a Caribbean ethic of self–help and its politics of self–determination. Anyone doubting this judgment need look no further than Farrakhan's attempt to broaden his leadership with the Million Man March.

While it may be difficult on the surface to discern Farrakhan's truck with Powell's moderate conservatism, the two men share a crucial assumption about the mechanisms of black improvement: pulling oneself up by the bootstraps. While Powell sees self–help as key to transcending race, Farrakhan sees it as key to translating race into the idiom of black self–determination. Undoubtedly, such an emphasis, as argued above, flows from their common ethnic roots. Farrakhan's roots are cloaked in virtually the same sort of secrecy that shrouds the internal workings of the Nation of Islam. To get a sense of his translation of race, and his appeal to millions of blacks, we'll have to understand where he came from and what forces shaped him.

Born in the Bronx in 1933, Farrakhan, like Powell, was the child of West Indian immigrants. He fed from his mother Mae Manning's Saint Kitts roots (Saint Kitts was formerly a British crown colony) and drank in his stepfather Louis Walcott's Barbados heritage. But from the beginning, there was trouble. Mae first fell in love with a Jamaican, Percival Clark, who quickly departed after their marriage. Still wed to Clark, Mae met Louis Walcott, who fathered Farrakhan's older half brother, Alvan Walcott. But Clark reemerged long enough to get Mae pregnant with another child, only to disappear again. The conflict was cruel: Mae was legally married to Clark but in love with Walcott. Her predicament was compounded by the fact that she and Alvan were dark. She was afraid that her baby would be fair-skinned, proving her infidelity. She tried desperately to abort the child three times with a coat hanger, according to Farrakhan biographer Arthur Magida. When her efforts failed, she decided to have the baby, born Louis Eugene Walcott, now Louis Farrakhan. Later, the elder Walcott would abandon the family, as well.

Farrakhan was brought up in Boston, in Roxbury, a black section of town permeated by West Indian culture. Showing early signs of musical promise, he took up the violin at the age of five, eventually gaining admission to Boston Latin, then arguably the most prestigious public school in America. He experimented with the guitar and the ukulele as well. He also played for the Boston College Orchestra and won the Ted Mack Original Amateur Hour. Reared as an Episcopalian, he was deeply influenced by the black nationalist teachings of his pastor, Nathan Wright, and the Garveyite doctrine of black self-determination, popular in his home and throughout Roxbury.

Although he had aspirations to attend Juilliard, Farrakhan's poor background (his mother worked as a domestic) placed the school far beyond his grasp. Instead, Farrakhan attended Winston-Salem Teachers College (now Winston-Salem State University) in North Carolina for a couple of years after graduating from high school. He moved back to Boston and married his pregnant high school sweetheart, Betsey, now Khadidja, in 1953. But his musical interests continued. Like his mother, Farrakhan was a fan of calypso. Many of the music's masters—including Lord Executioner, Growler, Attila the Hun, and Black Prince—found their way to the Walcott home in Roxbury. Similar to strands of hip-hop culture that would later celebrate Farrakhan as a hero, calypso fused art and politics. Like hip-hop, calypso was grounded in a specific cultural moment of black masculine expression: It grew from a Trinidadian Lenten festival in which men competed with one another to signify in clever ways on dominant culture and power. Calypso's lessons would certainly not be lost on Farrakhan. He ascended the ladder of power and influence within the Nation of Islam while doing rhetorical battle with white supremacy.

Farrakhan himself eventually gained local fame as a calypso singer, performing as Calypso Gene and as the Charmer. In the early fifties his night club career put him into position to meet Malcolm X, who was proselytizing in a Boston club. But it was in 1955, when he was in Chicago to perform, that Farrakhan was invited to a Savior's Day convention to hear Elijah Muhammad. He immediately converted to the Nation of Islam. When he returned to Boston, his charm was wrapped in a brand-new moniker that rivaled the intrigue of his stage name: Louis X.

Farrakhan's gifts in the secular world aided his rise in the Nation. He continued to write songs and penned two plays, one of which, *The Trial,* brought him fame among his fellow converts. The play also earned him notoriety outside the Nation when lines from it— especially "I charge you [the white man] with being the greatest liar on earth"—were featured in Mike Wallace's now famous late 1950s documentary of the Nation, entitled "The Hate That Hate Produced."

Farrakhan's first assignment was to Temple No. 7, in Harlem, where he soon became assistant to Malcolm X. Because of his organizational talent and oratorical gifts, he then became captain of the Fruit of Islam, the defense arm of the Nation of Islam, at the Nation's Boston mosque, and was named the minister shortly thereafter. Working his way through the ranks of the Nation, Farrakhan eventually became minister of Harlem's Temple No. 7, and then national representative for the Honorable Elijah Muhammad after mentor–turned–mortal enemy Malcolm X's bitter secession in 1964.

Since the late sixties, Farrakhan's reputation has continued to grow, even outside of the Nation. He draws thousands of blacks to venues around the country where he promotes a message of black rage at white supremacy. Despite his undeniable success in reviving and reshaping the Nation of Islam, however, he has been covered by a veil of suspicion that he cannot remove: that he had a hand in Malcolm's death.

Strangely enough, the shadow of doubt about Farrakhan's role in Malcolm's death is only increased by his denials. That has to do in part with the suspicion of those who "doth protest too much." Then, too, it might be because his denials of direct participation in Malcolm's death allow him to draw subtle benefits. Each time he admits that he whipped up the atmosphere that led to Malcolm's death, Farrakhan reinforces his good standing among Nation loyalists who still view Malcolm as a traitor. By consistently denying his direct participation in Malcolm's death, he pleases many who view Malcolm as a hero. So Farrakhan is able to satisfy Malcolm's enemies and many of his friends and followers with the same disclaimers. It is unclear whether Farrakhan's denials are genuine or shrewd calypso counterstrategies designed to deflect criticism.

His disputes with Malcolm aside, Farrakhan has proved to be a brilliant twin to the personality Malcolm shaped in the Nation of Islam. Farrakhan is one-half the fulfillment of Malcolm's divided mind about which route—separatist or limited solidarity with progressive whites—black folk should take to survive in America. If

Farrakhan is Malcolm's shadow self—at least the half of Malcolm that was disdainful of white folk while he was in the Nation and cautious about proceeding with their help once he departed— Farrakhan aggressively shields himself from Malcolm's brighter, perhaps blinding, other half. That half of Malcolm believed that caste and class should be attacked as well as race. That half of Malcolm believed that black folk should be open to socialist, humanitarian, and democratic strategies for racial uplift. That half of Malcolm believed that white folk really weren't devils. Farrakhan wears his contempt for the other side of Malcolm around his neck as a talisman. It wards off the amnesia that he believes clouds the minds of black prophets once they go soft. It is a reminder to Farrakhan of the price black leaders pay once they lose their way in a racial wilderness where they are lured by misty dreams of cooperating with the enemy.

If Malcolm is a burden to Farrakhan, representing both a past he seeks to forget and a potentially more reconciliatory future he prays won't arrive, Malcolm's presence is also, strangely, a blessing. Why? Because Farrakhan is able to spook white folk by reprising the nerve-rattling, fear-inducing, bogeyman act that Malcolm ingeniously put on as Elijah Muhammad's spokesman. Unlike Malcolm, Farrakhan won't foil the punch line by repenting in the end. It is a job for which he is supremely suited.

Like all of the Nation's great prophets, Farrakhan has a gift for painting the ugliness of white supremacy. In fact, it was the Nation's ingenuity for mining the resentments and unfulfilled fantasies of the black poor—a charm that worked even better for Marcus Garvey— that drew so many huddled, teeming black masses from skid rows, dens of iniquity, prisons, and enslavement to drugs to the Nation's statutes of liberty. The most shining example was Malcolm Little, later Malcolm X. Allah's Messenger Elijah Muhammad gave the Nation of Islam an institutional life that drew from the shadowy inspiration of founder W.D. Fard. Malcolm put the organization on the map and on the minds of Americans; his influence has reached far beyond the Nation's golden-era hundred thousand members in the sixties. Malcolm's orations, while built on the Messenger's teachings, brilliantly reworked the Nation's esoteric theology into a coherent assault on the absurdity of white supremacy. With Malcolm's loss, the Nation lacked a public moralist through whose intellectual arteries the blood of revelation from the Messenger might flow.

With Elijah Muhammad's death in 1975, the mantle of leadership fell to his son Wallace D. Muhammad, later Warithuddin Deen Mohammed. But the younger Muhammad led the Nation into orthodox Islam. Although his father had begun the process, Wallace's revelation to the Nation was even more radical: that its racialist outlook no longer squared with the religious beliefs of universalism and color blindness practiced by orthodox Islam. Plus, the increasing class status of many black Muslims—they jumped from poverty to the middle class in a generation—gave them a compelling reason to go mainstream. Their theology followed their pocketbooks. Thus, the Nation of Islam became the World Community of al-Islam in the West (WCIW) and a few years later, the American Muslim Mission.

Within three years of Elijah Muhammad's death, however, Farrakhan left Wallace Muhammad's mainstream Islamic group, which now had nearly three million members. He resurrected the Nation of Islam in 1978, awakening its members with his fresh interpretations of old Nation beliefs: that separatism is salvation; that black rage is righteous; that the poor are not mere pariahs; that prisoners are potential princes; and that black folk are God's real chosen people. These were the pillars of Farrakhan's translation of race into the language of black self-determination and resistance to white supremacy.

Farrakhan's three-year exile from the NOI taught him how easy it was for the Messenger's beliefs to be attacked or ignored. He set out to update and extend Elijah Muhammad's influence by pumping apocalyptic thunder into the Nation's eschatology. In Christian circles, eschatology has to do with the matters of ultimate importance: death, hell, heaven, the Last Judgment, the matters that come at the end of existence when God sums up human history and metes out punishment or reward. The notion of realized eschatology is the belief that those issues seep into time right now, that they cannot be put off by appeals to heaven or hell beyond history. Something like realized eschatology, perhaps more suitably termed a blues eschatology, is at work in the Nation's theological undercurrents. This blues eschatology drenches history in the crisis of black identity and gives the suffering and salvation of black folk a cosmic meaning.

For Farrakhan, black people are the world's Original People. What affects them affects the universe. The world is in Allah's hands. Black people, who are separated by degree, not kind, from Allah, are themselves divine. Hence, the judgment that black people declare, when they have been saved from their slavish dependence on the white world, is itself the foretaste, and the partial fulfillment, of a divine judgment. Under a blues eschatology, the events of black life take on an apocalyptic weight. Black suffering is placed at the heart of existence. The suffering of the black poor, victims of white racist violence, black males, and black leaders are all charged with a surplus of religious emotion. In fact, attempting to harm them is attempting to harm God.

Farrakhan has given the beliefs of Elijah Muhammad a face-lift. The white devil demonology has been largely replaced by blistering, bitter attacks on the practice of white supremacy. And while the Nation's apolitical stance has been replaced by strategic participation in black politics, Farrakhan has also extended Muhammad's reach into the Islamic world on the Nation's own terms. Farrakhan's coziness with a dictator like Iraq's Saddam Hussein is explained by Hussein's support of Farrakhan's relentless attacks on America's racist imperialism. It is also made possible by a solidarity forged by religious beliefs. Of course, one must question Farrakhan's embrace of Hussein in light of the exploitative manner in which Hussein, a secular nationalist, threw off the official anti-Islamic policy in Iraq to consolidate his power and influence by wooing the religious devotees of Islam.

During the fifties, Elijah Muhammad became friendly with North Africa's Gamal Abdel Nasser. Farrakhan has forged a controversial alliance with Nasser's star pupil, Libyan dictator Muammar Gadhafi. Both Gadhafi's political perspective and his patronage (millions of dollars since the late seventies) are important to Farrakhan. Gadhafi's famous *Green Book or Third Universal Theory* presents an alternative to both capitalism and communism. This partially explains Farrakhan's poor translation (or is it a good translation of Gadhafi's unworkable theory?) of Gadhafi's philosophy in Farrakhan's militant rhetoric against the state even as he supports versions of black capitalism.

Even in light of his forays into the Muslim world, Farrakhan's 1996 visit to Africa and the Middle East proved deeply problematic. He offered no public criticism of African nations and Islamic countries involved in unjust political practices, and that raises serious questions about his commitment to justice, his moral judgment, and his ability to provide the sort of self-critical leadership so sorely needed among black Americans. Farrakhan visited Nigeria, pleading with human rights advocates to give dictator General Sani Abacha three more years to make good on his promise to return civilian rule to the African country. Farrakhan overlooked the detention of hundreds of pro-democracy activists without trial and the execution of opposition leaders like poet Ken Saro-Wiwa. Farrakhan, it seems, sanctified the barbarous practices of an African nation for no other reason than that the nation is black. Farrakhan told Nigerians that stern discipline was sometimes necessary, and that Moses, like Abacha, had been a dictator.

In Tehran, Farrakhan vowed to help the mullahs in their bid to overthrow the "Great Satan," the United States. In the past he has been the guest of Sudanese leaders Bashir and Turabi in Khartoum. On his last visit to the Sudan, he heaped praise on the Sudanese government, lauding its "wise Islamic leadership." But there has been a recent surge of slavery in the Sudan. Farrakhan said nothing. Worse still, the Sudanese government has wiped out hundreds of thousands of its people in a bitter civil war. Farrakhan said nothing. Grievous, too, is the allegation that when Mohamed Athie of the International Coalition Against Chattel Slavery sought to speak for Africans enslaved in the Sudan at the Million Man March, his request was ignored.

Such behavior trumps Farrakhan's bid for mainstream black leadership. The tragedy is that his behavior occurred *after* the Million Man March, at which he made a credible if controversial claim to the leadership of millions of blacks. His actions after the march highlight nagging questions that emerged in the buildup to the gathering. Can a leader who has preached separatist dogma unite a broad spectrum of black Americans in their quest for social justice? Can the head of an authoritarian, some have said fascist, organization that thrives on racial conspiracies, bizarre gnostic beliefs, and religious charisma yield to the demands of a democratic constituency? Will Farrakhan's non-Muslim followers be free to criticize him? Or will they live in fear of being beat up or silenced by loyalists who consider such criticism blasphemous? These questions all point, perhaps, to a more basic question. Is race translation superior to race transcendence? Or, to put it another way, do the virtues of race translation outweigh the obvious deficits of a leadership built on race transcendence? The Million Man March provides a vehicle to explore the good, bad, and ugly aspects of race translation.

There are those who reviled the march as a "swamp of hatred." Others have romanticized it. I experienced a more ambiguous reality. The march embodied and cast light on complex cultural conflicts in black life over masculinity, ethnocentrism, responsibility, and atonement. It also highlighted the strengths and weaknesses of leadership built on race translation. Only a fool would fail to understand why many women, gays, lesbians, Jews, whites, and blacks were troubled by this march. I can also understand why they remain troubled by the place of Louis Farrakhan in black political life. In the lively contest to define the emerging black culture that the march symbolizes, this issue cannot be sidestepped.

The Million Man March is a logical extension and a brilliant summing up of Farrakhan's vocation of translating race. It clarified how his leadership has translated race with a heavy masculine accent. Masculine forms of experience. Masculine journeys to self-definition. Masculine quests for freedom. Masculine struggles for manhood. The Nation's genius—and its grave limitation, too—has always been its yen to redeem black masculinity. This is a theme that has only recently caught fire among pundits, practitioners, prophets, and public intellectuals. But Farrakhan was way ahead of the game. Another way of stating this is to say that the Nation's and Farrakhan's vice—a focus on men, leading to forms of sexism and paternalism—has been their virtue. That virtue is realized in Farrakhan's foresight that the problems of black male life would come to dominate the moral landscapes of black communities.

The Nation's singular focus on helping black men get their lives together is driven by its ideology of resistance to white supremacy. The Nation has worked diligently to make proud men out of black prisoners, those in jail or those whose self-image is distorted because they are captives to a worship of the white world. The Nation has always seen black male addictions—whether to violence, drugs, or white acceptance—as symptoms of a virus of lostness that infects the entire black community. The Nation holds that the lostness of black men leads them to abuse their wives and children; to abuse their bodies with alcohol and bad food; to maim and murder each other; and to embrace, like black revolutionary theorist Frantz Fanon, the breasts of white womanhood in search of the milk of affection and affirmation. Long before the decline of black male life became widely apparent; and long before black males were vilified and glamorized by both the cultural right and the left, the Nation of Islam preached its own brand of salvation for black males. And from the very beginning, the core of the Nation's message has not changed. NOI followers believe that black men can be saved only by being restored as loving leaders in black families where they receive and return adoration and respect.

With good reason, that message was strongly criticized by black feminists before the march as a thin cover for patriarchal posturing. Seeking to restore the black man as the head of the family devalues families where black women, by chance or choice, run the show. In the Nation's (and Newt Gingrich's) view, such families are defective until the black man returns to rule—and serve—in full glory by spreading his masculine splendor. And, no doubt, more of his seed. This deeply conservative vision of the black family, one held, perhaps, by millions of blacks, has blinded us to all sorts of nontraditional families where health and prosperity reign. This is no argument against the nuclear family's virtues, of which there are many. It is just a cautionary note against making it the only viable model for our communities. It is easy to see how feminist critics believe the language of black male restoration has only deepened the problems of black males and black communities. It makes women and girls minor factors in the equation of racial redemption. For such critics, the Million Man March would be business as usual. It would be a crude throwback to the times when women were expected to stay on the sidelines to cheer on men in the work of thinking, acting, and leading.

There is, however, a crucial difference between acknowledging the specific pains of black males—and hence drawing dramatic attention to the resources and remedies for their problems—and old-fashioned, if slickly updated, attempts to ignore the lives of black girls and women. Unfortunately, the two have often been collapsed. I agree with critics who argue that the rhetoric of black male suffering is often cobbled together from a distortion of black female troubles. Thus, the very language of black male crisis erases black women's faces and bodies from the canvas of social suffering. It is simply not true that black men's hurts are more important than the social horrors black women face. Too often, however, black male advocates behave and speak as if that's the case. What is undeniable is that the problems that hurt poor, young, black males affect the health and character of the communities in which those males live and, too often, die. It is the immediacy and impact of black male problems on our national life, not their greater importance, that justifies attention to their plight.

There is much to be said for black women standing side by side with black men to address the problems of black males. This is especially true because black women and children often bear the brunt of black men's rage. Black women's and children's bodies are often convenient targets for an aggression that black men fail to usefully direct toward the forces that cause their pain. Black women have energetically, and often without acknowledgment, fashioned solutions to the suffering of black males. They have done so as mothers, sisters, daughters, nieces, aunts, grandmothers, social workers, social critics, domestics, factory laborers, historians, doctors, civil rights leaders, and on and on.

Still, there are some things that black men have got to do by and for themselves. There exists among black men a great hunger for responsibility. That concept, often with good cause, is viewed with skepticism by the left, including feminists and black progressives. It's not that the left doesn't want people to be responsible. But it knows that for responsibility to make sense, for it to be a just way to judge individuals, we must account for the social forces stacked against those from whom we expect responsible behavior. In that light, there is truth to feminist arguments that calling black men to personal responsibility for problems that are largely not of their own making is confusing and harmful. The call for personal responsibility, without regard for its social contexts, can indeed be a way of letting off easy the society in which black men perish. For the most part, the march's organizers certainly downplayed the structural features of black male suffering. By linking morality to the personal, and not to the political as well, the march's organizers overlooked crucial social dimensions to black male problems. In some ways, the demand for atonement exaggerated black male responsibility by overestimating black male control. Plus, it gave solace to many on the right who have always said that personal responsibility is the cause, and, ultimately, the cure, for the problems black males face.

None of this means that we should ditch the idea of personal responsibility. It just means that we've got to come up with a more complex version of responsibility, the acceptance of which remains an important element in rehabilitating black men's lives. Without an acknowledgment of moral agency, the black male becomes the sum of the social forces that shape him. Such a construction denies the moral capabilities of individual black men. It also underestimates the capacity for black men to change themselves and their communities. Feminists and other progressives who ignore the question of personal responsibility deny the efforts of black men to behave humanely, especially toward black women and each other. It is true that a narrow conception of personal responsibility is harmful. But it is equally true that a failure to appreciate the moral dimensions of social transformation is destructive. The conservatives aren't, and shouldn't be, the only ones concerned about responsibility.

But other dimensions of the call to responsibility for black men at the march were offensive. For instance, Farrakhan and many of the men at the march failed to overcome their homophobia. The conservative view of the family held by the Nation, and by many blacks, also devalues the role of gay men (and lesbian women) in the history of black struggle. That conservatism discounts the intellectual contribution that gays and lesbians have made to the political and social health of black communities. Homophobia creates a form of intraracial apartheid. It was completely overlooked at the march, where a crude, simplistic view of racial unity prevailed. Similarly, the message of atonement, despite Farrakhan's oddly disjointed and esoteric oration on the subject, fell short of one of its most publicized aims: to communicate the failure of black men to treat black women right. There was nothing at the march to help black men atone for their misogyny, sexism, or patriarchy. Those plagues have ripped through our communities, including our churches and our mosques.

The charge of anti-Semitism against Farrakhan, too, plagued the march. It is a charge that has dogged him as long as he has enjoyed the limelight as a militant black leader. The disdain many Jews feel for Farrakhan and his heroic status among many blacks, in part for his sharp criticism of Jews, is a symptom of the hostility and confusion that thwart peace between the two groups. A lot of the tension between blacks and Jews centers in issues of cultural assimilation and class ascension. Jewish assimilation was largely aided by the ease, and eagerness, of many Jews to blend, physically and psychically, into the white mainstream. Black assimilation has been slowed by the inability to blend. Since we live in a culture where social goods and benefits are attached to color, Jews and blacks embody opposing features of our society's obsession with skin: *pigmentification* and *pigmentosis*. Pigmentification occurs when white-skinned outsiders like Jews are adapted into the dominant culture, extending the benefits of democracy. Pigmentosis occurs when dark-skinned outsiders like blacks are excluded from the dominant culture, curtailing the benefits of democracy. The tension generated by Jewish identification with the white majority, and the exclusion of blacks from that possibility, continues to plague relations between the groups to this day.

Although Farrakhan has been vilified by Jews for more than a decade—he was quoted as having called Judaism a "gutter religion" during Jesse Jackson's 1984 presidential campaign—he was even more widely attacked for the Nation of Islam's infamous 1991 publication *The Secret Relationship Between Blacks and Jews*. *Secret* purports to show through the heavy use of Jewish scholarship how deeply involved Jews were in the slave trade and how Jews continue to exploit black Americans. It is a horrible piece of scholarship and a prejudiced view of Jewish culture. It is tragic that the Nation of Islam covers its anti-Semitism in the robes of scholarly objectivity, a ruse perfected by white racists like William Shockley and Arthur Jensen.

Legitimate, mutual criticism between blacks and Jews is distorted by extremists on both sides. When Jewish racism is cloaked in sophisticated intellectual jargon, it is nonetheless destructive. And when black anti-Semitism is given a smooth gloss because of its mixture of half-truth and falsehood, it is nonetheless harmful. The Nation's obsession with Jews, the need to discover a Jew behind every problem that blacks face, informs its rhetorical assaults on Jews. Blacks and Jews must appeal to the humanist and religious traditions that we share: traditions that promote the democratic exchange of ideas and grievances without resorting to vicious name calling and immoral behavior. Blaming Jews, gays and lesbians, and feminists, though it assuages our hurt in the short term, leads us down a moral spiral that favors self-pity at the expense of true self-examination and social change.

Solving the problems of black men is but one element of coming to grips with the colossal problems that black folk confront. Of course, the much ballyhooed crisis of black leadership continues to seize the attention of black communities across America. Powell's emergence as a key figure in American politics has bolstered the appeal of leadership that transcends race. In the end, the transcendence that Powell symbolizes cannot successfully address the lethal persistence of race in our culture. The variety of ways that race, and racism, continues to dominate American culture will not be well served by a leadership whose success is pitted on suppressing key features of our racial malaise. Powell is right to focus on self-help, or bootstrap raising, as a prominent feature of black rehabilitation. But that's nothing new. Self-help has often been the only help black folk have known. But Powell also understands that you've got to have a good pair of bootstraps to lift yourself up. His vision of race transcendence is long on moral reconstruction, which is good. But it is short on social and cultural reconstruction. His vision fails to confront the structural features of American life that continue to harm black life. To take those features seriously—features like the maldistribution of wealth, the blight of capitalism, the material suffering of the impoverished, and class inequalities—is to challenge the deep conservatism of his political vision of the transcendence of race.

But neither will the race translation model of Farrakhan serve the best interests of black communities. Farrakhan is absolutely right to point out the continuing plague of white racism. He is right to accent personal responsibility. He is brave to preach to a spiritually hungry black America a message of moral and spiritual reconstruction. He is bold to articulate the forms of black rage that attract large segments of the black middle class. Farrakhan's appeal to the black middle class depends on the recognition that racism is not destroyed through higher class location or enhanced social status. The rage of the black middle class—a subject that journalist Ellis Cose brilliantly explored in his 1993 book—makes that group, perhaps, the most surprising constituency of Farrakhan's expanded leadership. (In Malcolm's day, the black poor and working class were drawn to his message. Now, with a full generation of mainstream access, the black middle class has rediscovered the need to deal with the sheer recalcitrance of racism in America. Farrakhan is deeply attractive because that theme, along with that of the redemption of black men, is his bread and butter.)

Then, too, the renewed appeal of Farrakhan—and Powell—to the black middle class is precisely because of black middle-class guilt and anxiety toward the black ghetto poor. There is a lingering sense among the black (and white) middle class that Farrakhan is "good for those ghetto people." The support of Farrakhan's social conservatism is, in many ways, a cop-out for the black middle class. (Praising his leadership for the black ghetto poor is a little like praising Mussolini because he made the trains work on time.) All of this suggests that we need not only bold leadership, but leadership that will allow for creative political alliances.

Farrakhan's fundamentalist religious orientation—one that continues to express a vicious homophobia and a thinly veiled sexism—limits his use to progressive black forces confronting the racial challenges of the next century. Moreover, the ethnic bigotry that flows from his forces undermines their ethical integrity in pointing out the evil of white supremacy. Farrakhan's brilliant but narrow translation of race fails to account for the nuances, the robust diversity, the rugged complexity, the multihued textures of black life in America. If black folk are to move into the next century with serious, committed, well-equipped leadership, we need to be able to call our leaders to accountability for their actions. The antidemocratic nature of Farrakhan's religious organization makes that a difficult task. His appeal proves that we need bold, visionary black leadership. But, despite its virtues, a race translation model of black leadership fails to express the broad array of interests contained in the grammar of black liberation and resistance.

Farrakhan and Powell are two of our nation's most important leaders, who, deservedly or not, have brought unique interethnic subtexts to the debate over black leadership in America. Their West Indian roots have sunk deep into the ideological territory of American debates over the best route to racial redemption for blacks. Farrakhan and Powell both offer intriguing, if frustrating, answers to our most persistent and painful racial predicament. In the end, what we need is a black leadership that attempts neither to transcend nor to translate race. We need a black leadership that *transforms* race. Race is transformed in such a model of leadership because it joins a compelling account of what race has been to an articulation of what race can and should be. A race-transforming black leadership, the kind we should develop in black communities across America, is able to do at least three things. It accents the persistence of white supremacy. It challenges black orthodoxies about racial struggle on the left and the right. And it links antiracist struggle to other forms of political resistance, including class and gender struggles. Still, it cannot be questioned that the brilliance of Farrakhan and Powell has intensified the national debate about the character of black leadership at the end of the twentieth century.

Inside Out: A Contemporary American Herstory

Fahizah Alim

FAHIZAH ALIM *is an award-winning columnist for the* Sacramento Bee (*California*) *and a former member of the Nation of Islam.*

Why would nearly one million black men from all walks of life heed the call of Louis Farrakhan, the Nation of Islam Minister hated by many Americans, to converge on Washington, D.C., on October 16, 1995?

The answer, obviously, is that Farrakhan is not hated by everyone. And if the numbers mean anything—whether you're taking the government's low estimate of 400,000 marchers or the Nation's optimistic count of almost 1 million—the man clearly has the respect and ear of a significant portion of black America. Answering the question of why he commands that respect may not be as easy.

Minister Farrakhan is as much an enigma to those who love and respect him as he is to those who hate him. And no matter how controversial you find him, he has emerged as a key player on America's racially-charged landscape, one capable of commanding the attention and support, if not the strict allegiance, of hundreds of thousands of black people who fill seats at almost every public appearance he makes.

Certainly, he is a postmodern black leader who knows how to attract media attention, better at it, oftentimes, than Jesse Jackson. Whether it's because of his castigation of black people, white people, or Jews, we all recognize that Farrakhan touches a raw nerve in America. I have seen this firsthand.

As a former adherent to the teachings of the late Honorable Elijah Muhammad, and through my work in the community economic and social programs run by the Nation of Islam, I know Louis Farrakhan. I first became aware of the organization during the tumultuous 1960s, after I enrolled as a freshman at the University of California in Berkeley.

Now, some thirty years later, I look back on my involvement in the Nation and am struck by how the cultural upheaval and political winds of that time so strongly forged the public perception of the group. Indeed, the social unrest in America coincided with my search for group empowerment, setting the stage for my conversion to the Nation of Islam. So, my story— and my political and personal evolution—begins in young adulthood, when I first encountered the philosophical and practical teachings of Elijah Muhammad and his acolyte Louis Farrakhan.

Like the majority of black students who entered predominantly white universities in the 1960s, I found myself pulled into a world that people of my color and economic class had little knowledge of. Although Berkeley and this elite world offered educational opportunity, it also was a world peppered with the cultural land mines of white rebellion and white supremacy.

In addition to the peace movement, the feminist movement, and socialist movements, there also was the Black Power movement, its presence manifested in many forms, from acts of nonviolent resistance to doctrines of black nationalism and separatism. After a decade's worth of sit-ins and riots as protests, we moved on to demanding breakfast programs and showings-of-arms. It seemed that the country had been forced to focus its attention on the victims of its bitter legacy of slavery and racial discrimination.

Before I entered Cal, I had not realized how my small-town California upbringing had protected me from the reality of the "two Americas"; it didn't take long for me to see how I was to benefit from the collective historical pain (and lately, the vocal protestations) of America's black masses. Earlier, my awakening to the plight of black people in the segregated South and the stratified northern cities came through the writings of James Baldwin and the televised expressions of outrage of black leaders like Stokely Carmichael, Dr. Martin Luther King, Jr., H. Rap Brown, and Huey P. Newton. Before becoming a recipient of the largess of the University of California, I attended a small high school in a small East Bay town. My mother's family had left the pine forests and slippery clay of Louisiana during the Great Depression, settling first in Arizona and then moving to California during World War II.

When they left the South, my parents also tried to leave the specter of Jim Crow and racial discrimination. Whether it was their own racially-mixed heritage or their haunting memories of racial strife, they rarely mentioned a person's race. If they were speaking among themselves about a white person, they would either show the palm of their hand to indicate that the person was white, or they would purse their lips tight and whisper "white," which came out as a sort of whistle.

I don't remember my mother or other adult family members using derogatory language when talking of other racial groups. And white racism and its impact on blacks was also not a topic of conversation in our home during my childhood. Years later I realized that this was the way they had chosen to try to erase not only the physical scars of racial discrimination, but also the psychological cuts. My way of dealing with racism was not their way.

At Berkeley, a literary-induced awakening to the condition of black Americans and the worldwide community of blacks helped prepare me to follow Elijah Muhammad. When Dr. Martin Luther King, Jr., was killed during my first year in college, I became fully empathetic to the struggles of the masses of black people, and—more important—fully committed to fighting the injustices. *How* to fight them was the big question, and I began to believe the Nation of Islam might have some answers.

My awakening began gradually, aided by the swirl of events at Cal during my early days at the campus. Many students, myself included, became increasingly aware of the dearth of information at Cal on black contributions to society. This is how the movement to include in university curricula accurate teachings of blacks' history (and the history of other nonwhites) began. By 1969, the movement had gained wide student support and some outside momentum. Some of us in those eventful months grew angrier and angrier when we realized how blacks' history, in particular, was being skirted or distorted through omissions. Widely viewed today as being on the vanguard of liberal education, Cal's curriculum and faculty during the late 1960s was considered by many of us too white, too conservative, too accepting of a limited portrayal of African-Americans.

Black instructors, and the personal perspective they might bring to their teachings, were rare during my years of secondary education. The first time I ever had a black instructor stand up in front of class and teach me anything was in a black history class I took while attending a junior college between high school and Cal. I didn't know how hungry I was for a black perspective on history.

Listening to a black teacher tell me about the struggles and triumphs of my people had a huge impact on me. I vowed that thereafter I would be a seeker of those truths. I came to see those stories, the truths of them, as weapons necessary to fight white supremacy and the common belief in black inferiority. They were weapons that white teachers had seen fit to keep from me.

I decided to begin educating myself. And as I began to read the Slave Narratives, the stories of Harriet Tubman and Sojourner Truth and the writings of Frederick Douglass, I became imbued with a sense of our true history. (I had taken the first step toward understanding the meaning of a verse in the Qur'an that reads, "Oppression is worse than slaughter.") I also grew large with pride and a sense of mission. I read into the quiet hours of the early morning, shocked and motivated by the stories of my ancestors.

Over time, my energies at the university became more political than academic. I saw no reason to continue following the rules of an institution whose very existence, as I saw it, was perpetuating the second-class citizenship of my people.

The only way I could continue being a part of the university was to work to change it. I got actively involved in the raucous, student-led group called the Third World Studies Strike. Our mission was to force the university to create an ethnic studies curriculum that included a Black Studies Department. Many other politicized students began to see our role as a privileged cadre of rabble-rousers, activists who viewed ourselves as being responsible for organizing and mobilizing the disenfranchised masses.

I began working as a community organizer in the inner city, passing out literature, organizing voter registration drives, and tutoring poor children in Alameda County's tougher neighborhoods.

Looking back, I know that my newfound empathy with my newfound inner-city brothers and sisters prevented me from focusing my energy on the educational opportunities that existed at Cal. I saw myself then as a liberator. When the Los Angeles Police Department broke into the Black Panther headquarters in Southern California, I joined a group of students from Cal and other local universities in standing all-night vigils at the local Panther headquarters, near the Berkeley campus.

Of course, during that period, police brutality was open and scandalously brutal. Even in supposedly "liberal" Northern California, it was no secret that the arms of the law regularly grappled with the openly angry "new Negro." Gone from the streets was the scared, obsequious Negro. In his place was the militant, proud-to-be-black youth, propelled by angry Black Power rhetoric and the horrific scenes of dogs being sicced on peaceful black demonstrators in the South.

I was one of those youths. I remember the black brothers on the Cal basketball and football teams taking up a collection so their favorite black girlfriends could trade in our straightened hair for the Angela Davis–type Afros or "naturals."

We wanted Cal and the world to know that this was a new Negro on the scene—one who was not going to assimilate and become a white person in black skin. We read Mao's Red Book. And Frantz Fanon's *Black Skins, White Masks*. Chancellor Williams's *The Destruction of Black Civilization,* and Cheikh Anta Diop's *The Cultural Unity of Black Africa. The Autobiography of Malcolm X,* all of James Baldwin; Richard Wright, Ralph Ellison.

We wrote revolutionary poems and met together to denounce the "pig" in loud, staccato prose. It was during one of those meetings of poetic defiance in a class taught by a popular black writer that I first encountered the life-changing teachings of Elijah Muhammad. My boyfriend at the time was a loud, angry Panther wannabe, a middle-class revolutionary stomping around in combat boots and sporting a wild Afro. Bright and extremely articulate, he wrote poetry that consisted most often of angry diatribes and ramblings about what Whitey had done and how he would one day pay. Most of the class offered similar writings.

But there was one student in that class who was different from us. I remember him as a quiet, neat, and somber young man with a thick mustache, bald head, and deep voice. He read a poem about his love and responsibility for his son and the role of the black man in creating a safe world for his family. His words and demeanor stayed with me and left a lasting impression as I sought to find my place in the black struggle.

The nonviolent tactics of Dr. King saw their heyday before the time of my political awakening, the epic marches, sit-ins, and demonstrations taking place just before my emerging activism. Though

I am not sure that I had the temperament to ever have employed King's nonviolent methods, my commitment to the black struggle also stopped short of using the Panthers' methods.

Also, the Panthers in our midst were often crude and unkempt. Their girlfriends seemed either too hard and masculine or too cowed and compliant. I supported the Panthers' grassroots approach, but I couldn't get ready for its rough edges, its vulgarity, its disorder. I wouldn't have admitted it for the world back then, but I guess I was just too middle class for it.

The turning point in my black activism came the Christmas of 1969, when I went to Chicago to visit my father and his upper-middle-class second wife, my stepmother. Away from the rhetoric and political agitation of Cal, I spent that Christmas break seriously reflecting on the nature of the black rebellion that was occurring across the country. I was uncomfortable with the radical methods of the Panthers, knowing that I could never carry a gun or let a man order me to screw his comrades for the revolution (as was rumored to happen to the Panther women).

My mind kept going back to the civil demeanor and the thoughtful words of the young man who had read the poem about his son in our black poetry class. I knew that he was a member of the Nation of Islam, because one day when I was hitchhiking to Cal, wearing a minidress, he gave me a ride to school. During the ride, he told me that my dress was short enough to be a blouse. He went on to tell me of the harmful effect of pork on my health. Rather than being embarassed, I was impressed.

Until then, I hadn't thought much about black Muslims. It was 1969, and they hadn't received much publicity since Malcolm X was killed, at least not in California. I believed them to be a weird, secretive, cultlike organization filled with members who thought Elijah Muhammad was God and allowed him to dictate their lives. But the young Black Muslim did not seem so weird. True, he was very different from the rest of the brothers at Cal but in a positive and reasonable way. He expressed the same anger and distrust of the white power structure as my other comrades, but he seemed directed toward building something and not just tearing something down.

When I returned to school from Christmas vacation and saw him again, I flooded him with questions about his lifestyle and his religion. He explained to me that his religious leader forbade his followers from drinking or smoking or using drugs, from eating bad foods or engaging in immoral or illegal acts such as adultery and fornication.

He started giving me regular rides to school and introduced me to vegetarianism, Islamic literature, and jazz. I was intrigued by this disciplined gentleman, who opened doors and called me sister. Then, one day after maybe a month or so of deep conversations, he dropped the bomb. Because he was married his "leader and teacher," Elijah Muhammad, frowned on our platonic relationship. I was outraged. Here I had found the self-determined, self-realized black man, and some old man in Chicago with a foreign name and a bow tie was standing between us? My naive sense of womanhood was offended.

Nevertheless, the next time a brother in a bow tie came to my door selling papers and inviting me out to the temple, I went. I wanted to prove to my friend that this man, this Elijah Muhammad, had no power to stand between us.

Ultimately, Muhammad had the power to stand not only between me and my new friend but between me and my family, me and my college education and the only lifestyle (distinctly radical-chic) and the only religion (Christianity) I had known. My first visit to the temple was like entering outer space. It was like no place I had ever been, located in a drafty, old, former church on Fillmore Street in San Francisco.

There I found a sense of order and peace and mutual respect I had never known. The Muslim brother had told me that I had to wear "something long" to the meeting. And since this was the mini-skirt era, the only long outfit that I had was a snake-print lounge number. I put it on, feeling self-conscious, but I wanted to see how this Elijah Muhammad could have so much control over my friend's life.

When I entered the temple, I was body searched. The woman who searched me was resplendent in white garb from head to toe. Her hair was covered with a flowing, nunlike scarf, and Australian crystal earrings sparkled against her smooth black skin. She explained to me that she would be searching me for my own safety. The Nation's administration did not want anyone to be able to come into the mosque with drugs or weapons. This procedure was also important to ensure that the police would not have a reason to raid the meeting under the guise of looking for contraband, she said.

She said also that sometimes the minister's message was so powerful that people would jump up and try to harm him or other members on the stage. She also confiscated my cigarettes, because smoking was not allowed in the meeting. Nor was chewing gum. I consented to the search, and she told me she would return my items to me after the meeting. Looking back, I wonder about my complicity. I guess my curiosity about these Black Muslims was greater than my resistance to the confiscations. And everyone, including Muslims who filed in with me, were undergoing the search procedure.

I later learned that the Black Muslims saw this as an important step in beginning to respect and submit to black authority without question. I believed then, and still do, that to promote more racial unity and strength, African-Americans must learn to respect other blacks who are worthy of respect. But that concept often was abused by unscrupulous members high in the Nation's chain of command, an abuse of power that proved to be, ironically, both the reason for its strength and the reason many faithful ultimately turn away from the Nation.

Inside the lecture hall, I was escorted to my seat by a regal, light-skinned woman wearing a silk, emerald-green long garment. She walked lightly ahead of me, her head erect as her scarf cascaded down her back. Her face, free of makeup, shined like a baby's, and her smile was dazzling white and infectious. She escorted me to a seat in the women's section. The men were seated across the aisle.

When I sat down and looked in front of me, I had to catch my breath. In front of the podium were three men seated. All were dressed in the FOI uniforms, suits that resembled military dress uniforms, except that they had stars and moons and other symbols that I was unfamiliar with.

All three men looked like someone had polished them for a portrait. Their skins were gleaming shiny and clean shaven. I could see that their hair was closely cut under their FOI caps, and they sat at attention, staring straight ahead, hands clasped to their sides and feet together. I had never seen such dignified-looking black men. Especially after two years at Berkeley, where the goal was to look wilder than the next person. Standing behind the podium, the minister also had on an FOI suit or uniform. And he greeted everyone in the Arabic words *As-Salaam-Alaikum,* which, he explained, meant "Peace be unto you." The audience responded in kind, *Wa-alaikum Salaam.*

He pointed to the men seated in front of him on stage and said that each of them had once been a troubled person. One had been a psychedelic drug user but now was a doctor. The other had been a philanderer but now was a happily married husband and father. I don't recall the other man's story.

What I remember most from that first meeting is that the minister said the trouble in our communities, in our families, and in our personal lives was because white people—the devil incarnate—had stripped black people of all "knowledge of self." "Our religion, our language, our culture, our names," he preached.

That was it! That explained it all: the reason that black people were stolen from Africa and brought across the Atlantic to suffer in inhuman servitude for hundreds of years. It explained why blacks couldn't vote in the South and had to sit in the back of the buses and drink out of dirty fountains. It explained why black men were lynched and black women were raped and found no justice in the courts. It explained to my young consciousness why black people were robbed of their property, their names, their religion, and their history and why my grandfather, who was three-fourths white, couldn't claim his white father's name.

These NOI members believed that the white man was the devil personified. As I saw it, this indeed explained why less than 1 percent of the students at the University of California were black and why white professors could ignore or malign any of the positive contributions that blacks had made in our history. It explained why my own mother had to stand on her feet nine hours a day in a drafty old cannery, packaging tomatoes and asparagus for $2,700 a year while a white "overseer" yelled at her to speed up the production. And why, with her hands aching and raw from the tomato acid, she cried herself to sleep many nights.

But most important, his words described how my ancestors were ferreted out of Africa, sold into slavery, and forced to serve a brutal, white slave master for nearly four hundred years while systematically being stripped of any sense of history, religion, culture, family, language, and civilization. Stripped clean of Identity. These were Elijah Muhammad's teachings, and they are now Farrakhan's teachings. The Devil. Who else could have done such a horrendous thing?

When the minister said he had the solution to free black people from the clutches of white supremacy, I was ready to listen. On that night, I looked at and listened to people who said they had been set free from mental bondage and second-class citizenship by the powerful teachings of the Honorable Elijah Muhammad. They were polite and peaceful. Neat and clean. They used no vulgarity and the men rushed to open doors for smiling women with healthy-looking babies.

I was hungry for more. I went back every night to listen to the local minister describe how slavery had stripped us of the knowledge of how to live a civilized life. He used constitutional references to show how black Americans were not considered full human beings, and he explained how what we had been taught by our enslavers—on the plantations and in the schools (once we were allowed to learn)—was designed to keep us powerless, disunited, and oppressed.

Pointing to Dr. King and Malcolm and Marcus Garvey, the local minister said that any leader who tried to organize and lift up the masses of black people was incarcerated or killed. Except his leader, the Honorable Elijah Muhammad, a man who had openly defied whites, and had publicly called them the hurtful name of devil for nearly forty years. It was a powerful message, a powerful demonstration of black independence, one that I wanted every black person to know about.

The local minister explained to the audience members that their dysfunctional families, their troubled communities, their ill health, their lack of political and economic power, and their love of white folks and hatred of themselves was due to the white supremacist indoctrination they had been exposed to during their entire sojourn in America. "You have been taught about yourself by someone who hated you and chose to exploit you for his benefit," he said from the podium. "How can you be expected to create a positive, secure world for yourself? You have been mistaught as to your nature and the nature of your oppressor. And you need to be retaught the nature of yourself and how to resist the hostile environment in which you have survived."

It all made sense to me. "How can you love yourself when the person who taught you about yourself hated you? First, you must be taught to love yourself and accept your own," he said. "You must stop trying to be like white people, straightening your hair, bleaching your skin, and trying to alter your African features. Then and only then," said the minister, "will you be able to come together as a people, throwing off the shackles that slavery had put on your mind and building strong families, communities, and nations." These words are the fundamental and practical teachings of the Nation of Islam.

Its more "mystical" teachings—including the legend of Yakub the evil scientist, and the supposed significance of unidentified flying objects—probably deserve criticism. But as I viewed them, their purpose was to encourage among black Americans personal liberation. I believed then, and still do, that all of the teachings espoused by Elijah Muhammad and now by Louis Farrakhan are mental vehicles designed to turn the black man's focus away from trying to reform his oppressor (the white man) and toward reforming himself.

The Nation of Islam is primarily a reform movement. It first went into the prison system, where men are captive audiences, freed from the daily struggles of survival in the streets and able to do some self-assessment and studying. Farrakhan addresses these men. He gives them, to use a term usually applied to the Christian ethos, redemption. But he has a message for all black men who feel that they have been victimized by white supremacy. And whether you and I agree with their feeling isn't really important.

When one who feels he has been the despised "black sheep" of society is told that he is not responsible for his self-hatred and powerlessness, you see a change begin. Many of us who turned to the NOI flourished after coming to believe that we are not responsible for the white man's negative actions and moral failures. When we began to learn that we have been deliberately mistaught and denied the "knowledge, wisdom, and understanding" necessary to live a civilized life, we were given a new lease on life, allowed a clean slate to begin to recreate ourselves and our future.

It's an empowering message. And it's one that rings true. That is why Farrakhan was able to command the attention of nearly a million black men from all walks of life in the fall of 1995. It's a courageous message that strikes the souls of black people with joy: A black man who talks as Farrakhan does and manages to stay alive.

White folks seem to hear only Farrakhan's anti-Semitic rhetoric, his description of them as devils, his vitriolic condemnation of them, but black folks hear a solution for their condition.

It's hard to worry about your friend's headache when someone is stepping on your feet. The Jewish pain is real pain. But it is not more important to black people than their own very real pain.

As James Baldwin put it, "Blacks are not anti-Semitic. Blacks are anti-white." Some Jewish people express dismay that blacks would use the term "holocaust" to describe what befell their ancestors who died crossing the Atlantic during the slave trade. But to millions of blacks, the African Holocaust is still going on.

Furthermore, when Blacks listen to Minister Farrakhan, they hear a black man courageously and skillfully criticizing the white power structure on their behalf. They see him taking on whites, and yes, those Jewish entrepreneurs who he believes malign, exploit, and distort the lives of Black people, the media owners who project worldwide images of us as animals.

They see a black man who has no white sponsors, who is educated, disciplined, economically independent, and who repeatedly demonstrates unconditional love and commitment to the Black Man, whether that man be Mike Tyson, convicted rapist, or accused child molester Michael Jackson, or O.J. Simpson—all famous and talented Black Men who Farrakhan says were "drawn out of the black community."

In the NOI, black Americans see a group of proud and fearless black men who follow Minister Farrakhan. Black men who will go into drug- and gang-infested public housing complexes and confront the lawless. And they see an economic plan to revitalize black families and black communities that have been abandoned by government and corporate entities.

I know Farrakhan's real-world impact on people. For example, when I started attending the University of California, Berkeley, I also started taking the birth control pill. I think it was included in the registration packet. I mention the birth control pill because at the time, it was the drug of choice for most single young women. Many who were still in high school and not yet sexually active were prescribed the potent drugs, allegedly to "regulate their cycles."

Moreover, marijuana, "drop out," and "free love" were the buzzwords of my generation. The Beatles, Jimi Hendrix, Sly and the Family Stone, our Pied Pipers of modernity, lured us into a dark and swirling hole of hedonism. And Farrakhan, espousing the teachings of Elijah Muhammad, brought me out of the tailspin. Until that point, I had been taking birth control pills to keep from getting pregnant. But after listening to Louis Farrakhan speak about how potent a drug must be to be capable of shutting down one of nature's powerful biological functions—that of reproducing itself—I stopped.

It took me another two years to ovulate or produce eggs again. And some years later, the pharmaceutical companies revealed that we had been guinea pigs and the pills prescribed to some young women were about ten times more potent than they should have been.

"You are poisoning yourself," Farrakhan has said. "Why kill the fruit of your womb and prevent maybe another great Black Leader from being born? Hasn't Pharaoh killed enough of our children?"

I'm glad I heard him. I stopped taking the pill. And now I am the proud mother of four children: a daughter and three sons. Minister Farrakhan's assertions may sound wild to those who believe society is making progress for blacks, but they make sense to hundreds of thousands of black folks "caught in the belly of the beast" here in what Farrakhan calls the "Wilderness of North America."

In the years since I first heard the words of Muhammad and Farrakhan, one can point to some advances black Americans have made in the professional classes, and we can point with pride to the growing black middle class. But the alarm must be sounded when one understands the weight of statistics such as: black men have a life span that is about equal to that of a man in impoverished Bangladesh; black infant mortality rates rival those of third world nations; and one in three black men is entangled in the criminal justice system in America. All these figures cause some black folks to conclude that justice means "Just us," to paraphrase Richard Pryor.

I write a column at a respected daily newspaper in Northern California that allows me to contribute my honest perspective on what it is like to be black in America. But to think that things are getting better for black people as a whole is to deny reality. Anyone who has older relatives can see that the quality of life is declining for them. Anyone who has children can see the pitfalls, the traps, and the shrinking opportunities that greet them in school and in their communities.

Gangs, drugs, homicides, unemployment, teen pregnancy, and single-parent homes are all indicators of a culture in decline. It's not just black culture, but American culture. And since black Americans are at the bottom of the socioeconomic totem pole, these ills are coming down upon our heads in disproportionate waves.

The social programs established during my youth that targeted black folks have made us the convenient scapegoat for America's economic woes, rather than the changing global economy.

Meanwhile, inadequate schools and lack of job opportunities propel young black males into an illegal underground economy that ultimately leads them to wholesale imprisonment. The massive buildup in the prison industry foretells of the new big business. The new high-tech plantations. In California and many other states, building bonds for prisons pass overwhelmingly in elections while those for schools fail miserably.

In major cities across the country, Minister Farrakhan is trying to build businesses, open schools, and teach black people how to pool their resources to build something for themselves. He has human flaws—he loves power; he loves drama; he loves to perform; he loves fancy clothes and even fancier digs. But, most important, he loves black people. Loves them more than he loves white people. And that is a rare black person to find. Most "black leaders" want to appease white folks. They need to have their intellect, their humanity, their worthiness validated by white people—the same people brought up to despise them. But not Farrakhan. That is his appeal.

As an NOI lieutenant during the early1970s, my task was teaching and training the women who joined the organization. I witnessed young chemically addicted female prostitutes come out of the drug culture and become good, loving mothers and homemakers. I saw former alcoholics and hustlers, wayward men and cheats become honest, dependable, and hard-working family men. I saw radical anarchists become community builders and schoolteachers. I even saw men involved in homosexual activity become satisfied husbands and fathers. This was made possible by a belief system and program that told them that their humanity did not originate in slavery or the jungles of Africa.

However, I soon came to learn, once again, that even the most well-intentioned movements have their downsides. As the Nation of Islam became more powerful and more economically viable—with its introduction of fish markets, factories, bakeries, and snack shops; its acquisitions of jets, farmlands, and growing newspaper businesses—a criminal element was attracted to the Nation.

The tens of thousands of religious, obedient, disciplined, hard-working, and tithing members acted like a beacon to hustlers, con men, and other provocateurs who tried to use the "believers" for their own nefarious plans. Many of these shysters-in-Muslim-garb came from the prisons, where many Muslim converts were found.

Over time, it became clear to me that some of the Nation of Islam officers were greedy, lying, and opportunistic individuals who did not share the Utopian ideal and moral discipline of the founder of the Nation of Islam. These individuals had themselves become oppressors and exploiters. Some of the mid- and high-level ministers became drunk with power, more concerned with fund-raising and sending large sums of money to Chicago (attempting to garner favor with the Honorable Elijah Muhammad and his staff) than in spreading the Messenger's word out in the provinces. They wore expensive suits and drove fancy cars. They became too dogmatic and intrusive in the personal lives of the followers. Power indeed proved corrupting to many of the ministers, as they created large, militarylike bodies within the organization, shadow societies of women and men designed to keep the rank-and-file members in check.

Those in higher command were quick to use the term "hypocrite" to describe a critic or anyone who disagreed with their dictates (much as Malcolm was called a hypocrite when he decided to leave the Nation). In the 1970s, as the Nation pulled in more money and expanded its empire, the abuse of power became more pronounced. I witnessed this spreading corruption, and I didn't like it. Furthermore, police scrutiny of the organization became more intense, as some members were linked to crime and violent confrontations with law enforcement.

Eventually, I started to pull away from the organization that had employed both me and my husband for several years. Initially, I kept my disaffection to myself, careful of not being labeled a hypocrite. But I became more and more disillusioned. Then, while I was on maternity leave in 1975 (women were encouraged to stay home and not attend the mosque while they were pregnant and during the first few months of the baby's life), Elijah Muhammad died. We, the rank-and-file members, were not prepared for that. Without saying it, many of us believed in Elijah Muhammad's immortality. We were not aware of anyone being groomed to take his place, and his Word was divine to us. We were distraught, for we were sheeplike in our devotion to him and in our adherence to his philosophy and code of living.

On the day of his death, I spent a fitful night with a dozen or so other Muslims talking about who would be Elijah's successor. And what would become of our Nation of Islam, already rife with power struggles and internal intrigues? Elijah Muhammad, the Messenger, as we called him, had died the day before the celebration of our annual Savior's Day event (which commemorates the birth of W. D. Fard Muhammad). Elijah's son, Wallace D. Mohammad, assumed the helm on that emotionally tumultuous day, hoisted on the shoulders of other ministers and his brothers.

It was a peaceful, albeit confusing transition, as Wallace (now known as Warithuddin Mohammed) had for years been publicly critical of his father's theology and was ousted from the Nation on several occasions. In fact, Wallace immediately began disbanding the militaristic arm of the Nation of Islam, the Fruit of Islam. He also eliminated hierarchical ranks and titles, took away the absolute power of the ministers, stopped the mandatory paper-selling and tithing, and loosened dress codes for the sisters. More important, he started explaining the symbolic teachings of his father and re-futed some of Elijah Muhammad's mystical theology, replacing it with mainstream Islamic doctrine.

Most important, at least to the outside world, Wallace stopped using the label "Devil" to apply to whites and even allowed them to attend meetings and join the organization, something unthink-able under his father. Wallace refuted his father's teachings as blas-pheming Islam. He said it was all that his father knew and that his intentions were honorable and well meaning, but it was not true Islam. He urged his followers to learn the traditional teachings and practices of Islam and promised them that this would give them a true spiritual, moral, and practical foundation for their lives. Thus began my transition from Nation of Islam to "mainstream" Islam. I began studying the Qur'an and praying in Arabic.

For a time, Minister Farrakhan tried to get with Wallace's pro-gram, too. But he eventually said that he found Wallace's methods wanting. He felt that the disenfranchised condition of his people required someone committed solely to their rise and to improving their conditions.

As I see it, both Wallace and Farrakhan provide insight into the problems of and solutions for African-Americans in this society and for society in general. I'm inspired by and learn from both men. True, I miss some of the structure, outward pride, and discipline fostered in the Nation of Islam that I joined in the early 1970s, but I eschew the dogma and the problems that can come from blind allegiance, which some NOI officials seem to demand. True,

Farrakhan's assessment of America's treatment of African-Americans is harsh and wilting for many mainstream Americans—but much of it is true. At the same time, I don't believe that his accounts of UFOs and the mother ship are any more outlandish than those of thousands of other Americans who believe in such things. (Heaven's Gate, a cult founded in the 1970s, led thirty-nine people to kill themselves in San Diego in March 1997. How many NOI members have ever killed themselves because they believed they would be united with a spaceship?)

I have met Minister Farrakhan on several brief occasions, and I have listened to him speak in gatherings since I was a young college student. I am often captivated by much of what he says, for he is a charismatic speaker. But I want from him less emotion and more teaching. I am impressed with what he and his followers have done to lessen crime in some public housing projects, and I have covered, as a journalist, his direct impact on reducing gang violence in Los Angeles.

For me, the Nation of Islam was a womb—to paraphrase Wallace—in which I was allowed to flourish and grow, to a point. It served as a womb that sheltered me and allowed me to develop and gain a knowledge of myself absent the presence of white supremacy. In America, blacks need a healthy framework by which we can shape ourselves. Some might identify the Nation's philosophy as separatist or black supremacist thinking, but I say that's a far pendulum swing from what we know to be true about white supremacy. And when the pendulum settles down, what we find is that the Nation's ideology has mellowed within many black Muslims, leaving us ultimately with a healthier sense of who we are, and with a more realistic view of society.

As we do when we emerge from literal wombs, I am still growing. I am proud of my experience in the Nation of Islam and glad for the personal evolution it provided me. Whatever you might think of the Nation, it freed me from the myth of white supremacy.

The Misunderstood Alliance:
Louis Farrakhan and the
World Community of Muslims
Aminah B. McCloud

AMINAH B. MCCLOUD *is an associate professor of religious studies at DePaul University and author of* African-American Islam.

When many Americans think of black Muslims living in the United States, they think first of Louis Farrakhan and members of the Nation of Islam. The term "Black Muslim" was coined some twenty-five years ago by African-American scholar and writer C. Eric Lincoln and refers specifically to members of the Nation of Islam. But how many Americans are aware that the community of African-Americans who follow the Islamic faith is large and dynamic, much larger and much more dynamic than the Nation of Islam? The finer points of Farrakhan's religious indoctrination and beliefs, and of the Nation's actual connection to the orthodox forms of Islamic faith, are rarely examined or disseminated along the primary tributaries of American consciousness: the media, the academy, and the home-grown grapevines of information. This intellectual void has created a widespread misunderstanding of Farrakhan's religiosity, and of his place within the domestic and international community of Muslims, which numbers near 100 million people. As many as 5 million African-Americans follow the Islamic faith in the United States, representing a religious minority among the predominantly Christian black population of more than 25 million. Best estimates indicate that the Nation of Islam's membership accounts for fewer than fifty thousand of the millions of Muslims in America. The majority of Muslims in America, immigrant and native, follow traditional or orthodox forms of the Islamic faith. This majority includes approximately 1 million native-born black Americans who have converted to Islam during the past two decades.

Beyond this religious demographic breakdown, the exact nature of the Nation's relationship to Islam is obscured by several factors, including creeping cultural ignorance and widespread American impatience with the details of non–Judeo Christian faiths. Furthermore, if one relied only on media reports of "black Muslims" during the past decade—which in large part have chronicled one or another racial conflict—it would be easy to arrive at the conclusion that all or most African-American Muslims living in the United States belong to the Nation of Islam.

So we have a reactionary response to the Nation of Islam, shaped by a twisting collection of misperceptions: It hardly seems to matter that Louis Farrakhan makes claims to Islam while failing to follow all the precepts of orthodox or traditional Islam. What registers with most of the American public is that Farrakhan's fiery presence is somehow linked to the religion of terrorists and "fundamentalist extremists." The mainstream American perception is that Islam produces militants who are scarily adept at transforming rhetoric into deadly action.

In reality, orthodox and traditional African-American Muslims have long considered the Nation of Islam and several other quasi-religious or nationalist African-American communities anathema. Representing the majority of African-American Muslims, the members of those traditional religions, (primarily Sunni and Shia) view the Nation of Islam's ever changing internal hierarchy and inconsistent descriptions of its founders beliefs with a degree of skepticism.

The Nation's inconsistencies, along with several other wrinkles unique to the NOI's expression of the Islamic faith, have drawn scrutiny, both public and private, from leaders in the world community of orthodox Muslims. Yet one could argue that while Farrakhan and the contemporary incarnation of the Nation of Islam rest fairly far afield of most traditional Muslims in America, philosophically and in practice, the Nation nonetheless holds a uniquely high profile in America. The reasons for this misassociation are many and include an uninformed media, scholarly myopia, and, during recent years, wild interpretations of Minister Farrakhan's meetings with Islamic leaders in the Middle East. Therefore, in examining Minister Farrakhan's place among African America's leaders, it is important to consider the Nation's position within the world religious community of Muslims.

To place Louis Farrakhan and the Nation of Islam in perspective, vis-à-vis Muslims worldwide, is to demystify a complicated relationship. But by pulling back the veil and reviewing the Nation's relationship to the world community of Muslims, perhaps we can begin to deconstruct the age-old model in which black religious leaders (usually but not always Christian) are unanimously graduated to the status of leader-at-large.

If Farrakhan is able to claim leadership status in black America in part because of his religious grounding, then it is only logical to examine his religiosity and furthermore its relationship to the international religious community he considers his own. Inevitably, what we find is that while Farrakhan and members of the Nation represent a small number of the larger community of Muslims, the Minister and his followers nonetheless adhere to the Islamic faith in measure enough to earn the respect and attention of many. It seems that the differences between Louis Farrakhan's brand of Islam and that of the majority of black Muslims in America hardly matters to those whom Farrakhan wants most to reach: black Americans, of every faith, who find themselves in need of a strong, morally sound Black Leader. Yet the departure points between the NOI and adherents of traditional Islam are intriguing.

Traditional Islam asserts the uncompromised unity of God and a very distinctive understanding of prophethood. By contrast, the Nation of Islam has its own understandings of both the unity of God and prophethood. During its first years (1930–1975), the Nation of Islam doctrine held that Master Fard Muhammad was God in the flesh and the Honorable Elijah Muhammad was variously his prophet and/or his messenger.

Now, twenty-three years after the death of the Honorable Elijah Muhammad, Master Fard is believed by NOI adherents to be alternately God in the flesh, a *mujedid* (renewer) or a *mahdi* (guided one), while the Honorable Elijah Muhammad is viewed as a divinely inspired messenger. This internal detail is important within the Nation's history but is little understood outside of the organization. It also has no direct counterpart in the Islamic faith as practiced by traditional Muslims.

Embraced for its truths and egalitarian treatment of all humans regardless of their color or ethnicity, traditional Islam attracts millions of African-Americans and, increasingly, Native and European Americans from all walks of life. Since the first half of the century, there has been a wide range of philosophically different African-American Muslim communities. Currently, there exist at least seventeen philosophically different communities that think of themselves as connected to Islam, including four incarnations of the NOI, the Darul Islam Movement, and the Five Percent Nation (a contemporary splinter that is made up largely of rap and hip-hop artists). The majority of African-American Muslims follow both Sunni and Shia beliefs, with a growing portion belonging to a wide variety of Sufi groups. All call God Allah, but they differ in some areas of Qur'anic interpretation, including their respective understanding of man's relationship to God,

God's relationship to His prophets, interdenominational gender re-lationships, and extra-scriptural references.

These communities also diverge on other key questions: whether one's faithful commitment should include the wholehearted em-brace of Islam (called within the Qur'anic doctrine the "complete affirmation"), and whether one will agree to accept the responsi-bilities of all Islam's disciplines.

Moreover, the various incarnations of Islam practiced by Afri-can-Americans differ with the NOI on the placement of required extra-religious focus, i.e., whether one should view the needs of the local community before the needs of the world community. This issue is a significant source of the tension between the Nation of Islam and the international community of black Muslims.

However, the first and primary source of tension between tra-ditional Muslims and the Nation of Islam is focused on the Nation's articulation of God and prophethood. Many African-American Muslims consider Islam the "original religion" of the African slaves. Although Western literature has encouraged the notion that most African slaves practiced traditional African religions and were first introduced to monotheism via Christianity, the areas in West Africa that were culled for slaves were in fact predominantly Mus-lim and had been so for six to seven hundred years prior to the ar-rival of the slave traders. Islam, as the traditionalists see it, provides a correct way of seeing the world, gives visionary guidance on human relations, and provides the only viable response to the rac-ism offered by the Judeo-Christian West. A strict orthodox read-ing of the Qur'an is not carried out wholly by the Nation of Islam, but the Nation's commitment to Islam involves observing enough of the traditional Islamic precepts to allow it to perhaps rightfully lay claim to the general description of the Muslim faith (in that the Nation includes prayers to Mecca, annual hajjs, and personal absti-nence as cornerstones of its religious expression).

In layman's terms, Islam is about the notion of surrender, or per-haps, as some Islamicists have put it, engaged surrender. It demands

God-consciousness in every facet of life, which in turn demands individual and communal responsibility. To achieve God-consciousness, the orthodox Muslim enters into a contract to embrace several disciplines. (The Nation follows some, but not all, of these.)

The initial contract is a witnessed affirmation (called the *shahada*) of the oneness of God and the prophethood of Muhammad ibn Abdullah of seventh-century Arabia. Along with *shahada,* the remaining disciplines represent the "five pillars": *salat*—five times daily prayer; *sawm*—fasting during the ninth lunar month of Ramadan; *zakat*—the payment by those eligible of a 2.5 percent tax on wealth owned for one year; and hajj—pilgrimage to Mecca, Saudi Arabia, at least once in a lifetime by those who can afford it. *Shalada* is the testimony of faith and is repeated by Muslims nine times per day. This affirmation and the disciplines focus and regulate orthodox Muslim life most everywhere on earth.

At the same time, a dilemma facing most African-American Muslims and followers of the Nation is a historical problem, one of attempting to balance the concerns of one's own people close to home with those of the ummah (the world community of Muslims). Arab nations have formed pan-Arab groups, for instance, as they recognize the unique problems of their people at home, while simultaneously organizing larger bodies to assist the umma. In Muslim African America, two responses to the dilemma can be seen in communities like the Nation of Islam and the Five Percent Nation.

These two communities say they prefer to keep the plight of African America on the front burner; while some other black Muslim communities, including Darul Islam, place their emphasis on the interests of the international Muslim community. Both manifestations, it is worth noting, pay attention to the concerns of the local and the international, but in differing proportions. And ultimately, when Islam comes to a community, it imprints its core beliefs at a fundamental level and stamps its worldview on the identity of the believer.

In a well-informed media world, we would see stories examining the similarities and differences between the Nation of Islam and the larger community of orthodox black Muslims, thoughtful explorations, for example, of the fact that African-American Muslims cannot and generally do not escape American racism despite their religions' non-American roots. Rather, Muslim religion as practiced by blacks, seems most often to draw dual condemnations in the forms of the well-documented miscoverage of black people by our popular American media, coupled with mainstream hostility toward (and ignorance of) Muslims. This contributes to a double-jeopardy effect that I will cover later in more detail.

But these public condemnations—the widespread, widely accepted anti-Islamic casts to many media "examinations" of Middle East religions—do not prevent African-American Muslims from responding to violence, abuse, homelessness, and discrimination both at home and abroad.

Indeed, a tightening of the ranks among Muslims worldwide is facilitated by such pervasive media criticism. Charity from the world community of Muslims is regularly given to shelters in American cities, and to relief funds for Kasmir, Bosnia, Somalia, and the Sudan. Muslims, due in part to the wildly inaccurate and inflammatory Western media view of Islam, have a broader understanding of patterns of colonialisms, imperialisms, and oppressions. Stateside Muslims see all too clearly how their condition, and the condition of the at-large African-American population, is no different than that of the Black South Africans, which is not too different from the class and racial issues facing Latin Americans. In this sense, the local experience for black Muslims in the African-American community is but one example of other race and class divisions in the world.

For African-American Muslims, American citizenship extends to having a say in the world—not just within the domestic community where they reside. Other Muslims in the international community are keenly aware of their obligations to and responsibility for American Muslims, and American black Muslims, including the NOI, have benefited over the decades from the fulfillment of this obligation.

Again, our lack of meaningful understanding of Islam in the United States (even in African America) is abetted by the fact that most researchers and scholars deny any significance in its presence. A dearth of American scholarhip on this issue has helped keep the religious waters of NOI and traditional Islam cloudy.

(Meanwhile, Muslim world support of African-American scholarship, both general and Islamic, is decades old; yet African-American scholars' understanding of Islamic faiths as practiced by blacks in America is shallow at best. Furthermore, there are no African-American Islamic scholars at Princeton, Oberlin, Stanford, Harvard, or Yale, which represent the hallowed halls of our American intellectual community. From the texts of most high-profile contemporary African-American scholars, one would know nothing of the competing influences of Islam and Judaism within the black American religious community.)

In truth, many African-American Muslims have made the international Muslim world their home, while others choose to go back and forth between the stateside Islamic community and the ummah. However, tension is created as one moves from the soul-killing effects of American racism and religious ignorance to the battering effects of colonialism found in the international Muslim world. This is exemplified by the experience of El-Hajj Malik el-Shabazz (Malcolm X). As a Nation of Islam convert to traditional Islam, El-Hajj found that his religious evolution did not play especially well back here at home among the NOI and Christian blacks, even as he saw his traditional Islamic education (with its attending non-Western cultural heterodoxy) as a necessary part of his religious growth. Now, in the last decade of the twentieth century, while the overall number of traditional black Muslims living in America continues to swell, the realities of the Muslim condition in the world community and the tensions between ummah and the domestic realm remain constant.

Minister Farrakhan is trying to bridge these two worlds—and link his at-home concerns with the greater ummah. This gesture, however clumsily executed, represents a larger, ongoing struggle for black Muslims in America, the balancing of domestic and international concerns. When Farrakhan visits leaders in Iran or Libya, an uninformed observer might see only that the Minister is willfully consorting with America's enemies, rather than recognizing the visit as an expression of his commitment to ummah.

That is perhaps why, in our popular American media, Louis Farrakhan seems to cut such a curious figure whenever he visits the Middle East. The phrase "cavorting with dictators" is rarely, if ever, followed by a discussion of ummah on the nation's news pages.

Consequently, the American media denigrations of Islam, the litigation and publicity surrounding persistent employment discrimination against Muslims, violence and harassment against Muslims, and desecrations of masjid (mosques) stateside during the last five years have brought Muslims together in ways and in numbers that have not been experienced before in this country.

In his February 1997 Savior's Day address, Minister Farrakhan punctuated his talk with the message, "We should worship no man." For many black American Muslims, that is a non-negotiable issue— an issue where there cannot be accommodation. Black American Muslims await a consistent articulation of Islam from Minister Farrakhan, even as they accept the values expressed when he speaks about the black American community. Most orthodox black Muslims see the "truth" in Farrakhan's words, in part because his observations fall within the worldview of traditional Islam and its concerns.

And while Farrakhan's adherence to Islam eschews secular winds (including the political variety), he should be seen as representing one of the many steps black Muslims must take if they are ever to move into the American political arena. (Farrakhan has spoken in recent years of wanting to initiate a "new political force.") An anti-Islamic sentiment is strong in America, stoked by historically unstable U.S.–Middle East relations and sparked by continual anti-Islamic rhetoric in Washington. Nonetheless, Minister Farrakhan's Islamic faith renders him immune to criticisms of political impropriety and anti-Islamic rhetoric—his religious determination supersedes most secular boundaries. He appears unfazed by the double jeopardy of his existence in America: As a black man and a Muslim, he is more likely than not to be viewed as a threat in many domestic quarters.

In its hundred-year presence in the United States Islam has not been tied to segregation, racism, and violence, in the way of American Christianity. In African America, Islam is the religion of ancestors, a religion of equality, a religion devoid of the racial depiction of God, and, foremost, a religion in which beings are judged by their obedience to God. For many African-American Muslims, the affront of authority lying only with black Christians is usually weathered with a sigh.

Most black American Muslims attribute the perception—that black leaders must be somehow linked to the Christian faith to the need of black Christian leaders to protect Christianity among black Americans; and the need of Christian leaders to protect a hard-built, hereditary consortium of authorized leaders of the black community from what they consider a threatening worldview—that of Islam. And again, tension derives from the overarching global sense of community that is central to the Islamic faith.

While Elijah Muhammad did not appear to engage the international Muslim community, his Islamic faith was viewed with suspicion by the black Christian leadership during his time. Farrakhan has made a great show of reaching out to the world community of Islam, and the response from Christian leaders has been accordingly apoplectic. Still, Farrakhan's outreach is not outside the rubric of orthodox Muslim practices, it only seems so because of the Nation's unorthodox interpretation of traditional Islam. As vice regents—i.e., trustees rather than owners of people or things—traditional Muslims engage each other without boundaries. The bond is cemented in the brotherhood or sisterhood resulting from the contract and the unity that results from the disciplines. In the same way that the five-times-daily prayers erase one set of class and gender issues, the notion of ummah obscures nation-state borders. This detail is critical in beginning to place some of Farrakhan's thoughts and actions within a larger Islamic context. For instance, by his continual condemnation of neocolonialism on the African continent and in the Caribbean, Louis Farrakhan demonstrates an understanding of the notion of ummah, however unorthodox his methods of expressing this understanding. All the same, the larger American community does not have a clear perception of the differences between traditional Islam as practiced by most black Muslims in America and that which is practiced by the Nation of Islam. Along with a dearth of scholarship on these issues, the popular media's continual conflation of the two and its general ignorance of Islam have further confused these distinctions.

Moreover, contemporary explorations of religion, politics, and social concerns in the African-American community have traditionally centered on the legitimacy—or, more specifically, on the authority—of the black Christian church.

Much of the canon, many texts on the black community, many recognized scholars, most politicians, for example, derive a stamp of legitimacy and authority from an intimacy with the black Christian church. While no one should deny the importance of the Christian church in the black community as one locus of black activity, it has never been nor will it ever be the only voice of authority in the black community. The spiritual status of black America is usually articulated purely from a Christian perspective, as are the black community's responses to social crises. As another worldview, Islam asserts non-Christian ways of knowing, non-Christian truths, laws, solutions, and, important particularly in the context of this text, another referent community of shared understanding. Our understanding of black American leadership cannot be complete until we reconstruct our understanding of religion's place in our history of black leadership.

Not surprisingly, then, the mainstream understanding of what constitutes "black leadership" in America has a hard time taking in the Muslim doctrine, whether traditional (as with Sunni) or unorthodox (as with the NOI).

When we turn to the complicated issue of African–American leadership, the ideological framework, the model most often used to define black American leadership in this century, is usually found in a duality model, one in which two figures, say W.E.B. DuBois and Booker T. Washington, are compared and contrasted. (This model type was designed by a group of "pragmatic activists," according to Harvard government professor Martin Kilson ("Paradoxes of Black Leadership," *Dissent* 42, no. 3 [Summer 1995]) pp. 368–372.

This duality model is limited and historically shallow, yet it persists. It presumes an either-or choice for African-Americans rather than a historic continuum of politically and philosophically diverse individuals whom we could describe as leaders. Yet, even though one might argue that neither DuBois nor Washington truly represented the concerns of the majority of African-Americans (working class, modestly educated), the two men, and the duality model they represent, have come to define the leadership paradigm in African America. Usually posed as two extremes, the duality model has been the blueprint for talking about all black leaders for decades. Most recently, the model has been used to contrast Louis Farrakhan with Colin Powell, a new twist on an old theme and one not without some merit. Still, it seems that the whole of African America can have only two points of reference on black leadership. In truth, the presence of Islam in the African-American community has for decades represented an overlooked departure from this model. African-American Muslim history is filled with leaders who sought and still seek to lift the veil of a particular African experience and reveal the global existence of oppression.

Farrakhan is only the latest in a long line that includes black Freemasons and Elijah Muhammad of those who have attempted to show how black Americans are linked to blacks around the world. For much of this century, thousands of American Muslims have made the hajj (the pilgrimage to Mecca), journeys that took place outside the mainstream of the national consciousness.

Hundreds, orthodox and nontraditional, Sunni and Nation of Islam members, have gone to universities in the Muslim world and returned to America to share their knowledge. African-American Muslims have understood themselves as active agents in many parts of the world. In the Islamic faith, a true leader is one who, among other responsibilities, effectively balances a commitment to serving the local and international brethren.

At home, however, contemporary black leadership has been identified by the mainstream as residing primarily in the Black Church, a specific kind of leadership sprung from an almost hereditary line. To be a "black leader" as we've come to understand the term today, one must be a preacher, or at least the son or daughter of a preacher, with demonstrable ties to the Civil Rights Movement. One must also offer proof of right thinking (being in favor of integration).

While other communities can debate the finer qualifications of leadership—including innovation, satisfaction of needs, and a varied definition of values—the script written for the African-American community seems to be narrowed to include only these so-called authorized black leaders.

These individuals, usually men, usually Christian, appear to have voice only on matters of race, which means that leadership as we know it is a questionable entity, anyway. By this I mean that the concerns of blacks have been carefully limited to protests on racial issues by both white liberals and authorized black leadership. (Few black "spokespersons" are made available in media to pontificate on subjects such as economics or the law or the environment; when the subject on the American radar screen is "race," however, you can expect to see a raft of black pundits.)

Yet we are seeing welcome signs of enlightenment where religion and black American leadership are concerned, including Harvard professor Henry Louis Gates, Jr.'s comment in a 1996 *New Yorker* special issue examining the state of African America that "a poll had to be taken to know that there is a remarkable gap between the views of the leaders and those of the led." Moreover, University of North Carolina professor Michael Eric Dyson's recently articulated model of black leadership styles as those of transcendence (Colin Powell), transformation (Jesse Jackson), and translation (Louis Farrakhan) makes it clear that attempts are being made to retain control of and revitalize the "scripted" model of black American leadership. Louis Farrakhan has begun the process of changing this dynamic with the conscious assistance of others such as Benjamin Chavis that is, he is attempting to facilitate the evolution of a constituency, the millions of black Americans who are questioning their role not only as citizens of America, but as citizens of the world.

This welcomed break from the traditional model of Christian-based black American leadership was most recently embodied by the October 1995 Million Man March. Farrakhan seems to speak more directly to the great numbers of black Americans who see themselves as outside the purview of traditional black Christian leaders, the somber, pulpit-thumping middle class that seems to berate a postmodern troubled soul more than it soothes.

Thus, the Million Man March affected people in many different ways. For the authorized black American leadership, the march represented perhaps its first large-scale public challenge. This was one event where speakers from the black elite found themselves relegated to the corners of the ring. Feeling left out, some of these traditional black leaders retaliated by using their long-trusted supporters—the liberal white media—to publicly condemn the notion that anyone but them could ever call black people together under any productive auspices. For African-American Muslims, indeed for many black Americans, this disdain was not unusual. And black American Muslims were not surprised that white and black Christians would demonize any face of Islam that tried inserting itself into the national debate over the future of African America.

At the same time, we would be foolish to think that only Farrakhan's Islamic association causes the demonization (his separatist rhetoric would draw intense criticism even were it shorn of religious trappings). But many black Americans say they agree with Farrakhan's socially conservative positions on everything from welfare to education. Indeed, some black Americans are drawn to Farrakhan and the Nation more for their social-political positions than for their religious beliefs. Nonetheless, Farrakhan's Islamic faith seems to bring detractors who fear or disdain that faith.

So we arrive at this place, where many Americans fear Farrakhan's religiosity, even as they fail to understand it and its connection to the international Muslim community. For black Americans to speak only from the narrow halls of the known—black Christianity in decades of old, predictable ways—is legitimate. Yet, regarding the myriad problems facing African America—drugs, unemployment, poor educational opportunities—the solutions offered by the black Christian elite, however inarticulate or even self-defeating, are usually accepted as accurately representing the "authentic" concerns of black America.

Any response to our shared condition that comes from the Muslim world (whether spoken by Farrakhan or Elijah Muhammad) is characterized by the mainstream pool of Christian intellectuals, black and white, as confused and inaccurate at best, its origin and motivation viewed as unfathomable or untenable. But, as the first Million Man March demonstrated, America's traditional "black leaders" are perhaps leaders only of themselves and of the increasingly disenchanted members of their congregations.

The African-American community—Muslim and Christian—is beginning to hear the beat of a different drummer. More black Americans are becoming more interested in participating in different parades, more receptive of finding new ways to solve their concerns. For growing numbers of black Americans, Islam, whether in the form of Farrakhan's Nation or in more orthodox shapes, provides a realistic road to solutions. And in the end, Farrakhan's Islam does not need the validation of whites or of black Christian leaders to appeal to African America.

Epilogue

During the weekend of July 3, 1997, I took part in an event called the International Islamic Conference. It was held in Chicago and organized by the Nation of Islam and the World Islamic Peoples Leadership Council. In several speeches given during the weekend of workshops and symposiums, Louis Farrakhan indicated a willingness to move the NOI more into "mainstream," or traditional Islam. He made it clear, at the same time, that NOI members would continue to worship only one god, Allah, and that they are expected to continue learning and observing the obligations of traditional Islam. He positioned himself as a leader-in-training and kindly deferred when some of the *shayks* and *imams* in attendance said they wished to name him an imam (in traditional Islam, an imam is a leader of prayers; while in America the term has come to refer to one who leads the community). Many NOI members present at the event, including Farrakhan's daughter, Donna Farrakhan, cried while discussing the complicated nature of making a transition to more traditional Islam. Overall, Farrakhan's lectures during this weekend reminded me of the talks Warith Deen Mohammed gave in 1975, as he was first beginning to lead his followers into traditional Islam. And, as when Mohammad first made those overtures two decades ago, Farrakhan's claims were met with outrage from some members of the immigrant Muslim community. In fact, the general tone of media reports following the weekend conference seemed to be doubtful of Farrakhan's stated intentions to "mainstream" the Nation. Time will tell. But clearly, Farrakhan has indicated a desire to put himself forth as a leader in the black community, and among some Muslims.

Farrakhan, the Hip-Hop Generation, and the Failure of Black American Leadership

Ron Nixon

RON NIXON *is a staff writer at the* Roanoke (Virginia) Times. *He has written for* The Nation *and* Southern Exposure *magazine.*

A follower of Farrakhan
Don't tell me that you understand
until you hear the man
—Public Enemy, "Don't Believe the Hype"

No black leader has had more of an impact on the Hip-Hop Generation than Louis Farrakhan. This is increasingly evident in the outward trappings of some young African-Americans, the post–Civil Rights Era blacks who came of age after the pitched struggle for integration and who have taken up rap music and black neo-nationalism as their preferred form of cultural expression. Pictures of Farrakhan and the words "Nation of Islam" adorn the postmodern uniforms of black and Latino youth in sparkling suburbs and dying cities alike: On oversized T-shirts, jackets, and clean baseball caps, the silk-screened image of Farrakhan often shares space with those of Marcus Garvey, Malcolm X, and Nelson Mandela. From portable CD players and thumping auto-speakers come the sounds of hip-hop artists, their song lyrics sprinkled with allusions to NOI teachings and tensions between blacks and Jews. Several hip-hop artists have joined the Nation, including most recently a young man called Q-Tip from the socially conscious rap group A Tribe Called Quest.

Less conspicuously, black students are the largest consumers of NOI publications, and Farrakhan is undoubtedly the most sought-after speaker on black college campuses. Thousands of black youth joined adults to fill an Atlanta hall in 1992 when the minister came to speak—many more, in fact, than turned out across town at Fulton County Stadium to watch the World Series game that took place the same night.

In Farrakhan, many black youths see a symbol of defiance and an alternative to established black leadership. Former Children's Defense Fund youth organizer Lisa Sullivan notices among some of these young adults "a strong rejection of both the white mainstream status quo and the post–civil rights middle-class (bourgeois) respectability."

Some youth use kinship language when speaking of Farrakhan, with words like "brother" and "love" helping them describe their feelings for the minister.

"I love Farrakhan without question or reservation," Jason Broom, a twenty-six-year-old African-American in Kansas City, told Newsweek magazine in March 1997. "He's a strong, stand-up black man. I don't practice his religion but I support him. He never turned on us on the street. He's for turning us to men." Indeed, the Newsweek cover story in which Broom was quoted focused on the generational rift between young African-Americans and their parents and grandparents, with hip-hop music, black neo-nationalism, and Louis Farrakhan cited as contraindicators of the divide.

When media pundits and civil rights leaders minimize Farrakhan's following among the Hip-Hop Generation, calling it simply youthful experimentation, they miss the point. Some of Farrakhan's appeal can be attributed to youthful experimentation by these young adults, and to their somewhat narrow embrace of 1960s-style black nationalism as expressed by Malcolm X, the Black Panther Party, and the Student Non-Violent Coordinating Committee (SNCC).

But the appeal must also be attributed to declining economic and social conditions of black youth. Their unemployment rates have been at epidemic proportions for some time. Educational and social structures have deteriorated. Affirmative action and other opportunities for advancement put in place to address past discrimination are in doubt because of conservative attacks.

Farrakhan has a rather unique ability to reach deeply into the souls of black youth, whether they are middle-class or low-income. Mattias Gardell, an associate professor of theology at Sweden's Uppsala University, writes in his book *In the Name of Elijah Muhammad: Louis Farrakhan and the Nation of Islam:* "Farrakhan seems to be able to talk to [young African-Americans] in a way that really makes them listen, even when he puts them down. This rapport enables Farrakhan to criticize and redirect destructive behavior patterns."

Nowhere is this rapport more apparent than in the controversy over so-called gangsta rap music.

During a 1992 congressional hearing, outspoken critic of gangsta rap C. Delores Tucker sat behind a table amid flashing lights and microphones fielding questions from members of the House Energy and Commerce subcommittee. This "pornographic smut" in the hands of our children coerces, influences, encourages, and motivates our youth to commit violent behavior, Tucker said, holding up the cover of *Doggy Style,* the album by California rapper Snoop Doggy Dog.

The words "thugs," "criminals," and "evil," flowed from Tucker as she described the music and the artists. Several young people seated behind the table near Tucker shook their heads in disappointment. Even after Yo-Yo, a popular woman rapper, testified that black leaders should attack the world in which rappers live, not the words they use to describe it, Tucker was unconvinced.

In short order, Tucker teamed up with conservative activist William Bennett to launch TV ads and a scorched-earth campaign against Time-Warner. The entertainment giant was part owner of Interscope Records, one of the most profitable companies in a growing field of rap music labels. It was not lost on the college educated, middle-class flank of the Hip-Hop Generation that Bennett and Tucker successfully pressured Time-Warner to drop Interscope.

Bennett is, of course, the same William Bennett who once stated that black youth needed to be "bathed in the culture of Western civilization instead of having their names carved" in their hairstyles; the same Bennett who led the late 1980s attack on affirmative action, an attack that a decade later continues eroding legal attempts to remedy historic discrimination in America; the same William Bennett who said during a Sunday morning network television political talk show that the racist, pseudoscientific 1994 book *The Bell Curve* "had some merit."

Shown side by side in ads attacking gangsta rap and Time-Warner, Tucker and Bennett compared gangsta music to propaganda which preceded the horrors of Nazi Germany and blamed rap music for most of the social ills that confront black America. As far as the Hip-Hop Generation was concerned, Tucker had joined up with the enemy in her crusade to "save" black youth.

"How can you call yourself a black leader and attack your children?" asks Julian Shabazz, a young man from Clinton, South Carolina. "What about the high unemployment, the breakup of our families, problems of low self-esteem, and the ready availability of guns, illegal drugs, and alcohol?", Shabazz said during an interview.

Karen Carrillo, a twenty-seven-year-old New Yorker, says Tucker and other old-school black leaders are way out of touch with 1990s reality. Furthermore, they are inconsistent and duplicitous—especially elected black leaders, whose donor lists deserve harsh scrutiny. "Blacks who call themselves leaders, like Tucker, seem to have a selective morality," Carrillo says during an interview. "They criticize hip-hop music for its violence and its demeaning portrayal of women, yet they will turn around and take money from the alcohol and tobacco industries. Have you seen how some of the alcohol ads depict black women? These folks have done more damage in our community than hip-hop will ever do."

Carrillo and other young hip-hop advocates say that unlike Tucker and other "leaders" who criticize the music and culture of the Hip-Hop Generation, Farrakhan criticizes destructive behavior—"Don't you call your mother no bitch or 'ho,'" Farrakhan told a student audience during an appearance at North Carolina Central University—without attacking the popular forms of expression preferred by the young. In that way, Farrakhan accomplishes the balancing act of avoiding alienating them even as he attempts to correct them. While many traditional black leaders have turned away from the so-called undesirable elements of black youth—gang members, drug dealers, prisoners—the Nation of Islam has extended to them a hand. Farrakhan has crisscrossed the country with a "Stop the Killing Campaign," a grassroots effort to end gang violence and black-on-black crime. In March 1997, after the shooting death of rap artist Biggie Smalls (a self-described "gangsta" born Chris Wallace and raised in Bedford-Stuyvesant), Russell Simmons, chief of Def Jam Records, asked the Nation of Islam to sponsor a forum to help end the feud between East and West Coast rappers.

This kind of youth outreach by Simmons and Farrakhan is taking a page from traditional black leaders and retyping it in a more streetwise script: In the late 1980s, the Urban League began sponsoring "Stop the Violence" campaigns that featured some hip-hop artists; Jesse Jackson's Rainbow Coalition has also attempted to reach out to black youth by enlisting some popular singers and athletes. Still, the old-school leadership suffers from a credibility problem with the Hip-Hop Generation.

For example, while Farrakhan was reaching out through public appearances in blighted cities and by calling for the 1995 Million Man March, other black leaders—including currently incarcerated ex-congressman Mel Reynolds—were holding anti-gang summits, and actively distancing themselves from marginalized groups of young blacks, the drug dealers and "gangstas" who represent a small but symbolically significant portion of the Hip-Hop Generation.

Moreover, many black youth see a contradiction between what black leadership does and what it says. In Farrakhan, young people see someone who is largely a product of the black community and who is sustained by the community. He is the freest black man in America, as he likes to say (some critics would probably question that, considering the loans reportedly received by the NOI from Libya during the 1980s). But in the more mainstream civil rights leaders and their counterparts within the conservative movement, many black youth see a leadership that is largely irrelevant and out of touch with their lives; they see a leadership more intent on keeping itself in power than in advancing the cause of black people.

Traditional Civil Rights leaders and black Democrats, many young people feel, are too concerned with symbolic marches and nostalgia for the 1960s, and far too dependent on ineffective tactics. Black Republican leaders, despite their Farrakhanesque rhetoric of self-determination, are viewed by many black youth as being "sellouts," political operatives more interested in currying favor with the white business structure than in uplifting the African-American community. Many youth also see both factions of this old-school leadership as being largely dependent on outside support for its power and prestige. From there it is easy to make the connection that black advancement seems to have become secondary to the needs of whites, whether liberal or conservative. For example, the Coup, a California hip-hop group, seems to chastise old-school black leadership for selling out black youth in its song "Fat Cats, Bigga Fish," in which a businessman tells a black mayor, "Don't worry 'bout the Urban League or Jesse Jackson / my man down at Marlboro donated a fat sum."

Furthermore, the 1992 pre-presidential election flap over Sister Souljah and the centrist position taken by President Bill Clinton is another example of the growing division.

In 1992, presidential candidate Bill Clinton, trailing badly in the

Democratic primaries, attended a Rainbow Coalition function at which he attacked Souljah, a young, black, female rapper, comparing her to ex–KKK leader David Duke for statements she'd made. (Souljah says her comments had been taken out of context by a news reporter.) Although Jesse Jackson and several other Civil Rights Era leaders criticized Clinton for the remarks, they nevertheless endorsed him for president. Many politically-aware young black people saw that as a pimp-slap in the face.

Meanwhile, Clinton as president has swung rightward and signed, among other things, a draconian welfare reform bill that will have a far-reaching detrimental effect on black children, according to the administration's own figures. That political shape-shifting did not keep most of the black, Democratic, Civil Rights Era leadership from lining up solidly behind him for a second term.

Another perceived failure of traditional black leadership and a reason many black youth embrace Farrakhan is the Ben Chavis–NAACP affair. The charges of Chavis's fiscal mismanagement of NAACP funds and sexual discrimination notwithstanding, many board members of the nation's oldest Civil Rights organization had already begun to express doubt about the wisdom of Chavis's attempted outreach to gang members, rappers, Farrakhan, and other black nationalists; the old-guard NAACP board regarded with suspicion his attempts to expand the youth membership in an organization where the average age during the early 1990s was forty. When several corporations and foundations threatened to withhold their funding from the NAACP until the Chavis fiasco was settled, it was obvious who really controlled the organization that supposedly speaks for black people.

And in February 1997, in a significant example of the ideological rift between traditional black leadership and the Hip-Hop Generation, Chavis announced that he had officially joined the Nation of Islam.

"There has been a conversion, and I have evolved into the Nation of Islam," Chavis told the Associated Press in Chicago.

Chavis's conversion, however arrived at, solidifies Farrakhan's standing with the Hip-Hop Generation as an appealing alternative to traditional black leadership. Chavis's short-lived and rocky tenure as executive director of the NAACP, with all its shortcomings, nonetheless marked the first time in the organization's eighty-six-year history that an aggressive outreach campaign to "troubled" youth had been undertaken. Chavis's late-breaking conversion to the NOI only underscores a sentiment shared by some black youth that the Nation is more progressive than mainstream black leadership. At the same time, it remains to be seen whether Chavis will draw from the Hip-Hop Generation the same kind of admiration that Farrakhan enjoys.

The Hip-Hop Generation is equally critical of the new so-called conservative black leadership that has become more prominent in recent years. While Farrakhan certainly shares with those black conservatives views on many issues—self-determination, capitalism, and family values, or the "Leave It to Beaver Syndrome," as media critic Makani Themba calls it—he parts company with the traditionalists by emphasizing black pride and black nationalism, Afrocentric culture, and rejection of integration as a realistic goal.

These are beliefs that originate in a reality that many youth find appealing. In contrast, the arguments of mainstream black conservatives are largely rooted in ideas and policies that originate outside of the community. Attacks on affirmative action by those who have benefited from it and an embrace of conservative and racist policies and allegiances with old-line segregationists like Jesse Helms and Strom Thurmond (who have in the past and present worked against the interest of black people) raise a red flag to the Hip-Hop Generation. Indeed, the fact that the Urban League once gave Strom Thurmond an award didn't improve that august organization's standing among black youth, even though by most definitions the Urban League is far from a "conservative" organization.

Within this void of credible leadership, Farrakhan appears for some black youth a viable alternative. For a generation attracted to

191

the teachings of Malcolm X and the Black Power advocates of the late 1960s, he stands out as the only leader speaking to the needs, the frustrations, and the isolation of young blacks.

In poll after poll, Farrakhan appears the clear favorite among young people asked to rank the effectiveness of black leadership. In a *USA Today* poll, respondents under age thirty-five ranked Farrakhan as the "most effective" black leader.

A 1994 *Time* magazine poll found that 53 percent of blacks of all ages viewed Farrakhan as a "role model" for black youth. There is, however, a downside to this appeal. Although Farrakhan has the ability to speak to the needs of many young African-Americans in a way that they believe is sincere, he and the Nation of Islam lack the organizational ability and capacity to effectively capitalize on the void in leadership in the black community. "Not a lot of young people are joining the Nation of Islam," says Lukata Mjumbe, political director of a community-based group in Atlanta called the Malcolm X Grassroots Movement.

The 1995 Million Man March provides a vivid example. Though the march drew nearly a million men (some say over a million) to Washington, D.C., Farrakhan and the organizers lacked the ability to expand on the event. For instance, no national database was created with the names of the hundreds of thousands who attended the march. Such a database could have been used in the same manner as that of the conservative religious Christian Coalition, which uses its database for fund-raising and to mobilize its members politically. Nor were specific programs for young people established nationally by MMM organizers to address the needs of black youth, even though many such networks had been established by local organizers. Such efforts, nascent and in many cases struggling in America's urban centers, have seen little support and follow-through from the Nation.

The NOI missed its chance to expand upon the work undertaken to mount the march. But perhaps the largest blow to Farrakhan's credibility is the remarkable direction he took following the march: In the spring of 1996, he took a high-profile, whirlwind tour of some African and Middle Eastern nations, and his bow-tied, smiling image was shown worldwide as he visited and defended the Nigerian dictator General Abacha, among other dictators. How, young black Americans might wonder, could the minister justify turning a blind eye to the enslavement and selling of African people that has been documented in the Sudan?

An editorial in the NOI newspaper, the *Final Call,* blamed the slavery reports on a Zionist newspaper. In the weeks following the MMM, during his visit to Africa, Farrakhan also defended the Nigerian government's hanging of writer Ken Saro-Wiwa and other political activists, saying, "You've hanged one man; how many have [the Americans] hanged?"

Politically active members of the Hip-Hop Generation, including many who had supported and attended the Million Man March, were disappointed. Others, like twenty-six-year-old Mjumbe of Atlanta, were disappointed but not surprised. "Farrakhan gets into trouble when he steps outside his [domestic] realm," said Mjumbe. "He is not qualified to deal with many of the problems facing us. His strategy is mostly rhetorical; it's neither revolutionary or progressive."

Ultimately, Farrakhan's appeal to black youth reveals a deep schism between youth and traditional black leadership. While liberal and conservatives seem to be arguing over what *Emerge* magazine during the 1992 presidential election called "the best white man for the job" of leading black people to the promised land, Farrakhan offers a vision that is more suitable. That vision is grounded in black nationalism and the tough realities of life for many in the black community. Yet, like the visions offered by traditional black civil rights leaders and conservatives, it is a vision built on style not substance, words not work. And finally, it is a vision that fails to address the critical needs of the next generations of African-Americans—hip-hop and otherwise—who will bear the brunt of the black community's continuing deterioration.

The Nation of Islam and Me

Salim Muwakkil

SALIM MUWAKKIL *is a writer in Chicago and an editor of* In These Times. *He is a former editor of* Muhammad Speaks, *a Nation of Islam newspaper.*

Minister Louis Farrakhan, leader of the Nation of Islam, is confronting a dilemma common to all fringe leaders making a bid for broader leadership: He must retain the allegiance of his core while reaching out. In the past his authority was dependent primarily on his fidelity to the doctrine of Messenger Elijah Muhammad, the NOI's late patriarch. The heart of that doctrine identifies white people as a race of devils and black people as God's seed, inherently divine. This eugenic theology is the foundation of a bizarre catechism that prevented the Nation from gaining either mainstream acceptance or Islamic legitimacy. But Farrakhan's role in organizing the Million Man March, the largest demonstration in the history of this country, has catapulted him into the top ranks of black leadership, and the success of that unprecedented assembly has provided him with a source of legitimacy beyond the reflected divinity of Elijah Muhammad. This offers him an opportunity to broaden his constituency beyond the NOI. But it also could erode his core following: Were Farrakhan to deviate too far from Elijah's message, he would provoke considerable discord within the ranks. Some of Muhammad's followers already accuse him of unconscionable revisionism. And since internal dissension is the NOI's most lethal enemy, Farrakhan must pay close attention to issues of doctrinal fidelity. That's why he's likely to disappoint those black activists who treasure his charisma and intelligence but gag on his belief system.

Even without widespread mainstream support Farrakhan probably commands the absolute allegiance of more black people than any other person on the planet. This is an enormous, perhaps unprecedented, amount of influence. And it's growing; for example, one of the less noticed results of his much criticized World Friendship Tour in 1996 was the way it expanded his international profile. He is among the most well-known African-Americans in places like Iran and Indonesia. The Nation of Islam's London temple is one of the group's fastest growing. Such international luminance is a long way from the Bronx, where Farrakhan was born Louis Eugene Walcott on May 11, 1933.

I met Farrakhan in 1975, right before we began a month-long stint in Uganda as guests of the Organization of African Unity and its host Brigadier General Idi Amin Dada. I was an editor of *Muhammad Speaks,* the Nation's house organ, and I accompanied the minister to record the results of the unprecedented invitation. I had been walking on the path that led to Farrakhan since the 1960s, when I, like many of my demographic cohorts, embarked on a serious identity quest. For African-Americans, this is an essential search because our hybrid identity is largely a creation of slavery; enslaved Africans and their progeny were forbidden from making ancestral connections while denied access to the society into which they were rudely deposited. Our dual identity is also a dueling one; we are socialized to debase—if not hate—our African selves—the naked savages from the heart of darkness.

But we've always known there was more to African-Americans, and since our arrival in the New World we have sought the ghost of what was lost between the Motherland and the plantation. Each generation mounts this search in its own image. The baby-boom generation that reached its teens in the 1960s launched one of this country's most energetic movements seeking black identity.

For me, born on the leading edge of that generation, most of the major events of my coming of age corresponded with the big moments of the sixties' Black Movement. In my early teens I heard Malcolm X speak many times at Harlem Square, on 125th and Lenox. For us, Malcolm almost single-handedly removed the stigma of "corniness" from intellectual achievement. He translated his hip, urbane, street-life sensibility into a kind of intellectual style we admired immensely. We wanted to talk like Malcolm; his meticulous diction, vast vocabulary, and knowledge of history sent us to the dictionary and the library, willingly. But the prospect of joining Malcolm's Nation of Islam was never seriously considered. The group's ascetic program required too much sacrifice for our young lusts. There was too much fun to be had, too many females to meet. In fact, the mere chance of meeting thousands of females at a 1963 gathering in Washington, D.C., sent me and four companions off to the historic March on Washington. During Dr. Martin Luther King, Jr.'s famous "I have a dream" speech, I was busy cultivating what turned out to be a lifelong friendship. I missed the speech, but I was there . . .

I was also in Harlem that next summer of '64, when it exploded in the first of the "long hot summer riots" of the 1960s. A companion, my cousin, was shot in the back by a New York cop during the disturbance; we were just watching the action when the bullet knocked him off his feet. Luckily, he lived. I joined the U.S. Air Force later that summer to escape the forboding future that most black male youth must eventually confront. Four years later, on August 31, 1968, a panicked white motel manager in a town near Macon, Georgia, shot me during a racially-tinged argument. Luckily, I lived. My convalescence lasted about five months past my scheduled October discharge date, and during that time I began nurturing a raging black militance. I linked my gunshot wound to my cousin's and identified white racism as the common culprit. Immediately after my delayed discharge in 1969, I became associated with the Black Panther Party through one of its most militant members. There was no doubt in my mind that the American "establishment," with its slavery-stained capitalism and its white supremacist biases, had to be overthrown in a revolution before true justice could reign. A socialist society, free of marketplace logic and scapegoating stereotypes, would follow in the wake of this righteous revolution.

This utopian vision was a part of the Panthers' ideological pull. But the group's most powerful attraction was psychological. The Panthers were catharsis personified; they were the organization embodiment of Dr. Frantz Fanon's argument that violence provides a path for the psychological liberation of an oppressed people. The party was designed to educate African-Americans about the nature of their historic oppression and also work within the community building institutions and delivering services to which the "masses" could relate.

Panthers also organized armed patrols to monitor cop behavior in response to continuing incidents of police brutality in inner-city U.S.A. This was a tonic for youth in the northern cities, like me and my peers, who were deeply embarrassed by images of civil rights protesters being beaten by rednecks and attacked by dogs. For us, the agrarian wardrobe and submissive demeanor of the southern preachers leading those civil rights crusades hit the wrong stylistic note. We were attracted to the Panthers—with their ghetto-honed militance, their swagger, their berets, leathers, and shades—because they embodied an attitude that explicitly reversed the sappy "we shall overcome someday" sentiments of the civil rights movement. After all, we were the children of Malcolm, and we wanted to overcome *yesterday*.

The Panthers also had an intellectual agenda. Huey P. Newton, as the minister of defense, precociously crafted a philosophical manifesto for the group. Combining elements of Marxist dialectics, the cultural materialism of Mozambiquan theorist Amilcar Cabral, Fanon's violence-as-therapy psychology, and Malcolm X's black nationalism, Newton fashioned a patchwork ideology and required his followers to engage in discussions about political philosophy. The Panthers cast themselves as intellectual warriors as well as physical revolutionaries.

But the lack of focus on concerns of culture and spirituality had seemed to me to be a serious deficit in the Panther Party. In my New Jersey town we instituted a breakfast program, a tutorial program for elementary school students and for older folks seeking GED diplomas; we operated a small-scale health clinic utilizing volunteer doctors and nurses who agreed with the Panthers that medical care should be more widely available to inner-city residents. In the process of providing these community services, I grew to understand the connections between self-discipline and group cohesion. And despite the Panthers' good intentions, our effectiveness was limited and sometimes undermined by a lack of discipline and mature dedication.

If we really were as serious about revolution as we claimed to be, then, I reasoned, we should have no problem completely submitting our personal preferences to the cause of black empowerment. That logic led me through cultural nationalism directly to Elijah Muhammad's Nation of Islam, better known at the time as the Black Muslims. I eventually became convinced that the Nation was the only organization doing the things that had to be done to change African-Americans' desperate condition.

This was an odd conclusion for me. I thought of myself as somewhat of an intellectual, attuned more to philosophical speculation than to the attitude of blind faith necessary as an adherent of an authoritarian religion. In fact, I once argued against the Nation's political quietism and its members' standardized rhetoric. The Black

Muslims were nothing but a bunch of brainwashed automatons who couldn't function effectively without Muhammad's strict discipline, I would argue, smugly; I criticized them for turning their backs on the struggle. Although I later changed that assessment, it turns out that my initial conclusion wasn't far off.

But at the time, it increasingly seemed to me that the Nations' program attended to what precisely were our greatest needs. I dismissed the problems I had with the theology (problems I'll outline later) as some of the "personal preferences" one needed to subordinate for the cause of black liberation. Theological technicalities were less important to me than the Nation's overall program: i.e., Muhammad's teachings emphasized discipline and personal responsibility, the very traits I had learned to recognize as essential to black progress. In order to be accepted among one's Black Muslim peers, one had to have eschewed the dissipating lifestyles that are such strong features of black American youth culture. One of the things that soured me on the potential of the Panthers was the susceptibility of too many members to those very dissipating practices; we would come up short on many missions because some behavioral excess landed our fellow revolutionaries in jail, in or under the wrong person's bed, hungover, too high, or something. The Nation, however, was all work and very little play. And if we were *really* serious about being black, that Spartan path was the one we should be walking—or so it seemed to me. I later understood how that same logic is also a ready ally of fascism.

One of the untold stories of those days, however, is that the fuse on the explosion of blackness was ignited by "Messenger" Elijah Muhammad (nee Poole), a lowly migrant from Sandersville, Georgia, with a fourth grade education. His Nation of Islam, formed in 1930, triggered the sixties Black Movement through the charismatic presence of Malcolm, who remained a dedicated minister of the Messenger from his 1952 release from prison until his break in 1964. And the era closed out with the soaring popularity of another NOI minister named Louis Farrakhan. In fact, during the so-called black power era, the Nation was a major influence on groups ranging from the Panthers to the Pan-Africanists, from SNCC (the Student Non-Violent Coordinating Committee) to the Black Studies movement, from the cultural nationalists to a host of indigenous Islamic groupings.

I also flirted with cultural nationalism, frequently visiting Imamu Amiri Baraka's Spirit House at the High Street headquarters of his Committee for a Unified New Ark in Newark, New Jersey. But soon it became clear that many nationalist operations merely mimicked the Nation, with dashikis and tikis substituting for suits and bow ties. The essential argument of the cultural nationalist is that black people were so badly damaged by being severed from their cultural roots we could only be repaired by reconnecting to African traditions. And since we didn't know from where on the African continent we derived, the nationalists proposed that we compose an African identity based on elements common to many African cultures—a composite Africa. To this end, Maulana Ron Karenga—with important contributions by Imamu Amiri Baraka—formulated a philosophy he labeled Kawaida. The Los Angeles–based Karenga made an audacious attempt to craft a coherent cultural nationalist ideology.

At the time, however, I concluded that Karenga had merely translated Elijah Muhammad's plain-spoken doctrine into intellectual exotica. Some cultural nationalists did this primarily to distinguish themselves from the Nation; antagonisms lingered between acolytes of the murdered Malcolm X and those who remained faithful to Messenger Muhammad. Many nationalists believed that Malcolm's assassination on February 21, 1965, was ordered by top-level officials of the Nation. And until a 1995 reconciliation, members of the Nation regularly condemned Malcolm as an apostate, totally undeserving of his popular acclaim. He was regularly referred to as "The Hypocrite" in the Nation's inner circles. I was in the air force when Malcolm was killed and antagonisms were hottest between the two camps. By 1970, an uneasy calm had settled on the dispute. Still, many nationalists maintained a studied distance from the Nation as a gesture of allegiance to the martyred Malcolm. But, I reasoned, if Muhammad's wisdom was the root, then why waste time with the branches?

When I began to understand our need for economic self-reliance, I realized that the Nation had been pushing that program since its inception c. 1930 in depression Detroit. And by the early 1970s, when I became involved, this group of mostly low-income black folks had accumulated an impressive portfolio of independent enterprises, including grocery stores, restaurants, bakeries, dry cleaners, and thousands of acres of farmland.

The social disintegration of too many black communities was traced easily to fracturing black families, and the Nation had always been firmly focused on family life. Most of the Muslim brothers I knew were married or on the way to the aisle. I knew no unmarried sisters.

The disproportionate violence and crime wracking too many black communities revealed an absence of cultural values that would situate our behavior within a larger code of social conduct. The Nation intended to impose such a code. The decay and Eurocentric biases of public education pointed to our need for independent educational institutions. Well, Elijah Muhammad had long established a network of schools, called Universities of Islam, in most of the country's major cities. The way I put it at the time was: "Elijah Muhammad must be the one, because he's doing what must be done."

I had problems with the Nation's religious doctrine, but I reconciled those differences by making metaphorical interpretations of the catechism's more outrageous elements. For example, the core belief that the "Asiatic black man is God, the maker, the owner, and the cream of the planet earth" was easily reconcilable with my more philosophical notions. If humanity arose on the African continent (as increasing evidence suggests), then black people were the first humans. And, if humans create phenomenal reality by perceiving it, as postulated by the logic of quantum mechanics—a logic I accepted as the perfect merger of science and mysticism—then, the first black humans "created" the universe by being the first humans to perceive it. Got it? Well, anyway, that's how I harmonized my own philosophical turn of mind with the Nation's genesis story.

Yakub's history was another of the Nation's doctrines that I translated into a more compatible intellectual language. In the Nation of Islam's peculiar theology, Yakub was the "big-headed scientist" who created white people on the island of Patmos in the Mediterranean through a five hundred–year process of eugenics. I transformed Yakub into a metaphor for the process of mass migration and environmental speciation. In a sense, I was cheating; true believers touted the literal truths of Elijah Muhammad's teachings. They argued that most people rejected Elijah's literal words only because of their undying allegiance to Western belief systems. Why, for example, is Yakub's history any more preposterous than the biblical story of Adam and Eve and a talking serpent? Why is it less believable than the biblical curse of Ham in which a son of Noah, and thus his "Hamitic" descendants, is damned to both blackness and eternal servitude for observing his father's nakedness?

All creation myths and most eschatological prophecies are, by their very natures, implausible. If we can suspend our rational skepticism to become Catholics, Buddhists, and Baptists, why can't we do the same for the sake of black unity and progress within the Nation of Islam?

And theological authenticity notwithstanding, the Nation presciently emphasized aspects of the black struggle generally ignored by other groups but crucial to our overall development. Here's one example: After leaving the Panther Party in late 1970, I entered Rutgers University's Newark College of Arts and Sciences and immediately got involved with a group that eventually occupied the dean's office to demand open enrollment and the naming of the campus center for Paul Robeson, Rutgers' most accomplished, yet seldom celebrated, black graduate. The campus was located in the predominantly black city of Newark, but the black student population was less than 1 percent of the total student population. We won our fight for open enrollment, but the black students who poured onto the campus were more interested in playing bid whist in Robeson Center than in toughing out a college education. Mere access wasn't sufficient, I soon discovered. There was a deeper cultural problem that few black organizations were addressing; the Nation of Islam, however, spoke to that issue strongly and clearly.

I got my "X"—and became a registered member of the Nation of Islam—in 1971 by copying exactly a letter, even down to the cursive handwriting, and sending it back to Chicago headquarters for approval. I was officially registered at Temple (or Mosque) No. 25 in Newark. This was also the mosque that headquartered the men responsible for Malcolm's assassination and, in fact, was well known in the Nation for its militant support of Elijah Muhammad. Among my duties was the sale of three hundred *Muhammad Speaks* newspapers per week. As the only Black Muslim on the Rutgers campus, this was a piece of cake; I had a captive audience of card-playing black students.

In September 1972, while still a full-time student, I was hired by the Associated Press as the first black journalist in the history of the Newark bureau. Under pressure to hire a black reporter in a city that was about 65 percent African-American, they were looking for a sufficiently socialized prospect with some writing skills. I was a student at Rutgers with several bylines in the campus newspaper and some sophomoric poems published in whatever publication was hard up enough to print them. After some tests and interviews, I was hired. The Nation required closely cropped hair and suited attire, so my editors probably thought they hired a clean-cut product of the black bourgeoisie. What they had in fact was an aspiring subverter. The Nation stressed the necessity of learning the skills of the "white man's civilization" and using them for the good of the black community. I tried to do that, though I was also a critic,

203

increasingly distressed by the racist mindset of mainstream journalism. I concluded at the time that what we termed "objective reporting" was essentially the ratification of the racist status quo. It became much clearer to me that African-Americans' perceptions of American life differed considerably from those of mainstream America.

I would write stories for the A.P. that followed the wire service's formula of writing "objective" news for the proverbial "milkman in Nebraska," go home and rewrite the piece for *Muhammad Speaks*. At the time, circulation at *Speaks* was about 800,000, and every black militant worth his or her salt was a regular reader. In 1974 I got the invitation to join *Muhammad Speaks* as an editor, and so I immediately quit the A.P. and moved to Chicago. For followers of Elijah Muhammad, Chicago was what Mecca is to orthodox Muslims. As an editor for the Nation's esteemed paper, I immediately became a celebrity.

I brought my family with me, which by that time had grown to four. It probably wouldn't have been my family had I not joined the Nation. My first daughter, Salima, was born in 1968. I chose not to marry her mother, even after we had another daughter, Rasheedah, in 1970. I quickly remedied that situation shortly after receiving my X. The stability afforded my two daughters by a solid nuclear family and the sense of self-regard instilled by the Nation's school system has served them in good stead throughout their lives. They are remarkably self-possessed young women who have avoided many of the traps into which many of their peers fell and easily maintain a positive direction. The foundation of their strength was laid in a family built largely by Elijah Muhammad's Nation.

Of course, I had not yet met Muhammad himself (I did meet him in late 1974). I knew him through his "National Representative" and Minister of Harlem's Temple No. 7, Louis Farrakhan. I first heard Farrakhan in 1969 and admired his intelligent eloquence; he was much like Malcolm in the early 1960s, even his vocal timbre. He was speaking regularly at the East, a black nationalist hangout in Brooklyn, so even then he was trying to heal the nationalist–Black Muslim breach. By 1971, I had heard him many times and become one of his greatest advocates. In 1972, police attacked Temple Mosque No. 7, and one patrolman was shot and another beaten. The news spread like wildfire, and within hours thousands of blacks gathered, including a contingent from Newark's Temple No. 25. The crowd shouted, "Leave the Muslims alone," and Farrakhan orchestrated the event like a maestro. In 1974, Farrakhan attracted nearly seventy-five thousand people to a Black Family Day rally on Randalls Island, New York.

When Elijah Muhammad died in 1975, I helped arrange general press coverage, as well as reporting myself on his huge funeral. It was an anxious, tense period for members of the Nation; we knew of no official succession procedure, and rumors were flying like debris in a tornado. However, most insiders were certain that Wallace Delaney Muhammad, Elijah's rebellious son and seventh child, would get the divine nod. Though he had been expelled from the Nation several times, his transgressions were downplayed because, according to Nation lore, W.D. Muhammad was divinely destined to become the group's next leader.

The contentious son was welcomed back into the fold by his father in 1974. Elijah was very sick at the time, and Wallace's return was greeted with unusual fanfare. Elijah spoke of him glowingly, and Wallace began attracting standing-room-only crowds at regular Thursday sermons. Although those sermons were more or less faithful to the Nation's peculiar catechism, it was obvious to all who heard him that Elijah's son had some new things to say. Nation officials began whispering that Wallace was teaching the "new wisdom of the second resurrection," a period that was long awaited and had been foretold by Elijah in the forties. W.D.'s prominence grew as Elijah weakened, and the faithful began reading Fard's doctrines on the wall. The feeble patriarch died on February 25, 1975, and his son and divinely designated heir took over with unanimous approval from the NOI's leadership on February 26.

My path personally crossed Farrakhan's during this time of turmoil. The popular New York minister had been touted by many as the only worthy successor to the deceased Muhammad, but he initially pledged fealty to W. D.'s new leadership. Within five months he was demoted from his position as national representative and began pulling away from the influential Harlem temple. Elijah's successor son directed Farrakhan to head a decrepit walk-up temple on Chicago's West Side and began taking other actions seemingly designed to humiliate Elijah's former representative. In June 1975, he sent Farrakhan off to lead a Nation of Islam delegation to the Organization of African Unity meeting in Kampala, Uganda, which then was headed by Idi Amin Dada. I accompanied Farrakhan and came to understand his anguish at the changes going on within his beloved Nation of Islam. Wallace Muhammad had begun changing the core beliefs of the Nation, bringing the group more in accord with beliefs held by the international Islamic community. Farrakhan's lectures started pushing the notion that Elijah's Nation was like the isolation ward in a hospital, where the afflicted are restricted to that ward and given special treatment until they're ready to join the general population. Wallace's ascension and the "second resurrection" meant it was time to join the general population. But even at that time, there were many former members urging the eloquent Farrakhan to leave Wallace's group and work anew at building Elijah's race-conscious nation. He confided in me his inner turmoil at being asked virtually to denounce a man he revered. He concluded that Wallace's way was the truest path to Islam.

Muhammad, the son, continued making drastic changes. In less than a year after his elevation he began criticizing Elijah for intentionally deceiving his followers about the divinity of Master Fard Muhammad and for pushing the eugenic theology that identified Caucasians as "white, blue-eyed devils." And since the core of the Nation's beliefs held that whites were grafted out of black people specifically to bedevil the planet, this change was a powerful blow to the heart of the Nation's doctrine. W.D. also abolished the Fruit of Islam security unit and eased the dress code that mandated closely cropped hair, suits, white shirts, and ties for men and long garments and headdresses for women.

In 1977, Farrakhan heeded the call of what had become a horde of disgruntled former officials to help rebuild the Nation, and he's been at it ever since. He is a remarkably gifted man. With his eloquence, his physical grace, and his flair for the dramatic, he is, by far, black America's finest orator. His considerable intelligence and organizing abilities combine in a rare synthesis of leadership that has placed him near the top of several black public opinion polls. He's addressed millions of people in the last few years and was the only one capable of pulling off the enormously successful Million Man March. His popularity among young African-Americans is even more unlikely. Although the Nation's message is as conservative and as antisensual as that of the most rigid Christian fundamentalist sect, he manages to attract the interest of the most testosterone-saturated segment of the African-American community—young men. Listen to some rap records these days, and you're likely to be startled by a stern Farrakhan sermon floating incongruously over a deep bass groove.

Farrakhan seems pretty much unparalleled in his ability to corral the raging energies of this hip-hop generation. One of the ironies of gangsta rap is that pioneering purveyors of the genre also are attracted strongly to Farrakhan's Nation of Islam (many, in fact, are members). But actually that's par for the course. The Nation traditionally has attracted the outlaw element among African-Americans. Keep in mind the gangsta pedigree of Malcolm ("Detroit Red") Little who later became Malcolm X. One of the major reasons Farrakhan's group is accorded such street-level respect is its historical connection to the black "underclass."

Although Farrakhan's fiery oratory is heavy with race-man swagger and challenge, he also urges self-discipline, family reverence, ethnic solidarity, hard work, honesty, civility, and all the other virtues held dear by Judeo-Christian civilization. The Nation's rehabilitative success among people utterly forsaken and abandoned by the rest of society recently has prompted mainstream black organizations to look more favorably in Farrakhan's direction.

This also was Malcolm's appeal. In fact, for a period, the stern figure of Malcolm X was exhumed and re-anointed as the preferred leader for the nineties. His X was everywhere, a product of both the marketing genius of filmmaker Spike Lee and the spirit of the times. But those who understood the absurdity of that "back-to-the-future" leadership urged that instead of embracing a dead martyr, black Americans could settle on a live Farrakhan as the most Malcolm-like of today's leaders. His status as a modern-day Malcolm X is a development rife with irony: Farrakhan was one of Malcolm's most persistent detractors during the late firebrand's bitter feud with patriarch Elijah Muhammad. In fact, Farrakhan wrote that Malcolm was "worthy of death" in the December 1964 edition of *Muhammad Speaks*. Two months later, Malcolm was assassinated, almost certainly by NOI members. But there also are many similarities between the two: Both men were devoted students of the late Muhammad; Farrakhan once served as Malcolm's lieutenant in the NOI's Boston headquarters. It's obvious that Farrakhan fashioned his speaking style from that of his former boss. Both held the post of Elijah Muhammad's national representative. More important, Farrakhan's positions on most domestic and international issues virtually echo those of Malcolm.

But the Malcolm X analogy also reveals the limitations and perils of this appeal. Malcolm's assassination by members of Newark's Temple No. 25 should have cautioned Farrakhan about the dangers of cultlike adoration. It should have educated him to the need for democratic expressions of dissent within the Nation as well as for some accountability to interests outside the group. But, if leadership has a divine connection, what right do mere mortals have to dispute it—democracy notwithstanding? If all the questions are already answered, why continue to ask them? These were some of the questions that ultimately led me away from the Nation and its successor. Wallace Muhammad's slow destruction of his father's dogma had the effect of releasing me from the sway of all dogma, including that of orthodox Islam.

It's also likely that Farrakhan has learned the lesson of Malcolm's murder all too well. He may have concluded that his veneration by adoring acolytes is in the Nation's best interest. Had Elijah not inspired such transcendent devotion, the Nation surely would have disintegrated following Malcolm's assassination. There were dozens, perhaps hundreds, of deaths triggered by the resulting internecine feud. As a reporter in Newark during the early 1970s, I covered some of the ritualistic murders still reverberating from Malcolm's 1965 assassination. My reflections on the ease with which disciples can commit even the most heinous acts, as long as it's in the name of their particular deity, began reviving my skepticism of temporal figures seeking religious devotion. That, coupled with my realization of the similarities between the NOI's devotional, "fatherland" nationalism and the mystical Aryan nationalism of Nazi ideology, helped speed my exit from the Nation and its varied offshoots.

But Farrakhan also seems to have learned a lesson from the experience of Wallace D. Muhammad, who now is referred to as Imam W. Deen Mohammed, Muslim American Spokesman for Human Salvation. He spells his name differently to further mark the theological distinction between his practice of Islam and that of his father. But Mohammed's utter rejection of Elijah's Islam provoked widespread anger and disenchantment among many former members and has deeply tarnished his image among militant young blacks who are the de facto arbiters of movement authenticity. Farrakhan has been careful not to alienate the young turks within the Nation—represented primarily by Khalid Abdul Muhammad, the former aide whose rabidly racist speech at a New Jersey college provoked a stern rebuke and demotion from Farrakhan—as well as from the group's legion of militant admirers on the outside. Farrakhan's status among the "no sellout" Hip-Hop Generation is largely a function of his uncompromising persona. The public focus on politics and conciliatory black leadership has whetted an appetite among black youth for the kind of outspoken leadership embodied by Farrakhan. The canny NOI leader thus far has managed to maintain this street credibility while making subtle alterations in doctrine.

But that is Farrakhan's tragic dilemma. He's trapped between the eugenic, authoritarian message of his mentor and the promise of wider and more consequential influence that would follow a repudiation (or at least a serious reinterpretation) of that message. He must maintain an uneasy equilibrium. If he loses his balance, everything could go up in smoke. Literally.

Farrakhan Fever:
Defining the Divide
between Blacks and Jews

Derrick Bell

DERRICK BELL *is a professor of law at New York University. He is author of* Faces at the Bottom of the Well: The Permanence of Racism; Gospel Choirs: Psalms of Survival in an Alien Land Called Home; *and several other books on race, class, and the American legal system.*

It is a source of constant wonder that black people in this country remain such a threat to whites, despite our relative powerlessness and our reluctance—except under severe provocation—to use what potential power we have. The belief that we represent a serious danger is deep, historic, and beyond cure. Initially, there was the fear of revolts during the slavery era, then in the post-Reconstruction period, it was the fear of black competence, the real motivation for the literally thousands of blacks lynched for failing to "stay in their place." Then, today, fear rather than either logic or justice is a key part of crime policies that have ensnared a third of young black men.

A minor but significant contemporary evidence of this "black threat" phenomenon is the alarm-filled attacks aimed at Minister Louis

Farrakhan whenever he speaks harshly about whites, particularly Jews. The facts are that his negative statements about Jews border on the bizarre and that they constitute only a small portion of Farrakhan's enormous vocal outpourings and, when made, are usually followed by efforts to explain them or put them in a larger context.

But none of that makes any difference to the full-court, rapid-action response that places Farrakhan as public enemy number one. I have sought explanations from my Jewish friends, but they are no help. They may not adore Farrakhan, but they readily agree with me that the retaliatory blasts are both unnecessary and counterproductive. So, in what may be an excess of tolerance, I have been trying to comprehend by comparison the reasons for the periodic and always highly publicized reactions over the hostile statements about Jews made by members of the Nation of Islam and a few black scholars. There may be a parallel between the reaction of some Jews to the inflammatory statements made about them and my rather excessive response to an incident that happened to me.

It was a lazy afternoon during a long, quiet summer, when, without students or the pressure of classes, law teachers can get some serious research and writing done. In response to a knock on my office door, I interrupted my work. A somewhat seedily dressed black man opened the door, put his head in the doorway, and seeing my questioning look, said, "Excuse me, Professor, but I am looking for someone, and I think you are the person who can help me." As it turned out, I was unable to help the young man. Indeed, by the time he left my office a few moments later, I was chilled to my core with a sense of personal and philosophical dread.

The young man, whom I will call Nat T., said he was searching for a character I had created for one of my books, an allegorical figure named Geneva Crenshaw. When I explained that Geneva didn't really exist, Nat became agitated.

"Get me straight, Professor. She thinks like I do," he said. "I will find her, and together we will lead an uprising like nothing this damn country has ever seen."

I looked at him hard. Nat returned my stare without blinking. He did not seem mentally disturbed, just scarily purposeful. "You are not the first black person to give up on the system," I suggested, "but taking the law in your own hands is dangerous and . . ."

"Don't talk to me about the law," Nat interrupted. "I know it firsthand." He explained, "Yeah, I may not look like it today. It's been ten years, but I worked my way through college and got into a half-ass, night law school. They flunked me out. Didn't like me questioning what they were teaching, said I was too angry to be a lawyer, didn't have the right attitude." He continued speaking, his story of personal loss (a wife and child killed in a car wreck) wound through with repeated references to how "the system" and whites had done him wrong. He traced his present, intinerant-but-militant position to that humiliating law school failure. And he insisted he was serious about executing an extreme means of balancing the scales in America.

"With all your anger," I ventured, "you have a lot more faith that this society will respond rationally to your plans than I do."

Nat T. ignored me and began describing in more detail how he was going to organize the black community and build an effective retaliatory force. He obviously had given the matter of revolution a great deal of thought—a fact that made his schemes seem even more insane to me.

I told Nat T. that I really had to get back to work, but he kept pressing me on Geneva Crenshaw. Again, I told him that she did not exist. He shook his head. "Don't you know that when you deny Geneva Crenshaw's existence, you are denying your existence. There is no hope for you, man. No hope."

Nat T. headed for the door, then turned and told me that he would be coming back.

"And once Geneva Crenshaw and I link up and get our revolution started, one of my first missions will be to return and blow your head off. As a black agent of the enemy, you are as dangerous and more damaging than the real enemy."

"So," I said, my anger rising, "your racial revolution will begin at home."

"It will begin with the enemy," he responded. Then, as suddenly and as resolutely as he'd come, he left.

My encounter with Nat T. was traumatic. And, given their vigorous response, the attacks by CUNY Professor Leonard Jeffries, the Reverend Louis Farrakhan, and his former spokesperson Khalid Muhammad frighten some Jews as much as Nat T.'s threat frightened me. And, I suggest, for three quite similar reasons. First, statements filled with so much venom are distressing in themselves. Second, the individual statements remind us of group hostility in the society aimed at us. Third, by lashing out and seeking to trounce a rather vulnerable enemy, we nourish our denial of the major enemy we dare not challenge. I want to examine each of these responses.

First, the hostile statements are distressing in themselves. The automatic response to a verbal attack is defense and then counterattack. In my case, after Nat T. left, I called the campus police. I was teaching at Harvard Law School at the time and had them in my office and searching the campus within minutes. I got them to involve the Cambridge and Boston police departments. The Boston police found him at a homeless shelter and warned him to stay away from the university. I was not relieved. At that point, I felt some guilt for "turning in a brother" but insufficient sympathy for the cruel hand that fate had dealt him to simply ignore his threat on my life. To tell the truth, I had rather hoped the police would arrest Nat T. and put him away. Here, my good sense, or rather lack of influence, kicked in. What charges could I bring? A threat to kill me at some time in the future? Likely, Nat T.'s threat was scary, but in the context of crime in today's world, who would take it seriously?

In the face of verbal abuse by Minister Louis Farrakhan and his former spokesperson Khalid Muhammad, some Jews react in a fashion quite similar to my reaction to Nat T. "After all we have been through," they seem to say, "we are certainly not going to accept gratuitous insults by demagogues using hate tactics to gain power at our expense. We know the tactic and have been victimized by it over the centuries. But no more. The place to draw the 'never again' line is right here."

Of course, the Jewish response to what they deem anti-Semitic attacks makes my call for police action seem mild in comparison, but no less futile. The Nation of Islam has been castigated in full-page ads and dozens of opinion columns. The U.S. Senate has voted a resolution condemning Muhammad's speech at Kean College. But like Brer Rabbit after being tossed in the briar patch by Brer Fox, the Nation of Islam spokespersons are glorying in the condemnations, gaining great acclaim from their followers, who hail them less for what they said than for their willingness to upset white people. It appears perverse, but not to blacks who spend their lives carefully censoring their comments to whites to protect their jobs, keep their apartments, save their lives.

Nation of Islam speakers are not the only blacks who have had to face the consequences of saying harsh things about Jews. Some Jewish groups supported a major, though unsuccessful, effort to remove Professor Leonard Jeffries from his teaching post at the City University of New York (CUNY). Citing first amendment and due process violations in the process, Professor Jeffries sued and obtained a judgment of $400,000, an amount lowered substantially on appeal. Jeffries had been espousing an "Afrocentric" curriculum that CUNY administrators found unacceptable.

According to Wellesley College Professor Tony Martin, college administrators and Jewish groups have tried to have him removed as a result of his use of a book deemed disparaging of Jews.[1] He has written a book, *The Jewish Onslaught: Dispatches from the Wellesley Battlefront,* detailing those efforts.[2] As with my calling in the police on Nat T., these attempts to use position and influence to punish our attackers tend to encourage rather than discourage the abuse from which we seek relief.

The second reason for our actions likely prevents us from hearing, much less heeding, advice about restraint. The threatening statements remind us of a broad range of hostility in the society that is aimed at us. Thus, my fear of Nat T. was less from what he said than from what he symbolized. He reminded me that he is neither alone nor entirely inaccurate in viewing successful blacks as the enemy—no matter how hard we may work for the progress of all blacks. Our success has served to separate us from the great mass of our people.

We live and work apart; our children are not in the same schools. We attend different places for shopping, recreation, and even worship. Middle-class life is not without its problems, but those problems pale beside the daily dangers and wrenching frustrations of the black poor and working class. The presence of achieving blacks provides a convenient excuse for society's failure to give these victims of racism the aid we offer so readily to those harmed by natural disasters. Regrettably, there are a few blacks—thankfully few—who are quite willing to grab a tainted fame and fortune by giving a corrupted "racial legitimacy" to such views. Given this climate, it is a wonder that there are not more blacks who, like Nat T., believe we "black tokens" are their enemy. As economic conditions worsen for poorer blacks, the numbers of those who share Nat T.'s opinion will increase.

I speak of the isolation of successful blacks—and the sense of unease based on that isolation—based on experience. My reading of and discussions with Jews indicate that many share my sense of isolation. As Paul Berman puts it: "The styles of Jewish New World success follow patterns that were established in the Old World ghettos, and the successes themselves are fated now and then to call up, out of the creepier depths of Christian civilization, the old paranoid accusations about conspiracies and evil."[3]

Acknowledging the miracle that has taken place merely by the act of Jews fleeing from the Old World to the New, Berman says: "Even the fat-and-happiest of American Jews has to shudder at the spectacle, which is always taking place, of some eminent person, not only spokesmen of the Nation of Islam, standing up to give the ancient libels a fresh new airing."[4] For many Jews, Louis Farrakhan and the Nation of Islam evoke those fears. Unlike blacks, most Jews are successful in all the ways this society measures success. And yet there is justifiable concern that their very success has heightened rather than reduced the hostility vented against them—simply because they are Jews.

Thus, openly expressed, racial-religious epithets revive the never-far-from-the-surface fear that, as writer-activist Letty Cottin Pogrebin puts it, "the dominant majority may suddenly turn against the Jews (as some Americans did during the energy crisis and the Gulf War), fear of possible peril to the state of Israel (every Jew's haven of last resort), and fear of the slippery slope that propelled another 'civilized society' from spewing hate to building gas chambers."[5] Pogrebin acknowledges that one cannot compare the current suffering of blacks with the fear of potential suffering, but, she explains, "for Jews one generation removed from the Holocaust, the fear is real and the vulnerability deeply felt."[6]

The third explanation for our response is a form of aggressive denial. We hope that by soundly squashing the relatively powerless individual whose words upset us, we are symbolically defusing the major powers in the society that we fear to upset and refuse to challenge. Those are the forces that are far more capable of doing us in—when the time is right. Again, my fear was less of Nat T. himself, or even all the Nat T.s our society has embittered. Rather, I fear the power of those who have to be aware of the policies on schooling, unemployment, poverty, welfare, crime and crime fights, that are the direct and indirect cause of so many black deaths that they render capital punishment, at least as administered in this country, both a slower and a far less certain method of death.

I wonder. Do any of those who demand that black spokespeople drop everything and denounce the rantings of a few blacks have any sense of what is happening to black people in this society? Does it mean anything that in most urban areas, 80 to 85 percent of black men will be caught up in the criminal justice system before they reach their thirtieth birthday—if they reach their thirtieth birthday? The number of black men in prison now exceeds 800,000, the largest number of black men in prison in any country in the world. And what is this country doing about it? The Congress has offered up a crime bill that the president was all too anxious to sign. It will provide billions for new prisons and create new categories of crime to fill those prisons.[7]

If the nation's policies toward blacks were revised to require weekly, random roundups of several hundred blacks, who were then taken to a secluded place and shot, that policy would be more dramatic but hardly different in result than the policies now in effect, and that most of us feel powerless to change. Nat T. knows this, and he views me as a danger precisely because I don't see or, rather, don't want to see it. How much easier it is to rail against Harvard for failing to hire a few more people of color for its faculty. Or, in the context of this essay, how much easier to rail against the anti-anti-Semitic excesses of the *New York Times* columnist A. M. Rosenthal or the Anti-Defamation League (ADL).

Like writer and scholar Michael Lerner, I "can't stand the hypocrisy from a white media and white establishment that does everything it can to exploit and degrade blacks, then looks on in pretended horror when pathologies start to develop in the black community."[8] And if my ranting and raving is loud enough, for a time I may block out the awful truth Professor Delores Aldridge will not let us forget, namely that "both Jews and blacks occupy a somewhat precarious position in American society and culture. Neither group has the power to determine the destiny of the other. They both warily monitor the mood of the White American mainstream." Then she adds, "Allies do not have to be good friends."[9]

True, but any alliances are hard unless the allies agree on the identity of their common enemy and do not lambast each other in a futile effort to deny a truth that is too scary to acknowledge. The more vocal elements of the Jewish community are committed to denunciation and retaliation as the appropriate means of combating black anti-Semitism. Black spokespeople who refuse to join in the denunciation are deemed to have sided with the anti-Semites. Few blacks will join in a response so broad based that it includes all of us. Just as Nat T. is not a unique individual, Minister Farrakhan is not alone in his view that hate, rather than love, marks the road to power. Indeed, as has happened with so many outspoken black leaders before him, Farrakhan could be removed violently from the scene tomorrow, and the danger would remain and might worsen. Farrakhan draws tremendous crowds to his three-hour speeches, but in addition to castigating whites and countless other groups, he preaches quite conservative messages of nonviolence and self-help, messages with special significance for young blacks living in a society that tries its best to deny that they even exist.

In commenting on Farrakhan's book *A Torchlight for America* for its back cover, I observed, "Unlike those conservatives, black and white, who only preach self-help to the poor as a crowd-pleasing abstraction, Farrakhan's formulas emphasize the Nation of Islam's experience in educating black children, rehabilitating black prisoners, ridding black communities of drug dealers, and rebuilding respect for self—the essential prerequisite for individuals determined to maintain the struggle against the racism that burdens our lives and, unless curbed, will destroy this country."

I certainly don't expect many Jews to agree with this assessment. They despise Farrakhan, probably for all three reasons discussed above. When he attacks, their reaction is retaliation. This proactive response is likely satisfying, but as with my hope that Nat T. would be jailed, it is not very rational and often seems counterproductive. Entities deemed supportive of the Nation of Islam or its spokespeople have been threatened with economic reprisals, and black leaders and groups—though they have no more in common than color with the Nation of Islam speakers—have been urged to condemn the speakers.

During Benjamin F. Chavis's brief tenure as NAACP executive director, he warned his ADL counterpart, Abraham Foxman, that continued ADL attacks on Farrakhan could create precisely what Jewish leaders say they fear: black anti-Semitism.

Foxman acknowledged the risk but said he was willing to take it, warning on his part that if African-American leaders do not clearly distance themselves from views such as Farrakhan's, "it will undermine the moral underpinnings of a coalition."[10]

This pattern of hard-line responses to blacks and civil rights policies deemed threatening to Jews did not begin with Louis Farrakhan. While some Jews helped establish the NAACP early in this century and provided both financial support and legal acumen to black educational programs and the Civil Rights movement, the Black Power Movement in the late 1960s and the widespread adoption of affirmative action policies in the 1970s alienated many formerly supportive whites. Their number included a great many Jews, some of them later called neoconservatives, who sensing the ebb of public support for racial remedies, became highly regarded spokespeople for opponents of school busing, affirmative action, welfare, and most of the causes their former civil rights colleagues espoused.

They also supplied a most effective chorus of condemnation when former UN ambassador Andrew Young was discovered to have met secretly with the Palestinians. The Jesse Jackson case is, of course, the classic example of the retaliatory response. Jackson has done everything but offer to jump off a tall building to explain his position on Israel and Palestine and to atone for his mid-1980s "Hymietown" remark, all, seemingly, to no avail. Despite Jackson's position as the leader many blacks respect most, many Jewish groups will not forgive him. As one Jewish friend who opposes such tactics put it, they are "demanding penance without hope of forgiveness."

Jews should respond vigorously to statements they deem anti-Semitic. On the other hand, it seems to me an example of "piling on" when Jewish groups ignore efforts by blacks like Jackson to apologize for their statements; it seems to me that they use their greater influence in the community to block political aspirations and other activities not connected with the statements or actions that offended them. In addition, there is the use of economic clout to threaten business enterprises of those deemed dangerous to Jewish interests. Thus, some Jewish groups are seeking to prevent the Nation of Islam from obtaining or holding contracts with public housing authorities to provide the projects with much needed security. While, according to a *Time* magazine story, the Nation of Islam has not always been successful in reducing crime in its public housing security businesses, it does provide jobs and build entrepreneurial skills in communities much in need of both.[11]

Regrettably, the pressures exerted against the Nation of Islam adhere to a pattern.

The writer, teacher, and publisher Haki R. Madhubuti recalls years ago mounting a protest against John Johnson, the publisher of *Ebony, Jet,* and other black publications.[12] The protest followed Johnson's discontinuance of *Black World* and the dismissal of the magazine's editor, Howard Fuller, a highly respected journalist. Madhubuti reports that a large group set up picket lines around Johnson's new, multistory building on Michigan Avenue in downtown Chicago. Within the first hour of the demonstration, Mr. Johnson himself appeared and invited the group inside for a talk. There, Johnson told the group that he had halted the publication of *Black World* and fired Fuller for refusing to cease publishing the Palestinian side of the Middle-East struggle and the African support for that struggle. He did so, he said, "because Jewish businessmen threatened to pull their advertising out of *Ebony* and *Jet* magazines and would have convinced their gentile friends to do the same if the Middle-East coverage didn't stop."[13] Madhubuti confesses to this reaction by the display of overwhelming power. "We were stunned into a weakening silence. Our responses were few because we knew it was both an economic and political decision and as an astute businessman, Mr. Johnson did what he felt was best for his company."[14]

How, one might ask, do Jewish boycotts or their threat differ from those blacks have used since the 1930s to get jobs in white-owned and—more recently—Korean-owned businesses located in black communities? The difference may seem more lawyer-like than real, but I think there is a distinction based on the relative power of the protesters. Blacks resort to boycotts as a substitute for political and economic power in an effort to pressure businesses to treat blacks fairly. Jewish groups utilize their superior economic power to intimidate blacks into halting actions that Jews find offensive, whatever the value of those actions to blacks.

Jews may certainly do what they feel is necessary to protect the image of Israel. But it should not be a surprise that many blacks resent the use of Jewish political clout in this way. It serves, among other things, to heighten the antagonism toward Jews rather than—as I assume is the purpose—to lessen it. Many blacks, including myself, have been all too reticent about expressing publicly our resentment at pressure tactics of this type. There is, to be frank, the same silencing character of economic clout that Madhubuti's group experienced. And there is also the rationalization that we have more important priorities demanding our energies. But we blacks should find the courage to speak out, as Michael Lerner did in a 1994 essay for *Time* magazine condemning "some in the Jewish world who for decades have used the Holocaust and the history of our very real oppression as an excuse to deny our own racism toward blacks or Palestinians."

In the frantic effort to make it in America, Lerner writes in *Time*'s Feb. 28 issue, "We also began to buy the racist assumptions of this society and to forget our own history of oppression."

Had we blacks been more forthright in the past, there might not be the current consternation among Jews about the reluctance of some of us to step forward and publicly condemn the disparaging statements made about them. The frequently posed question "Whatever our differences, should we not stand shoulder to shoulder in opposing racist statements?" must be answered, as New York State Senator David A. Paterson explained, in the light of the tolerance of pervasive racism against blacks. With such figures as Jesse Helms in the Senate and Rush Limbaugh as a national media icon, blacks are very suspicious of white efforts to focus our antiracist efforts on any black political leader—including the appalling statements of Khalid Muhammad.[15]

Paterson acknowledges the historical reluctance of blacks to engage in public criticism, adding, "For generations, whites have called on black leaders to denounce other blacks' actions or statements they find offensive. Many black leaders have actually been denounced as a result of such pleas, leading to crippling battles among black political leaders. Betrayals and self-defeating efforts to exclude rival leaders have undermined hard-fought efforts to gain and hold political power all across the country."[16]

Blacks complain, with some justified bitterness, that spokespeople of other ethnic groups are not asked to stand and condemn anti-Semitic statements made by individuals within those groups. Thus, Senator Edward Kennedy is not required to condemn the clearly anti-Semitic rantings of Pat Buchanan at the 1992 Republican National Convention. It would be ludicrous to insist that John Kenneth Galbraith denounce the anti-Semitism of David Duke simply because both men are of Scotch ancestry. Whether or not it is a conscious action, it demands that blacks condemn hate speech and its propagator even when they have no connection beyond race reflect recognition of blacks as society's "other," a role of societal subordination that Jews have had to play as much as any other people in history. In the status of "other," there is no distinction among members of the group. The unsettling statements of one can be "canceled" by the denunciation of another.

Letty Cottin Pogrebin, a long-time civil rights activist, would disagree. She says that "the need to hear reassuring words from blacks can be read as a measure of the high regard Jews have for the opinion of the African-American community," and that "the demand for a response from black voices bespeaks a greater recognition and respect than the rest of America extends to the authority and power of black leadership."[17]

I am certain that Ms. Pogrebin speaks sincerely for herself and, likely, for many other Jews. The chapter on black-Jewish relations in her book *Deborah, Golda, and Me* is one of the most objective and thorough I have read on this subject.[18] But blacks have been down so long that they recognize demands based on dominance when they hear them.

First, the demands are unilateral. That is, blacks must condemn statements deemed by Jews to be anti-Semitic, but there is no similar willingness of those Jews to condemn any racist statements and actions by Jews. For example, Michael Lerner must not be the only Jew ready to acknowledge the hypocrisy among "Jewish neoconservatives at *Commentary* magazine and Jewish neoliberals at the *New Republic* [who] have led the assault on affirmative action (despite the fact that one of its greatest beneficiaries has been Jewish women); have blamed the persistence of racism on the victims' culture of poverty; and have delighted in the prospect of throwing black women and children off welfare as soon as possible."[19]

Second, the demands are limited to blacks. Where is the pressure that Jewish groups should be placing on right-wing groups and their leaders who are ready to match anti-Semitic words with deeds?

Micah Sifry, a *Nation* editor, noting that the Anti-Defamation League comes down far harder on relatively powerless blacks making anti-Semitic statements than on those whites in high positions, writes: "There is no question the A.D.L. takes its minority anti-Semitism seriously, as well it should. But what about anti-Semitism elsewhere, among the white majority and by the powerful?"[20] Sifry makes the point that as some Jewish groups have turned more conservative, they tend to excuse the anti-Semitism of those on the right while bearing down on blacks. Sifry's long article offers impressive support for his position, but it is not one likely to influence ADL leaders who sat out the David Duke races in 1990 and 1991 for senator and governor, allegedly because of ADL's tax-exempt status, but quietly circulated a nineteen-page memo to reporters detailing Jesse Jackson's past statements regarding Jews, even before the "Hymietown" furor broke."[21] In the 1980s, when the "Hymietown" remark was made, Sifry reports, "A.D.L. officials leapt at the opportunity to nail [him] as an anti-Semite. Apologies were of no use. 'He could light candles every Friday night, and grow sidecurls, and it still wouldn't matter. . . . He's a whore,' Nathan Perlmutter, then the A.D.L.'s director, told *CBS News* reporter Bob Faw."[22]

Andrew Young suggested recently that the Jews' quite understandable determination expressed in the phrase "never again" is not inconsistent with a willingness to forgive. Of course, forgiveness works both ways. My determination to speak out more vigorously about Jewish statements and policies I find upsetting should not prevent me from getting beyond those actions once I have been heard. It also means that I am simply not going to join my Afrocentric colleagues who find of great seriousness the percentage of Jews who engaged in the slave trade or who are responsible for Hollywood stereotypes of black people. There is enough to debate in the present without digging up centuries-old challenges that, even if proved, would not alter our current difference.

For a host of reasons in addition to those discussed here, the tension and enmity that have marked and marred black-Jewish relations since the mid-1960s are likely to continue. I am confident though that my relationship with Jews who make up what is likely a majority of my friends and associates will also continue. They will agree with much in this essay, and, from time to time, we will join in projects that serve our interests. No doubt, other groups of blacks and Jews will do the same. That may be as close to an alliance as any of us can get, and it may be enough to frustrate those in power who must enjoy the battling between the two groups most likely to be sacrificed "in the nation's interest" if the need arises.

In the effort to avoid the fate of all societal scapegoats, many Jews will support the statement by Albert Vorspan and David Saperstein, two leaders of the Reform movement, who write in their book *Tough Choices: Jewish Perspectives on Social Justice:*

> We can find no safety in turning inward upon ourselves, severing our links with the general community. We can find safety only if we help America deal not only with the symptoms—hatred, rage, bigotry—but with the root problems of our society—slums, powerlessness, decay of our cities, and unemployment, which spawn the evils of bigotry and conflict. Our task as Jews must go beyond the defensive job of countering the attacks of anti-Semitism, to helping bring about a just and peaceful society.[23]

Similarly, many blacks will agree with Cornel West's view when he writes:

> My fundamental premise is that the black freedom struggle is the major buffer between the David Dukes of America and the hope for a future in which we can begin to take justice and freedom for all seriously. Black anti-Semitism—along with its concomitant xenophobia, such as patriarchal and homophobic prejudices—weakens this buffer. In the process, it plays into the hands of the old-style racists, who appeal to the worst of our fellow citizens amid the silent depression that plagues the majority of Americans. Without some redistribution of wealth and power, downward mobility and debilitating poverty will continue to drive people into desperate channels.
>
> And without principled opposition to xenophobia from above and below, these desperate channels will produce a cold-hearted and mean-spirited America no longer worth fighting for or living in.[24]

Notes

1. The book, *The Secret Relationship between Blacks and Jews,* was prepared by the Historical Research Department, Nation of Islam. It contains a quite controversial history of Jewish involvement in the transatlantic slave trade and African slavery. This book was subjected to severe criticism by Professor Henry Louis Gates, Jr., in a full-page, op-ed article titled "Black Demagogues and Pseudo-Scholars," published in the *New York Times* on July 20, 1993. A series of responses to that article, several of them quoted in this essay, was published in *16 Black Books Bulletin: WordsWork* (Winter 1993–94), published by the Third Century Group, P.O. Box 19730, Chicago, IL 60619.

2. Tony Martin, *The Jewish Onslaught: Dispatches from the Wellesley Battlefront.*

3. Paul Berman, "The Other and the Almost the Same," *The New Yorker* (February 28, 1994): 61, 63.

4. Ibid.

5. Letty Cottin Pogrebin, "What Divides Blacks and Jews," *New York Newsday* (March 2, 1994): 48.

6. Ibid.

7. Andrew Hacker, *Two Nations: Black and White, Separate, Hostile, Unequal* (New York: Ballantine Press, 1992).

8. Michael Lerner, "The Real Crisis Is Selfishness," *Time* (February 28, 1994): 31.

9. Delores Aldridge, "Henry Louis Gates' 'Black Demagogues and Pseudo-Scholars': A Response," *16 Black Books Bulletin* 3 (Winter 1993–94): 15, 16.

10. Lynne Duke, "A Continuing 'Dialogue of Disagreement,'" *Washington Post* (February 28, 1994): A6.

11. William Henry III, "Pride and Prejudice," *Time* (February 28, 1994): 21, 23.

12. Haki Madhubuti, "Blacks, Jews and Henry Louis Gates, Jr.," *16 Black Books Bulletin* 3 (Winter 1993–94).

13. Ibid., 8.

14. Ibid.

15. David Paterson, "White Outrage, Black Suspicion," *New York Times* (March 20, 1994): E17.

16. Ibid.

17. Pogrebin, "What Divides Blacks and Jews."

18. Letty Cottin Pogrebin, "Ain't We Both Women? Blacks, Jews, and Gender," in *Deborah, Golda, and Me* (New York: Crown Publishing, 1991), 275.

19. Lerner, "The Real Crises."

20. Micah Sifry, "Anti-Semitism in America," *The Nation* (January 25, 1993): 92, 93.

21. Ibid., 96.

22. Ibid.

23. Ibid., 99.

24. Cornel West, *Race Matters* (Boston, MA: Beacon Press, 1993), 81. See also West, "How Do We Fight Xenophobia?" *Time* (February 28, 1994): 30–31.

A Ham, a Violin, and

Ohhhh Those Psychic Blues

Itabari Njeri

ITABARI NJERI *has been a writer and editor at the* Los Angeles Times Sunday Magazine. *She received the American Book Award for her memoir,* Every Good-Bye Ain't Gone. *She is also author of the 1997 book,* The Last Plantation—Color, Conflict, and Identity: Reflections of a New World Black. *She lives in Brooklyn and Los Angeles.*

We are driving toward his chateau-like home on the outskirts of Detroit. The vehicle of choice this day is his late-model red Porsche, which shares a garage with a Range Rover and a BMW convertible. He didn't inherit wealth. He earned it, the hard way, through smart investments in the stock market and as the owner of several fast-food franchises and car dealerships.

"Louis Farrakhan represents the *mainstream* of Black America," Eddie tells me with passion.* He is thirty-something and one of my favorite cousins. Unlike many Black people who feel they must de-

*Eddie is a composite of several relatives. I use Black and White as ethnic designations and therefore treat them as proper nouns.

fend Farrakhan against the assaults of a racist culture, and even more Whites who are obsessed with this fringe character and have inflated— nay created—his threat to the Republic, I rarely give a thought to the man. He does not, as my grandmother used to say, get my bowels in an uproar. But comments like this do generate some peristaltic action. Still, I am fond of Eddie. He is charming and bright, though I have often considered him politically naive. He doesn't read—unless it's books about spiritual growth or how to make a buck or the sports section of the newspaper. Of course, he thinks I am an elitist intellectual and out of touch with "the people."

"Mainstream Black America? I don't think so. Why do you think so?" I ask him.

I look straight ahead and try not to overreact while Eddie, who regards Malcolm X as one of his great heroes, tells me, "If Black people were really honest and said what they really felt—without being concerned with how some White people were going to interpret it—yeah, he represents mainstream Black America. He's beholden to no one and the only Black leader with the courage to tell White folks, to their face, their crimes against humanity. I love him."

I knew Eddie had been to New York recently and hadn't been able to get a cab.

"The man is sexist and anti-Semitic," I reply.

"Are those the only reasons you are against him?"

"Wouldn't that be enough?"

Later, I call a friend of mine, a married woman with children and a prominent writer and editor—very pragmatic and more mainstream in her political orientation, I feel, than I.

Representing the mainstream? "I don't really believe that," she says. "First of all, I've never forgiven Farrakhan because I do think he had something to do with killing Malcolm."

"Amen."

"Fundamentally, I don't trust him. But beyond that, I think most Black Americans are far more conservative in their social thoughts and actions than people think they are. They are some of the most conventional people in America. They are some of the most church-going people in America, we already know that; and Christian church-going, not in the Nation of Islam."

"Well," I put in, "Farrakhan quotes the Bible more than the Qur'an anyway."

"Exactly. And I think that most Black people do not have a desire to be segregated again. Most Black people want the American dream more badly, more desperately than most White people want it—meaning material wealth in more deep-in-the-heart ways than White people." (Last I heard, Eddie planned to trade in his Range Rover for a Hummer.) "So we have bought into this place that we are in. We don't have any desire to pick up and have our own homeland and leave luxury and comfort. Black women don't have any desire to put scarves back on their heads and walk behind their man."

But given the intellectual and moral bankruptcy of Black leadership generally, she believes Farrakhan's great appeal is that "he tells a certain sort of truth. There is a certain clarity to what he is saying about Black folks taking responsibility for themselves morally. He doesn't attempt to put it in some sort of package that everyone can accept. It's not shaded. Now, some of what he says is nonsense. But some of it is clear-headed."

"For instance."

"That kind of self-help stuff that he has been talking about for years—you can't rely on the White man for anything—is quite clear, and a lot of people respond to that."

Yes, they respond to that. But the notion of severing economic ties to a White-dominated society and the implicit stance of alienation from the values and practices of European-American culture that the Afrocentrism of the Nation represents to many are myths. The Nation of Islam has always embraced capitalism and bourgeois, middle-class values with a vengeance. Farrakhan lives, of course, in the same house that Elijah Muhammad inhabited—a grand, yellow-brick, neo-Mediterranean structure in a professional, integrated

Chicago neighborhood. Members of the Nation call it the Palace, a symbol of what every Black man might attain through his entrepreneurial efforts—the kind of labor epitomized in a *Mad TV* comedy skit. You may have seen it. Pity if you didn't.

In the skit, staged like an infomercial, Farrakhan and an imperious bodyguard suddenly appear in the home of a White high school student; the boy is fretting with his mom, over his inability to master calculus.

"Billy, what's wrong?"

"I can't get this math."

That's when Supermath Supremacist Farrakhan rushes into the suburban kitchen.

"Don't worry, Billy. We are here to guide you."

"Wow, Louis Farrakhan."

"All right, Billy, to solve the problem that you have here, what you have to do, what you must do—"

His bodyguard issues an Amen-corner-style "All right."

"Is take the height of the Washington Monument—"

"Preach on."

"Subtract the age of Billy D. Williams, fifty-seven."

"Go ahead."

"Then add the average number of actors in a Spike Lee film."

"Oh, tell it like it is."

"Divide by 1,947—"

"Make us proud."

"Which is the first year they let Black men play in the major leagues—"

"Ah-huh."

"Then take the square root of sixty-four—"

"Yes, sir."

"Which is eight. Which is how long the slave chains were that bound the children of Africa. And your answer will be twenty-seven, which is exactly how many years ago Martin Luther King was assassinated."

"Eh-eh-eh," the bodyguard mutters mournfully.

"I think I get it now," says Billy. "You mean in this example here, I need to take the average length of Snoop Doggy Dog's braids, multiply it by eight, which is how long *The Cosby Show* lasted—"

"Go ahead."

"Divide it by the number of Black hockey players—"

"Make us proud."

"Then add four hundred years of oppression, and the answer is twenty-four. And the twenty-fourth letter of the alphabet just happens to be "X," as in Malcolm X, the man you k—"

"Close enough, Billy," yells Farrakhan. "But you still have much to learn."

"Yes, indeed."

"I'm so proud of you, Billy," says his blond mom.

"Yes, it's that simple," says the actor, doing a dead-on imitation of Farrakhan. He looks into the camera with that high-beam, excruciatingly hammy (my Egyptian, Muslim husband agreed it didn't look halal to him) smile that gave Farrakhan the moniker the Charmer back in his calypso-singing days. "With my new math-made-easy videos, pretty soon anyone, Black or White—we're not here to discriminate—will be able to take an entire calculus exam in less than ten minutes without the use of a calculator."

"I can't wait to take that math test tomorrow," Billy tells him. "Thanks, Louis Farrakhan."

"Right on, Billy, right on. So if you want to get into the *mind*set of math supremacy, call: 1–800–555–0199. That's 1, as in won our freedom; 8, as in I just ate, but I'm still hungry; 555, as in *Five on the Black Hand Side,* a very *fine* Fred Williamson film; and 199, carry the five, which gives you 19.95, exactly what this video costs, shipping and handling not included."

Besides the subtext of ambivalent mutual regard—the love-hate but inevitably intertwined Black-White dynamic in America—the *Mad* skit not only satirizes the Messenger of God's esoteric numerology, it's a parody that suggests how deeply Farrakhan and the

Nation are entrenched ideologically and practically in the American economic system. To that extent, he is very much a part of Black and White mainstream life. Not only are Whites at the helm of this system, but the American entrepreneurial spirit was very much a part of the tightly knit, business-owning, Caribbean immigrant community in the Roxbury section of Boston Farrakhan knew as a youth, the bootstrap nationalism of the Nation of Islam hailing back to Booker T. Washington and a continuing current in African American life.

But the skit also conjures up for me an aspect of the self-reliance theme that has become part of a reactionary mantra, one pushed by an indifferent government whose retreat from social and economic justice is rationalized by asserting that government can't do everything, then blaming the victim by telling the hungry and homeless, the unemployed and marginally employed, the unwed teenage mother—often knocked up by a man twice her age who refuses to pay child support—and her baby, to embrace personal responsibility and pull themselves up by straps attached to thin air.

Perhaps in another skit, *Mad TV* will get to satirize the patriarchal worldview that underlies the Nation of Islam and its leader's view of family values promulgated at the Million Man March. As the Northwestern University political scientist and writer Adolph Reed, Jr. made plain in *The Progressive,* beneath "the unctuous, proforma tones of apology and tender concern for Black women's need for relief" was a "resurgent demand for pride of patriarchal place" as a priority in community life.

Black nationalist organizations have always been incubators of virulent sexism masquerading as deferential, Madonna-like elevation of women—coupled with homophobia. (I remember when I was in the Congress of African people as a teenager, led by the then nationalist Amiri Baraka, the party line was that homosexuality was a European form of degeneracy alien to African people. My first week in Tanzania, however, I went dancing with a large party of friends and was hit on by three lesbians, two of whom got into a

fist fight over another woman.) So when I hear two Black, gay female friends complaining at the top of their lungs that they are sick
and tired of White people—Jews in particular—telling Black people
who can and can't represent them, then defending Farrakhan and
his positive leadership primarily because White folks are *agin* him,
their lack of clear-headedness elevates my blood pressure.

"Now, you think about two dykes living in a homophobic,
patriarchal, theocratic state run by Farrakhan," I tell them. "You
want your plane tickets now? So he verbally jacks up White people,
salvages some of the most marginalized among us, and pushes economic self-reliance. Mussolini, you will recall, made the trains run
on time. Your butts would still be among the first whipped, im-
prisoned, and worse."

In the name of fighting White hegemony, my friends are, as
Reed points out, identifying with Farrakhan in much the same way
many African Americans have identified with O.J. Simpson. "Both
replace direct civic action with the passive, vicarious investment of
group aspirations in the fate of some individual who is held to be
under racist attack. Both beckon us to disattend to the public deci-
sions being made around us and instead embrace oceanic good feelings and empty symbolism."

Farrakhan's "a leader in the sense that he can gather people to
him, but they don't go anyplace when they leave him," Julian Bond
says. "You know, that Negro didn't even vote until 1984."

But we know he gets White folks riled up, as apparently was
the case with a Jewish acquaintance of long standing. "Well," she
says when I tell her I am writing this essay, "I certainly would like
to know what *you* think of Louis Farrakhan." Though she tells me
this over the phone, she says it with the unmistakable tone of one
whose eyebrow is raised with doubts about my place on the moral
continuum. Given my documented embrace of the Miscegenated
American Experience, in books and articles with which she is familiar, her challenging tone surprises me.

"What I think about him? I don't give him much thought at all, unless it's for a paying writer's gig like this."

I have distilled the essence of his message and found it wanting. I have lived through one twentieth-century incarnation of Black Nationalism in the early seventies while in the Congress of African People, a group whose social organization—women bowing to men as they backed out of a room, puritanical sexuality, at least in theory, no reading of the *New York Times* because of its corrupting influence—was profoundly influenced by the Nation. I don't need to repeat the errors of the past, among them: the ethnic chauvinism that makes a static prison of the self by constricting the meaning of Black identity.

Do not misunderstand. I often make the point that my romance with jazz and Bermuda nights and the unmistakable high, round curves of a dark man's moonlit posterior undulating to the Godfather's declaration, *I'm superbad,* intoxicates me with all its endlessly inventive pleasures. These things cannot but make me healthily ethnocentric. Such emotional attachments, however, are no ground for asserting cosmic moral, aesthetic, and intellectual superiority. I am no Afrocentric.

I wore my African garb and sandals in the snow—proclaiming, "Hell, no, I'm not cold. I'm an African"—during much of the seventies. And I taught people how to celebrate Kwanza before anybody trying to out-Afrocentric me today ever heard of it. I also learned much that was valuable from my experience with brilliant people, such as Baraka, when I was in CAP. But ultimately, I took what was most significant and ran with it: the nationalist imperative to define one's self instead of being defined by others—whether the definitions are imposed by a White supremacist culture, or those derived from the compensatory, esteem-boosting ideology of Black nationalism that is a response to white supremacy.

White America, for instance, expects me to define myself by a slave master's rule: one drop of blood makes you Black, what I call the Little Dab'll Do You School of Genetics. It was designed, of course, by a plantocracy to ensure that no child fathered by a White man—usually the master—and born to an enslaved Black woman inherited the free status of the father. This economically motivated definition of identity was meant to perpetuate the South's population of human chattel and rationalize, on the basis of the alleged inferiority of "Black blood," a continuing caste system after nominal emancipation.

Forced to make a virtue out of a necessity, African-Americans, one of the most heterogeneous ethnic groups in the world, have embraced this initially imposed definition. We wisely asserted that we would not let our diversity render us politically dysfunctional, as has been the case in Brazil, for instance, with its color-stratified population of African descent. But there are so many tests for "authentic Blackness" in the African-American community that it often promotes serious internal group conflict. You're too light. You listen to the wrong kind of music. You don't speak Black enough. As one brother from South Central L.A. told me, "I read your work about being Black in terms of ethnicity, culture, but understanding the stuff that goes into that comes from a lot of different places. And I have to admit—because I consider myself to be, and the people around me are, Afrocentric—that I have denied my complete heritage: some White blood, some Indian, and just say I am pure African." At least he didn't say that he claimed to be descended from royalty. You notice how nobody who claims to be "African" in America is ever descended from the village thief or even the village blacksmith.

I define myself as a typical New World Black. An ordinary, everyday, walking-around-Brooklyn Negro. African, East Indian, English, Arawak, and more I don't know about. I am the child of a first-generation Jamaican-Guyanese American mother who was a nurse, and the daughter of a doctor; he was killed one night in Georgia by drag-racing crackers who never even got a speeding ticket. I am the child, too, of a brilliant, African American drunkard and Marxist scholar who was fathered by a White preacher who raped his mama. Still, I embrace the Miscegenated American Experience—as one does the rose with its thorns. I come from a people whose music and dance define what is most distinctive in America's culture. And through our struggle for justice, we have extended the meaning of democracy for others in this place and inspired world admiration and emulation.

Though Americans usually act like a dysfunctional family denying kinship to each other, we are tied by culture, history, and blood. There is little here that does not bear the imprint of the Black presence, whether subtle and sweet, or bludgeoned into the ground and tainted with blood and tears. I embrace this history of survival and creativity. I am no stranger in a strange land—the essence of the nationalist cant the Nation of Islam has promoted for decades. I and people like me define this place.

Further, while no Hitler, Farrakhan is the leader of an organization whose fascistic bent views miscegenated blood as a cesspool and singles out Jews—among all Whites—as the disproportionate source of Black exploitation, as opposed to the disproportionate source of support of social justice for Blacks, as they have been.

And speaking of fascist tendencies, the Nation of Islam is notorious for, at the very least, threatening to suppress opposition through force. I must admit, however, that the flip side of their muscle, represented by the Fruit of Islam, is that they are the closest thing we've got to the Mafia—without the same degree of corruption—and in the real world, sometimes heads have to be cracked. Hey, it's the Brooklyn in me. I wish I'd had a little FOI muscle behind me in the days I was singing on the road, in clubs, and didn't get paid, among other indignities. But such thoughts usually come during house party chatter after a few drinks.

Knowing that this Jewish woman was aware of my views, I retracted my head and neck in one of those funky chicken moves, but froze it in the back position—while, I assume, her eyebrow was raised—astounded that she was looking for some sort of Farrakhan litmus test from me. But her attitude simply underscored another of Reed's points. Farrakhan "has become uniquely notorious because his inflammatory nationalist persona has helped to center public discussion of Afro-American politics on the only issue (except affirmative action, of course) about which most Whites ever show much concern: What do blacks think of whites?"

As dismissive as I may seem of Farrakhan, I am profoundly aware that he articulates and seems, for many, to have a prescription for the moral decay and drug- and gang-related carnage that has laid waste to so many African American communities.

My friend the Black woman writer and editor asserts, "No other Black leader is saying: Yes, there are ways we are being screwed over by the government. But let's not protect, in our community, drug dealers and murderers and gangbangers because 'Oh, well, they just had a rough life.' That's not acceptable. I can't believe that we basically accept the fact that we have little old ladies in every Black community in America who live behind drawn blinds, who are afraid to leave their own house because they might be attacked by one of their grandson's best friends."

I know that Farrakhan's message resonates, especially, among the most marginalized Black folks—convicts, prostitutes, drug addicts—many of whom can put the prefix "ex" before those labels because of the salvation they found through the Nation's program of self-reliance and self-respect synthesized with racial chauvinism. And, more broadly, no matter how assimilated a Black person may be in this land, there usually exists within her some deep, unassuageable pain associated with the American crucible of race. This is a psychic blues that Farrakhan, virtuoso violinist and demagogue, knows the words and music to and plays on exquisitely with the compensatory rhetoric of nationalism: The White man is evil, we are kings and queens, our history was stolen, we are the inventors of everything, etc., etc. And when, after a particularly bad day of jousting on the nation's racial battlefield, and White folks have worked my last nerve, I catch Farrakhan raising hell with them, I chuckle and nod my assent—as most Black folks do. Because in many ways, we are a people without land but a nation within a nation, psychologically tired of having been, through most of our history, symbols of powerless morality thwarted by immoral power.

It is, therefore, easy—though dangerous—to be cynical, to embrace a reactionary militant like Farrakhan because he seems to be speaking for "us" in a nation that demands law and order but refuses to control guns and then murders presidents, rock stars, and nonviolent Christian martyrs in public with numbing regularity. But he is an entire package. You can't take him, or be taken in by him, because he plays on those psychic blues so well.

"I don't understand why you don't trust him," my cousin Eddie says. "People keep calling him an anti-Semite, but he has said he is willing to come to the table and talk with Jews. Why aren't they willing to sit with him? And what is he doing that's hurting Black people? What's in it for him?"

"Power," I explode. "He wants to be a major power broker in the Black community. And since so much of what he says squares so nicely with conservative ideology, the only thing increasingly keeping him from gaining mainstream White support is his anti-Semitism."

The White media and conservatives of all stripes were fawning over Farrakhan for rallying these thousands of Black men at the Million Man March and asking them to publicly beat their breasts for sins against their family, community, and nation. Of course, if the men we saw were the immoral, irresponsible—sometimes brutal—beasts of the American imagination, the well-mannered, generally well-educated and working brothers out there would not have been so effective at busting—as they did—the negative stereotypes generated by the media.

But as the late *Newsday* columnist Murray Kempton put it, in a column printed a few days after the October, 1995 march, Farrakhan adroitly seized the hour to frame a self-serving *Message to the White Man:* See, I am the one to tame these ignoble savages. "It did not matter that there was nothing uncivilized and much that was noble about the assemblage he had called up, so long as so many White Americans see men of color as owing them no end of apologies and entitled to none themselves. The powerful could not ask for a more convenient servant than a prophet who abjures his faithful to get off the streets and into the pews."

Of course, the day after the march, Kempton reminds us, Congress went back to "hacking at the working poor in Farrakhan's audience by cutting Medicaid, raiding their taxes and ridding the social budget of $20 a week for feeding and clothing each baby born to an unwed sister."

A Black scholar I've talked to laments that the "rhetoric of the Black leadership in this country is on the whole fifty years behind the times. It is anachronistic in terms of its binary, Black–White construction of race relations, and lacks any serious comprehension of the place of African Americans in a social landscape transformed by vast demographic changes." I consider that an understatement.

Farrakhan is the worst thing that could happen to Black people at the dawn of the twenty-first century. He is taking us back at least a quarter century to a narrow nationalism some of us experienced then and outgrew. While many did not have that experience, it is tragic that, in regard to this and much else in Black life, we have too few institutions that can document the limitations, as well as what was valuable, about the nationalist experience and disseminate that information broadly. We are chronically plagued by a lack of historical memory. We should be building on lessons learned from the past and moving beyond it. Instead, too much of Black America is enamoured with one of the most vulgar variants of nationalism we have ever seen: Afrocentrism, which views everything through the prism of race and eschews all class analysis. When I was in CAP, we read Lenin, we read Mao, we read Nyerere. We at least paid lip service to socialism. The current Afrocentric mood finds its roots in—in part—and is fueled by, the racial chauvinism and capitalist ethos of the Nation of Islam.

"How can you say that Farrakhan is the worst thing to happen to Black people? I don't believe that," my cousin says disgustedly as we, at last, enter his four-car garage. The passion in his voice is directly correlated to his need to see himself, and be seen, as authentically Black.

"Well, let me tell you something," I say as I climb from his shiny car. "I don't want to live in a community where he has anything to do with shaping our political future. National Black leadership is bankrupt, but there are leaders at other levels who don't get the national spotlight because the media do not seek them out. They want to keep the camera on whomever they perceive to be an inflammatory Negro.

"And anyway, I'm never going to forget about Malcolm, though you seem willing to. The twenty-fourth letter of the alphabet should be branded on Farrakhan's head."

Of Malcolm, Farrakhan,
and the Politics of Rage

Leonard Pitts, Jr.

LEONARD PITTS, JR., *is an award-winning syndicated columnist for* The Miami Herald. *He is based in Washington, D.C.*

It is the necessary thing that was never said, the needed rebuff that went unuttered, choked back behind pieties, platitudes, and thankful prayers. Nobody said it. Not Frederick Douglass or W.E.B. DuBois, not Booker T. Washington or even Marcus Garvey, not through the years of redemption, Reconstruction, or Renaissance. Never said this harsh, but needed thing:

Fuck you.

Not for shock value or gratuitous offense, but because this was something that required saying, a thing personhood demanded. After chains. After the whip that cut crevices of blood into the tissue of a weary back. After rape. After waking up before the sun for 246 years and working past the dark to enrich someone else. After having to ask some man for permission to have a wife, grow a garden, or hold your own child. After being told salvation meant you would become white in the afterlife.

Fuck you. Because rage needed a vent.

If you are to understand Louis Farrakhan or even to effectively criticize him, if you are to appreciate the hold he has on the imagination of African America, you must first come to grips with that truth. Get past the beatific smile and the baiting of Jews and middle-class blacks, go beyond the invocation of Allah and the preaching of self-help, and realize that fuck you is the thing that has made this man. Whether you think him demon or angel, the unalterable fact is that both perceptions issue from that place, from his native understanding that sometimes you need fuck you to remind yourself that you are a man.

Have you ever read the Slave Narratives, the interviews with former slaves that were conducted for the Roosevelt administration in the 1930s? They are remarkable for their lack of rancor, their matter-of-fact recounting of the horrors and humiliations that beggar imagination. Indeed, the ex-slaves, products of a system that ingrained their inferiority, viewing the past from a perch of Depression, dependency, and infirmity, not infrequently waxed nostalgic for what some called the "good old days" of enslavement.

And if that sounds too startling to be true, remember that rage was pushed to subterranean levels in the search to make ourselves acceptable to white men. Their approval had always been our barometer of self worth. But pushing rage down ignored the urgency of that thing that needed to be said.

Fuck you.

Free at last, and fuck you.

We shall overcome, yet fuck you.

I have a dream, but first, fuck you.

Which is not to deny or belittle the sweet promise of freedom, overcoming, and dreams. But rejection had to come first. An airing of grievances and through that, a staking out of new personhood. Yet that moment never came (though Garvey was close), and instead the rage was swallowed down like a cod liver oil tonic that made smiles queasy and uncertain.

Then came Malcolm X and he said fuck you, and rage found its vent. He said it with anger, said it with intellect, said it with the cold-bloodedness of an assassin, said it without reverence, *boomed* it like a loose cannon, rolling this way and that on the deck of American democracy, immolating icons and shattering shrines and sending everyone ducking for cover. Never said it in words, of course, but ever and always in actions that rejected, emphatically, white mores and milieus, white approval and acceptance, even white understanding.

If white folks were shocked, blacks were scarcely less so. This was a jolt that cleared the eye and stiffened the spine. Some of us feared him. Some rushed to condemn this dangerous man who spouted reproach like a broken sewer pipe. Some of us wanted white people to know in no uncertain terms that we didn't condone this. Oh no, not at all.

Malcolm scared every Negro who spent his days aspiring toward a sepia rendition of the white middle-class ideal. He was not a hero in my house, his image obvious by its absence from that mantelpiece shrine where Martin Luther King and John F. Kennedy kept watch over us as we dined.

My folks and those around them were covetous of white people's acknowledgment and respect—I'll never forget the look in Mama's eye, the stony fix of her jaw, when she was marching forward to set straight some white man who had dared treat her as less than she was. So Malcolm and his Nation were a threat to her and to Negroes like her who placed significance upon what whites thought of them. Those Negroes in turn ridiculed the Nation for its bow ties, its bean pies, and its strictures against pork and cigarettes. Each side, I guess, gave as good as it got, but it would take twenty years or more before each could hear the truth of the other.

Malcolm *expected* mistreatment from whites, took it as a given and in so doing, mitigated it. For many blacks, this was a revolutionary revelation, the notion that we could simply *be*, without white people.

But people like my folks knew the long-term truth that belied the short-term celebration. In America, one can never quite *be* without white people. Not for long, anyway. Sooner or later, they must always enter the equation. Thus, what they think, understand, and believe about blacks must matter, if only as an issue of self-interest.

So black people who disdained Malcolm were right. But also wrong. Because yes, Malcolm's invective was ugly, unpleasant, unrealistic, and maybe even unfair. But we didn't understand how *needed* it was. Didn't hear rage hissing through the vent like steam, grateful for release. Didn't realize that Malcolm X and our own beloved Martin King were less opposite members than flip sides of the same coin—rage and redemption—and neither could be quite whole without the other. Which is why, though King's legacy is more concrete and easier to discern—voting rights, civil rights, integration—Malcolm's is no less crucial or real.

He said fearlessly what needed to be said and in so doing, returned our lost sense of self, challenged us to be who we were, free standing and unapologetic. He renewed our pride.

And now, thirty years later, some would say the same is true of Farrakhan. Indeed, in many ways he seems to serve the same function Malcolm X once did. But that's puzzling. Not just because we've seen this before but rather, because we still seem to *need* it so badly.

Rage, then redemption. Wasn't that the formula? How did rage vent and then rebuild?

The answer is depressingly simple. The Civil Rights years were followed by an angry lurch toward conservatism, an era of racial codifying and scapegoating that told us with overt brazenness and covert insistence that black people were what ails America.

It wasn't true, but America was no longer much interested in truth. It wanted expedience. It wanted the unpleasantness over. So the battle for freedom was declared won, the battlefield cleared, and black people, as they had been in the wake of Reconstruction a century before, were left to contend with abandonment. Can anyone be surprised at what happened next? Families imploded, bonds corroded, cities turned foul with decay, and we seemed, for an awful, apathetic moment called the 1980s, to throw up our hands and accept it all. Remember the big items on our agenda in that decade? We crusaded for a Martin Luther King holiday and the right to be called African-American.

But MLK Day sometimes seems little more than an excuse for a car dealer to throw a sale. And have you ever heard a bigot say African-American? It sounds remarkably like nigger.

And yet as we fought for those things, our children were beginning to die. The soil was fertile for Louis Farrakhan, rising out of relative obscurity in the 1980s like a specter from white America's nightmares. And he, with a generation of young rap stars as his Greek chorus, brought us a renewal of the rage that had once felt so good. The surprise was that it still did.

It should have felt redundant. We had already said, "Go to hell, whitey," already worn our Afros and dashikis, and raised our clenched-fist salutes, already wallowed gleefully in the wickedness of bad-ass attitude. Did we really need to do it again?

Apparently so. We left the apathy of a dead decade behind and traveled full circle to a place we had already been. Welcome back to rage.

Nothing wrong with rage, mind you. It beats apathy any day. More, it is a natural human response to unbearable circumstances. But rage is not an end unto itself. Thus, it becomes incumbent upon black people to acknowledge anger once and for all, confess its validity and righteousness.

And then get over it. Or at least, *beyond* it.

Because if anger without release is a time bomb, anger without resolution is an endless orbit that goes nowhere and accomplishes nothing. At some point, a person must ask: Anger in the service of what? Anger toward what end? Louis Farrakhan has yet to formulate a compelling answer.

In any event, we were supposed to have been past this by now, striding swiftly toward higher ground. When the people sang "We shall overcome, someday," *this* was the day they had in mind. A day when, if we had not actually achieved equality, we would at least be well on the way. Instead, we got sandbagged by the same cycle that smashed us back to earth after the Civil War: optimism, conservatism, obstructionism, defeat. The death of dreams.

And so, we return to rage with Minister Farrakhan as our guide.

"What do you think of him?" asked a young colleague not long ago.

She seemed taken aback when the answer was, "Not much." I applaud his philosophy of black economic self-empowerment, I said. And his Million Man March was a transcendent experience. But on the whole, on balance? Not much.

"Well, *I* think he's a great man," she said. Pause. And then, the inevitable caveat. "Of course, I don't agree with everything he says."

Which is the preferred euphemism for: "Of course, he gets really crazy sometimes about the Jews."

We toss it aside as though it were a little thing, these acts of mass slander, these episodes of lump sum libel of which he is so fond. But it is not a little thing. It is wrong.

And wrong not just because it defames and insults Jews, but— and I daresay this is even more important—because it defames and insults *us*.

We require scapegoats?! *We* need a common enemy?!

Is that all that tethers us one to the other, sister to brother, tomorrow's bright child to yesterday's scarred and weeping slave? Yes, tethers are crucial to a people whose history is dislocation and rupture. But, God, aren't the chains enough? Doesn't the blood suffice? Can't we make do with a common history of lynch mobs and fear, jazz and jump blues, Langston's poems and Muhammad's fists, the sweet mysticism of soul and the intricate rhythms of our language? Do we have to hate the Jews, too? Is this our tie that binds?

And if the answer is yes, Lord have mercy, what does that say about who we are?

Of course, this has been the defining question of our existence since before slave shackles were struck away. Who are we? African or American? The answer was never easy.

African, yes, but place a black American man in a village in Gabon and you will quickly discover him to be as bewildered and disoriented as any Volvo-driving, checkered pants–wearing, golf-playing white man would be.

American, sure, but place that black man on Rodeo Drive in Beverly Hills and you will quickly discover him to be an object of white suspicion, consternation, and confusion, an automatic and eternal outsider.

African or American? The obvious answer is both and neither. We are a new creature, looking for a place to fully belong.

May I suggest the United States of America.

Because though Farrakhan and his Nation of Islam talk separatism talk, none of us will ever walk the walk. The notion of blacks emigrating from this place, a notion embraced by Abraham Lincoln, Marcus Garvey, the Ku Klux Klan, *and* the Nation of Islam, by the way, is logistically impossible.

Likewise, the federal government will never, even on the occasion of an ice storm in hell, surrender any of its land for our exclusive use. Just ask the white separatists in the Pacific Northwest who've been demanding the same thing for years.

But it's not just logistics that render the notion absurd. It's the whole weight of our history, our every guiding notion of decency and justice. The bottom line is this: We belong here. This is our country, by right of suffering and toil. We aren't going anywhere. We stand now and tomorrow in the land of our birth. And we need to stand with something more than anger.

Once upon a time, yes, we needed to say, fuck you. Once upon a time, we needed—for decency's sake—to reject the white man and put him in his place. Perhaps on occasion we still do.

But for that to be the engine of a leader's agenda, for it to be the tether that unites us, is troubling and sad. We have returned to this pass, circled back to this place, but it's time to move on—for good. We don't need this any longer.

We need to rebuild our families and renew our communities.

We need to educate our minds and raise our spirits.

We need to defend selfhood and dignity.

We need to fight white folks who try to drag us down.

We need to fight black folks who try to drag us down.

And we need to save our children.

Because they are watching us. Needing direction. Sensing our confusion. Drawing from our rage.

What are we to say to them? How are we to resolve the conflict for them when we can't even do it for ourselves? How do we make them understand this contradictory impulse we have to be in America, but not of it? Within, but also without?

And most important, why give a child this rage? Love, yes. Awareness, yes. Nourishment for the hard road ahead, definitely.

But rage? *Why?*

Save the children. From white people. And, God help us, from us. We owe them so much more than the bitterness of wrath. We owe them hope. We owe them a way. We owe them the thing that lies beyond rage, the thing Malcolm found when he went to Mecca.

He said the kinship he saw there shocked his race-weary soul, dissipated the rage, leaving him only the clean, bright hardness of his truth. Malcolm grew from rage. Into what, we will never know because the rage, spurned, reached out and killed him.

Louis Farrakhan, it must be said, is no Malcolm X. He shows no sign of growing from rage, few signs of growing at all, which is why his claim as a great man falls short. But that's his problem.

Our challenge is to move on like Malcolm. Perhaps to become that thing he never got a chance to be, resolve the dichotomy he was struggling to fix: African *and* American.

It is a deceptively simple task. It asks us simply to release and unclench. To open and let possibility in.

Deceptively simple. Which means, hard as hell. But we owe it to ourselves. Moreover, we owe it to our children. It is time to take them by the hand like elders do and lead them to a place we've never truly been, to the horizons beyond rage.

Farrakhan, 1985 to 1996:

The Consistency of Calypso Louis

Stanley Crouch

STANLEY CROUCH *is a cultural and jazz critic in New York. He is author of* The All-American Skin Game, or the Decoy of Race, *and* Notes of a Hanging Judge, *from which the first half of this essay is adapted; the addendum was written in 1996 following a post–Million Man March speech Minister Farrakhan gave in New York.*

Nationalism of Fools
October 29, 1985

There again were the black suits and red ties, the bodyguards in blue uniforms, the women in white, the aloof cast of the eyes and the earthy manner: the Nation of Islam. Twenty-five years ago it was Malcolm X's show, though he could never have filled Madison Square Garden. On October 7, twenty-five thousand people turned out to hear Louis Farrakhan.

They queued up outside—the poor and the young, the unemployed and the gang members, the middle-class Negroes. They were anxious to get in and hear someone attack the people they felt were responsible for their positions in the burgeoning illiterate mass; or they were there out of curiosity, intent on hearing for themselves what Farrakhan was about. Many came because they were happy to support a black man the "white-controlled" media unanimously hated. Or because Mayor Koch had called Farrakhan "the devil," usurping the Muslims' term for the white enemy—if Koch hated him, he might be lovable, an understandable reaction given the long-standing antipathy between the mayor and New York's black community. I also think many were there, especially the young, because they had never been to a mass black rally to hear a speaker who didn't appear to care what white people thought of him, a man who seemed to think their ears were more important than those of Caucasians.

The atmosphere at Madison Square Garden was unusual. Though the speeches started two and a half hours late, the audience was patient, partly out of respect and partly out of awareness that the Fruit of Islam doesn't play. A fool and his seat would soon have parted. I overheard one young black man saying that he could look at the Muslims with their neatness and their discipline, their sense of confidence and their disdain for white privilege, and understand their appeal: "They look like the last thing they ever think about is kissing some white boody." After repeatedly telling a blond female photographer that she couldn't sit in the aisle, one of the FOI said, to the joy of the black people listening, "Miss, I asked you three times to *please* not sit in the aisle. Now you will either get your behind over or you will get your behind *out.*" And there was something else. As one woman put it, "Well, what can you say? Nobody looks better than a black man in a uniform. Look at all those handsome black men. I know I wouldn't want to be in the Nation, but I wouldn't mind it if they lived on *my* block. I bet there wouldn't be any mugging and dope dealing and all of *that.*" From the outside, at least Farrakhan's group projects a vision of restraint and morality. It's about smoothing things out, upholding the family, respecting the woman, doing an honest day's work, avoiding dissipation, and defining the difference between the path of the righteous and the way of the wicked. At one point the commander of the FOI came to the microphone and said that he could smell reefer smoke. He asked that anyone who saw those guilty parties report them to "the nearest brother." Wherever the puffing was going on, it stopped.

Beginning in 1959, when the press started bird-dogging Malcolm X, the Muslims' disdain for white people seared through the networks, eventually influencing the tone, the philosophy, and the tactics of black politics. The Nation of Islam offered a rageful revision that would soon have far more assenters than converts. Though it seemed at first only a fanatical cult committed to a bizarre version of Islam, Elijah Muhammad's homemade Nation was far from an aberration. The Nation fit perfectly in a century we might appropriately call "The Age of Redefinition." Its public emergence coincided with the assault on Western convention, middle-class values, and second-class citizenship that shaped the sixties in America. The whole question of what constituted civilized behavior and civilized tradition was being answered in a variety of wild ways. So Elijah Muhammad's sect was part of the motion that presaged transcendental meditation, sexual revolution, LSD, cultural nationalism, black power, the Black Panther Party, the anti–Vietnam War movement, feminism, and other trends that surely appalled the Muslims as thoroughly as the Nation did its roughest critics. As much as anything else, those angry home-grown Muslims foretold the spirit of what was later known as "the counterculture."

But Elijah Muhammad's counterculture was black. Where others explained the world's problems with complex theories ranging from economic exploitation to sexism, Muhammad simply pinned the tail on the white man. In his view, black integrationists were only asking for membership in hell, since the white man was a devil "grafted" from black people in an evil genetic experiment by a mad, pumpkin-headed scientist named Yakub. That experiment took place six thousand years ago. Now the white man was doomed, sentenced to destruction by Allah. If "so-called American Negroes" separated themselves from the imposed values of white culture, then moved into their own land, black suffering would cease. In calling for five or six states as "back payment for slavery," Muhammad reiterated a Negro Zionism rooted in the "back to Africa" schemes of the middle nineteenth century, which had last fizzled under the leadership of Marcus Garvey.

In the context of prevailing media images and public racial struggle, this was all new. Here were Negroes who considered *themselves* the chosen people. They proclaimed that the black man was the original man, the angel, and that since the first devils to roll off Yakub's assembly line were the Jews, the idea of *their* being the chosen was a lot of baloney. By embracing Muhammad's version of Islam, his followers stepped outside of Judeo-Christian civilization, asserting their African roots at exactly the same time Africans were coming out from under colonialism and remarkable shifts in world power were in the offing. They declared the white man a thief and a murderer: he had ripped off the secrets of science from Africa. (Muhammad's ministers taught that Egypt was an acronym for "he gypped you.") Using the Africans' information, the blue-eyed devil went on to steal land all over the world, including America from the Indian. The Muslims "exposed" Christianity as no more than a tool to enslave black people, a way of getting them to deny their origins and worship a "white Jesus" (when the Savior was described in Revelations as having skin the color of burnished brass and hair akin to pure lamb's wool). They spoke of dark skin and thick lips as beautiful, charging that the mulatto look of light skin, thin lips, and "good" hair was the mark of shame, of rape on the plantation. In attacking the Caucasian standard of beauty, the Muslims foreshadowed the "black is beautiful" buttons and revisionist images of race and gender we would soon hear from all quarters.

Though most of what they said was no further out than the mythological tales of biblical heroes, their explanations lacked poetic grandeur. But their exotic integrity made that irrelevant. Just as there is a beauty in a well-made club or knife or rifle, there is a beauty in those who yield to nothing but their own ideals and the discipline necessary to achieve them. The Muslims had that kind of attraction, particularly for those who had known the chaos of drug addiction, prostitution, loneliness, abject poverty. Suddenly here were all these clean-cut, well-dressed young men and women—men, mostly. You recognized them from the neighborhood. They had been pests or vandals, thieves or gangsters. Now they were back from jail or prison and their hair was cut close, their skin was smooth, they no longer cursed blue streaks, and the intensity in their eyes remade their faces. They were "in the Nation" and that meant that new men were in front of you, men who greeted each other in Arabic, who were aloof, confident, and intent on living differently than they had. Now the mention of a cool slice of ham on bread with mayonnaise and lettuce disgusted them. Consuming the pig was forbidden and food was eaten once a day because a single throe of digestion "preserved the intestines." Members didn't smoke, drink, use drugs, dance, go to movies or sports events.

The Muslims' vision of black unity, economic independence, and "a true knowledge of self" influenced the spirit of black organization as the Civil Rights Movement waned. Few took notice that it was much easier to call white people names and sneer at voter registration drives from podiums in the North than to face the cattle prods, the bombings, and the murders in the South. Since the destruction of America was preordained, the Muslims scorned efforts to change the system. Theirs was the world of what the French call "the total no."

Though they were well mannered and reliable, the Muslims were too provincial and conservative to attract the kind of mass following that would pose a real political threat. Yet as chief black heckler of the Civil Rights Movement, Malcolm X began to penetrate the consciousness of young black people, mostly in the North. While his platform was impossible, a cockeyed racial vision of history that precluded any insights into human nature, young Negroes loved to watch him upset white people, shocking them no end with his attacks on their religion, their history, their morality, their political system, and their sense of superiority. He described nonviolence as nonsense. And he said it all with an aggressive, contemptuous tone that had never been heard from a black man on the air. What we witnessed was the birth of black saber rattling.

Malcolm quickly became what is now called a cult hero. But for all the heated, revisionist allusions to history and exploitation, Malcolm X's vision was far more conventional than King's. Where the Southern Christian Leadership Council and the Student Non-Violent Coordinating Committee were making use of the most modern forms of boycott, media pressure, and psychological combat, revealing the werewolf of segregation under a full moon, Malcolm X brought the philosophy of the cowboy movie into Negro politics: characters who turned the other cheek were either naïve or cowardly. The Civil War had cost 622,500 lives; the Civil Rights Movement had brought about enormous change against violent opposition without losing 100 troops. But you could never have told that listening to Malcolm X, who made each casualty sound like 100,000. He talked like one of those gunfighters determined to organize the farmers against the violent, vicious cattlemen. One of his last speeches was even called "The Bullet or the Ballot." Hollywood had been there first.

In the wake of Malcolm X's assassination and canonization came the costume balls of cultural nationalism and the loudest saber rattlers of them all, the Black Panther Party. Both persuasions rose from the ashes of the urban riots, each dominated by egomaniacs who brooked no criticism, defining all skeptics as Uncle Toms. They gathered thunder as the Civil Rights Movement floundered. The remarkable Bob Moses of SNCC abdicated following the murders of Schwerner, Goodman, and Chaney. The organization became a shambles as white support was driven out. Stokely Carmichael and Rap Brown devoted their efforts to inflammatory rabble rousing, encouraging the anarchy of urban "revolts." King was felled in Memphis. America then endured the spectacles of Ron Karenga and LeRoi Jones, Eldridge Cleaver and Huey Newton. Hollywood didn't miss the point: it turned pulp politics into pulp films. Black exploitation movies saved a few studios as Negro heroes moved from scene to scene beating up white villains, usually gangsters, in chocolate-coated James Bond thrillers. It all wore thin as would-be radical black youth discovered that romanticizing Africa and wearing robes or calling for the violent overthrow of the American government led to little more than pretentious exotica and the dis covery that the police weren't paper tigers.

When Elijah Muhammad died in 1975, Louis Farrakhan was a member of the Nation's upper echelon. He had seen the organization survive Malcolm X's defection in 1964. So it must have been rough on him when Muhammad's son Wallace repudiated his father's teachings, opting for regulation Islam. Suddenly, Farrakhan was back in the world without a filter. Elijah Muhammad's vision had created an extended family of believers destined to come out in front when Allah gave the word and evil was struck down. Now Wallace was spurning seclusion from society and the guarantees that come with apocalyptic prophecy. And there was another problem. Elijah Muhammad had explicitly aimed his teachings at the downtrodden black man in America, not Muslims in their own countries. When charged with distorting Islam, he had explained that this was a special medicine for a special case, a people who had "no knowledge of self." Submitting to conventional Islam meant giving Middle Eastern Muslims the inside lane. But Louis Farrakhan wasn't about to become just another one of millions of Muslims. The Charmer, as he was known when he was a singer, wanted to lead. And he did: He broke with Wallace to carry on Elijah Muhammad's teachings.

Now, after thirty years of watching others chased by reporters and interviewed on national television, Farrakhan has his moment. Malcolm X is dead, King is dead, the Panthers have been declawed, Eldridge Cleaver is born again, Ron Karenga and LeRoi Jones are college professors, and the factions devoted to urban guerrilla warfare have been either snuffed out or chased into hiding. Now it is all his, the mantle of extreme militance, and the media hang on his words, no matter what they make of him. He is a national, if not an international, figure, a man who can draw turn-away crowds, get $5 million from Gadhafi, and surround himself with a surprising array of supporters.

The appearance of Louis Farrakhan at this time seems a comment on the failures of black, liberal, and conservative politics since the Nixon era, when cultural nationalists started putting on suits and Marxist revolutionaries sought the great leap forward of tenured professorships. Though black mayors were elected in more and more cities, and many millions were spent to eradicate obstacles to Negro American success, the thrust of these attempts at social change was no more accurate than Chester Himes's blind man with the pistol. The epidemic proportions of illiteracy, teenage pregnancy, and crime in Negro communities across the nation tell us what went wrong. The schools became worse and worse, the salaries for teachers less and less; there were no serious efforts (including welfare cutbacks) to discourage teenage parenthood; and the courts were absurdly lenient with criminals. The result is a black lower class perhaps more despairing and cynical than we have ever seen.

But conservative programs have been equally deadly. While the administration chips away at the voting rights of black Southerners and panders to religious fundamentalists, it ignores human nature by deregulating the business sphere with such vengeance that the profits of stockholders take precedence over the environment. In this atmosphere, Farrakhan's broad attacks are political rock and roll—loved more for the irritation they create than for their substance.

★ ★ ★

The guests who filled the podium gave the impression that Farrakhan had a broader base than assumed. They included Christian ministers, American Indians, Palestinians, Stokely Carmichael, and Chaka Khan. Of Khan's presence, one young man said, "She shouldn't have done that. Her record sales are going to go down. Those Jews ain't going to like that. She might be through." I wasn't so sure of that, but if black people were in equivalent positions in the record business, I doubt they would think lightly of a white star sitting on a podium with the Ku Klux Klan.

When things finally kicked off, a Christian choir opened with a song, and Stokely Carmichael spoke first. He bobbed and flailed, often pushing his head past the microphone. The sound went up and down; some sentences came through clearly, others were half heard. He attacked Zionism, calling for war against Israel and recognition of the "sacredness" of Africa, where Moses and Jesus were protected when in trouble. The intensity was so immediate and Carmichael got carried away so quickly that the address seemed more a high-powered act than anything else. In his white robe and white hair the lean and tall West Indian looked much like the ghost of Pan-African nationalism past. As Kwame Touré, he carried the names of fallen idols, African leaders who resorted to dictatorial control when things didn't go the way they wanted, whether that meant throttling the press or subjecting the opposition to the infamous "black diet." But then much of what Carmichael has had to say since the black power years has been itself a black diet, a form of intellectual starvation in which the intricacies of international politics are reduced to inflammatory tribalism.

A Palestinian, Said Arafat, attacked Zionism as "a cancer" and called for "the total liberation of Palestine." Russell Means, one of the founders of the American Indian Movement, gave a predictable address about an Indian taking his tomahawk to an insulting white man. Then a golem popped out of his bandana: "When we were in Los Angeles the Jews did a number on Mr. Farrakhan." He concluded by saying, "I want you all to remember that Hollywood has denigrated and debased every race of people, but there are no plays or movies denigrating the Jewish people." (Half right, half wrong. As J. Hoberman points out, many movies with Jewish stereotypes were made during the silent era, but the moguls backed off when sound came in, yielding to community pressure. And though Hollywood's contribution to "negative images" of ethnic groups is unarguable, it is also true that revisionist Westerns such as the classic *Fort Apache* started appearing long before AIM was founded.)

All the speeches were short and made their points. Then the featured attraction was introduced. The audience rose to its feet and burst forth with a heroic sound, filling the Garden with a gigantic chord of collected voices. Very soon, Farrakhan proved his shrewdness, highhandedly using the rhetoric of social movements he would have opposed twenty-five years ago. When the applause ended, Farrakhan called attention to the female bodyguards who surrounded him and claimed that Elijah Muhammad was the first black leader to liberate the woman. Point of fact, the Muslims used to say, "The black woman is the field in which the black man sows his nation." But after all, the past is silly putty to men like Farrakhan, who used the subject of women as the first of many themes he would pass through or over. "The world is in the condition it is," he said, "because it doesn't respect women." Growing bolder, Farrakhan attacked the separation of the sexes in traditional Islam, saying women should be allowed into the mosque. That will no doubt be quite a revelation in the Middle East, when Farrakhan goes on his promised third world tour.

Farrakhan went on to be consistently incoherent for three hours, embodying the phrase "Didn't he ramble?" He circled many topics, always ending on his favorite subject: Louis Farrakhan. He talked about how good he looked, how he should be compared to Jesus, how the Jews were after him, how he was on a divine mission, how he would go to the Southwest and die with the Indians if necessary, how "examples" should be made of black leaders who criticized men like him, how black people needn't worry if they were called upon to go to war with America, since Allah would do for them what he did for David when the boy fought Goliath. He piled his points in Dagwood sandwiches of contradiction, moving from the "fact" that whites were invented devils to the observation that if America is hell, then those who run it must be devils; then obliquely referring to the *Annacalyptus,* an occult history, with the remark that we have never seen races evolve from light to dark, further proof that the "Asiatic black man" must be the father of all races. To finish off that run, Farrakhan dug out the anthropological findings in East Africa, which suggest that man originated there. Rounding the bases of absurdity, metaphor, and the occult, he hook-slid into science.

When Farrakhan wasn't talking about himself, he most frequently baited Jews. When he does that, he plumbs the battles that have gone on between black people and Jews for almost twenty years. He speaks to (though not for) those who have fought with Jews over affirmative action, or have felt locked out of discussions about Middle East policy by Jews as willing to bully and deflect criticism with the term "anti-Semite" as black people were with "racist" twenty years ago. I'm sure he scores points with those who argue that Jewish media executives are biased in favor of Israel; who say that films like *Exodus,* TV movies about Entebbe, Golda Meir, Sadat, the stream of documentaries, docudramas, and miniseries given over to "the final solution" are all part of a justification for Zionism; who were angry when Hollywood saluted Israel's thirtieth anniversary with a television special, and cynically wondered if "those Hollywood Jews" would salute any other country's birth.

I don't know of any other country Hollywood has saluted, but a propaganda ploy by a few executives does not a conspiracy of six million Jewish Americans make. (You can hear them whispering into the phone at your nearest deli, "Hey, Murray, I just got word we'll have another special coming up; spread the word in your block. But make sure no goyim are listening.") If such a conspiracy exists, how has it allowed South Africa, Israel's ally, to get such an overwhelming amount of bad press?

Of course, Israel's relationship to South Africa complicates the question. For all its moral proclamations, the Israelis supply arms to Botha's gang and refuse to cooperate with sanctions. This convinces certain quarters that Israel and its sympathizers support racial injustice and antidemocratic regimes, angering those who had a sense of international black struggle hammered into their minds by Malcolm X and his emulators. That sense of collective black effort was a sort of political evangelism, bent on saving the third world from white savagery and exploitation, a racial variation on international revolutionary Marxism. (It was this sense of foreign destiny that inspired the back-to-Africa movements, which eventually led to the founding of Liberia, Israel's true forerunner—a country begun for free ex-slaves to the resentment of the sixty local tribes. One wonders how much Herzl and associates knew about Liberia and whether or not they were inspired by its example.) At present, however, it seems to put more emphasis on the interests of a foreign country than on the conditions of black Americans, a tendency I doubt we would see in the Jewish community if it had the same degree of social, educational, and economic problems that burden millions of Negroes.

But screwed-up priorities are nothing new to black politics, nor, unfortunately, are anti-Semitic attacks loosely using that most dangerous article of speech: "the." Those three letters fan conspiracy theories and push us back to the 1960s, when LeRoi Jones brought a grotesque refinement to anti-white sentiment by reading poetry that baited Jews on college campus after college campus, to the cheers of black students. Such tours probably had more than a little to do with intensifying the Zionist fervor of many Jews who had been told to get out of civil rights organizations.

The failure of Jones, Karenga, and other black nationalists to realize their separatist dreams made for a jealousy that floats to the surface in the speeches of Louis Farrakhan, their heir. When Farrakhan makes references to Reagan "punking out" to the Jews or the Zionist lobby having "a stranglehold on the government of the United States," he is projecting the kind of power *he* wants onto the American-Israeli Public Affairs Committee (AIPAC), commonly called the Zionist lobby. In his version, however, Farrakhan feels free to make threats on the lives of black reporters, politicians, and anyone else who criticizes him.

The envy of AIPAC's influence reflects a nostalgia for the days when so much of the national dialogue was given over to the racial question and the quality of black life in the country was an issue at the front of the political bus. During those years, desegregation and racial double standards were the primary concerns. There was little room for anti-Jewish or anti-Zionist feeling, regardless of how deep they might have run in black nationalist circles. Now the judas goat of Jewish conspiracy is trotted out again as an explanation for the loss of concentrated attention on black problems.

Yet it would make more sense to emulate the efforts of activist Jews that have made AIPAC, as Paul Findley's *They Dare to Speak Out* documents, such a force on Capitol Hill. Obviously, black leaders have failed to create a comparable force to lobby for the interests of Negro Americans. The nationalist rhetoric backfired and made black problems seem more those of a group in a self-segregated world than central to the country at large. As one black woman, infuriated by Farrakhan, said, "We should be putting our feet in the pants of these politicians. Get this dope out of here. Get these schools working. Clean up these neighborhoods. Do what we need done." The Jews who work in Israel's interest know the secret: hard work, fund-raising, monitoring voting patterns, petitioning, telephoning, writing to elected officials. It's difficult and laborious work, but it can get results. As that angered black woman concluded, "We can get all this up off our backs if we want to do something besides listen to some fool who hates ham talk like he's bad enough to exterminate somebody."

But for all his muddled convolutions, Farrakhan's vision isn't small. He wants it all. The world. Who else would feel free to promise that he would tell the Muslims of the Middle East how they had distorted Islam? Who else would claim to be single-handedly raising a people from the death of ignorance and self-hatred?

Though Farrakhan's address was supposed to reveal his economic program, his ideas about black-produced mouthwash, toothpaste, and sanitary napkins took up only 10 or 15 of his 180-minute montage of misconceptions. They were cheered now and again, as was almost everything he said. I doubt, however, that the black people there rising to their feet, screaming themselves hoarse, roaring as though he was scoring baskets as he bounced his ideas off their heads, followed his content. What clarity there was had little connection to a black American point of view. Though his look and his podium style owe much to the black church, his ideas were dominated by a bent Islamic fundamentalism that might get him more money from Arabs. But whatever the underlying goals, Farrakhan's cosmology has little chance of overthrowing the strong tradition of Negro culture, custom, and thought improvised in the "wilderness of North America," as Elijah Muhammad might say. Few black people will ever believe that Farrakhan is so divinely significant that if the Jews try to touch him, Allah will bring down the blood of the righteous on America and they will all be killed outright. As a guy sitting near my row pointed out, "Anybody who uses the first person pronoun as much as he does can't be saying anything. If they were, they would just say it, not keep telling you how great the one who is *about* to say it is."

But Farrakhan isn't just your garden-variety megalomaniac. "Louis Farrakhan," said a woman editor who lives in Harlem, "is a creep. He is a fascist and has nothing to say. Whenever people try to defend him by saying he's speaking out, I always wonder what the hell they mean. He has nothing to offer but half truths, he tries to intimidate the black press into a cheering squad or a bunch of silent lampposts. His exterior is clean and neat, but his insides are dirty and his talk is pure sloppiness. How can educated people like him? It's just laziness. All they want is to anger some white people, or pretend he's angering them in any way serious enough to warrant the attention he's getting. Nowadays if you try to bring up a serious topic in a lot of middle-class black circles, people want to change the subject and treat you like you're causing trouble. This kind of thing is crazy."

The real deal is that few intellectually sophisticated black people are ever seen on television discussing issues. Reporters seem to prefer men like Louis Farrakhan and Jesse Jackson over genuine thinkers and scholars. Farrakhan obviously reads little that gives him any substantive information, and Jackson admitted in his *Playboy* interview that he hates to read. As Playthell Benjamin, one of Harlem's finest minds, says, "There is a ban on black intellectuals in the media. As the sixties proved, if we were allowed back into the area of discussion, the nature of the social vision would be radically changed, from politics to art. There are all kinds of men like Maynard Jackson, David Levering Lewis, Albert Murray, and others who could bring this sophistry and nonsense to a halt. They could make the dialogue more sophisticated." Benjamin is absolutely on the money. We rarely get to hear the ideas of black people who have spent many years studying and thinking and assessing their American experience and the policies of this country around the world.

By and large, those were not the kinds of people who came to hear Louis Farrakhan, roaring and cheering until the evening was finished off by an overripe Chaka Khan singing, strangely, a song called "Freedom," a cappella and quite beautifully. Beyond the podium and not far from Farrakhan's white limousine were the young women bodyguards, who had stood through the entire three-hour address, hardly moving and constantly scanning the crowd for assassins. They were hugging each other and crying, releasing the tension that had percolated through the long watch. Some were thanking Allah that their leader hadn't been harmed. All of them were brown and their skin had a luxuriant smoothness, their eyes the clarity of those who don't dissipate, and behind what I'm sure was experience in martial arts, was the same tenderness a man always notices when women feel deep affection.

Yet one image remained in the front of my mind: this light-skinned young man wearing a camouflage shirt and pants, brown fringe sewn across the shoulders, studded black leather covering his forearms. Whenever Farrakhan said something about "the Jews," that young man screamed or shouted, pushing both fists into the air, frequently leaping to his feet. Near the end of the evening, when I had moved down toward the stage and was preparing to leave, I looked up and saw him once again. The front of his eight-inch-wide black belt bore a large Star of David formed in studs.

Farrakhan from 1985 to 1996

While Louis Farrakhan's appearance as the final speaker at the first anniversary of the Million Man March at the United Nations was short about 950,000 people, it was very similar to the show he brought into Madison Square Garden on October 7, 1985. But he didn't call that one a "Day of Atonement." At that time Farrakhan was elbowing his way into a media not yet fully aware of who he was or what the Nation of Islam stood for.

The press was caught not napping but showing off how quickly it forgot all the stuff Malcolm X spouted when he was the spokesman for the cult—white people being "blue-eyed devils" invented six thousand years ago by a mad black scientist, the animosity toward interracial marriage, the demand for separate states on the

American continent, and the tales of spaceships filled with black scientists ready to destroy America "when the word is given."

Mistakenly thinking he had achieved a coup for his 1984 presidential campaign, Jesse Jackson had gotten Farrakhan and his cult to register to vote, something that broke with their tradition of staying out of politics. Thusly pulled out of the shadows, Farrakhan became so outraged during that campaign year when Milton Coleman of the *Washington Post* reported Jackson's "hymietown" remark that the bow-tied minister was recorded threatening Coleman's life, promising to "deliver" death to him some day.

At the Garden in 1985, Farrakhan's point was the same one he tried to make with his political medicine show at the UN in October 1996. Then, as now, Farrakhan was intent on proving himself not just a black leader but a rallying force for third world grievances against white people, America and the American government, Zionism, and those black people unwilling to line up behind him.

It doesn't matter what Louis Farrakhan does, however, because he will forever remain a long-winded, self-celebrating bore whose speeches lurch and stumble from one topic to another like a blind man walking through the walls of a paper house and tripping over the furniture. Still the West Indian calypso singer overheated by his audience, he cannot get off the stage. Beyond that, Farrakhan is as incapable of using one standard for his observations as he is of being cogent.

At the UN, he ranted about the American government, took credit for the drop in national crime, demanded recognition of Palestinian sovereignty, and demanded that the U.S. lift embargoes on Cuba and Muslim countries, but he never attacked the present-day problem of slavery in Africa—which is well documented—nor has he ever been particularly bothered by Libyan leader Muammar Gadhafi's contemptuous writings about sub-Saharan Africa in his *Green Book*.

This is very important to understanding him and how he is used, for there are interesting reasons that Farrakhan vociferously denies the presence of the ills in the countries he visited during his Middle East and African tour following the Million Man March. However haughty and self-righteous he might be when defending those dictators, their corrupt regimes and barbaric practices, Farrakhan is actually no more than a shill, Uncle Tomming to those who might help him get some headlines, make loans to his cult, and pretend that they take him seriously as a major force in America—which is only possible if they don't do any research into his actual position.

What we have here, at least as far as the anti-American part of the Arab world is concerned, is an incredible degree of condescension for the purposes of using Farrakhan as an irritant they can push further under the skin of the United States' political leadership. After all, the kind of Islam that Farrakhan practices and teaches his followers is so far removed from tradition that it would have provoked holy war were it to have been started in the Middle East, where much blood has been shed by warring factions preaching the "true" Islam.

Once Farrakhan leaves their quarters, the Arabs must have a long, loud laugh at this self-important buffoon whose hatred of the press because it will not celebrate him reveals that he, like Ronald Reagan, thinks he's being reviewed. The poor man is still the entertainer hoping to someday dominate showtime at the Apollo.

As usual, there is more.

It also seems quite true that there have been good responses to the initial Million Man March in terms of community involvement and so on, but we seem to forget that the appearance of those many thousands in Washington on October 16, 1995, was the result of the work of more than three hundred black organizations nationwide, including fraternities, sororities, churches, community organizers, radio stations, and newspapers. The reason we forget that has much to do with our media. Their perpetual interest in "discovering" Negro bogeymen took them far afield of the facts as they discussed what Farrakhan had supposedly wrought. In actuality, the Nation of Islam (by itself) had neither the troops nor the outreach to bring off that monumental gathering. A combination of our American luck and the leader's character saved us from an expansion of his cult's membership. By the time Farrakhan got to the microphone in Washington, he blew the biggest recruitment opportunity he's ever had, exhausting the audience with a typically rambling address. Whew!

I firmly believe that as responses to the Negro American problem become progressively sophisticated, Farrakhan will probably fade back into the cult world where he belongs. People will begin to see him as Kareem Abdul-Jabbar does. Speaking like every true Muslim I've ever talked with about Farrakhan, Jabbar said of the minister in a 1996 *New York Times Sunday Magazine* interview, "He uses racist demagoguery instead of trying to deal with real problems with real solutions. And I don't respect his constant attempts to make people angry at each other. Besides, what the [Nation of Islam] is talking about is not Islam. I mean, it uses some Islamic trappings. But [they] want us to believe that there are black scientists driving around the universe in a spaceship called 'the mothership.' I don't take them seriously."

From where I sit, that clearly slam-dunks the issue in the interest of reality.

Big Persons and the Littles

Gwendolyn Brooks

GWENDOLYN BROOKS *is a Pulitzer Prize–winning poet in Chicago. Her ground-breaking works include "*A Street in Bronzeville," *an essay collection; and* Annie Allen, *a poetry collection. This essay, a collection of thoughts and impressions on Farrakhan and African-American leadership, was first read as part of the 1994 Jefferson Lecture, an address by Brooks at the Kennedy Center in Washington, D.C., and has been adapted from her 1996 book,* Report from Part Two.

Farrakhan. We don't have tea. I have met the Avidly Assaulted One once. About a quarter century ago, a woman poet, then a Muslim, brought him to meet my husband and myself. He was impressively relaxed. He brought no guards, no guns. We were impressed by his warm eyes, his kind patience, flexible dignity. He listened to our ideas. He listened to every word we said. He waited for us to finish our sentences. He never interrupted. (Today, interruption is an Art.) He did not feel the need to pastor. At least, he did not pastor. He did not ask us to join anything.

This man I have not seen since. He is, however, a member of the Black Family. He is a Family Picture. I look at the picture. I don't want to forget that this individual has saved a lot of sick-souled, gasping, bare-footed Blacks no one else cared to save. He has fed them, medicated them, detoxicated them, schooled them: thus making many of <u>our</u> lives, homes, and little children a <u>SMIDGEN</u> safer. Sometimes, where there is Mess, and he is called, Mess is stomped upon. He is not Malcolm. But do remember that <u>Malcolm</u> could be called, <u>would</u> come, would lift that one open hand, and—mirabile dictu—<u>WONDERFUL</u> to tell of—Mess would be mesmerized and shorn.

Remember also Martin, Medgar, Fannie Lou, Ida B. Wells, Chicago's Haki, Jesse, Carol, California's Maxine, others, others. Without this Sweet Sentience—the difficult strainings—many of us who are still living would not be. We would be <u>missing</u>, or stiff in strict and restricted little lives. We should keep those names, and memories of what those names <u>meant</u>, and mean, as companions, richly with us as we walk our streets, breathing in our previous air, and symbolically spitting on a few of the Homeless.

Those leaders, their acts, their influence, their belief in the power of affirming decency, keep many of the wild and beastified <u>some</u>-what hopeful, willing to wait a <u>little</u> longer, willing to be watchful, willing to forswear those calm deliberate walks up aisles of trains or planes with guns a-blazing.

I Use them all. I appreciate <u>all</u> the Radiance.

But I must supplement.

I do not <u>wor</u>ship <u>any</u> Big Person. A long life has taught me that rigorous worship of Big Persons is not an intelligent management of my time. A long life has taught me that many of the Lit-tul people are large enough to merit my salute, my practical gratitude.

Middle-aged Martha Steward in a class at Chicago State University improves her classmates every Thursday night without once indicating that she considers herself superior to them in any way.

No pastoring, but warmth, clear wit, bread-and-vegetables wisdom, kindness. (Kindness is not popular.)

A "word" about Big Persons:

> I shall tell you a thing about giants
> that you do not wish to know.
> Giants look in mirrors and see almost nothing at all.
> But they leave their houses nevertheless.
> They lurch out of doors—
> to reach you, the other stretchers and strainers.
> (Erased under ermine or in loud tatters, oh
> moneyed or mashed, you matter.
> You matter, and giants must bother.)

Well, I shall not join the Muslims or any other Passionate Purity. But: instead of popping all these pebbles at the Purposeful pastor, why are we not surveying with seriousness a mightily impressive and altering tumor of your day?

Vladimir Zhirinovsky hates the idea of "all these Blacks" running around in his country, with "all this Power." And the complete population of the Jews, he opines, should settle in Israel. (Isn't THAT resented?) He affirms Manifest Destiny, believes that it was right to strip the Indians (I can't remember his bothering to use the name Native Americans) of most of what was theirs. Zhirinovsky is media-manager, hostility-heater, malevolent Player. Few want to talk about him. Few admit. Fear. I feel I'm back in the late Thirties. I am not a social scientist, I am not a fluent Politico. But when I look at Zhirinovsky I think of John Donne's Bell. It tolls for Thee. "Never ask For Whom the Bell tolls. It tolls for THEE."

I am sure that one of Zhirinovsky's admirations is Niccolò Machiavelli, author of The Prince. Surely Zhirinovsky squealed and dampened himself when he read: "A Prince should disregard the reproach of being thought cruel where it enables him to keep his

Subjects united and obedient." Surely it was a while before Z was dry. And likely he was again visited by difficulties when he went on to read: "Fortune is a woman, who, to be kept under, must be beaten and roughly handled; and we see that she suffers herself to be more readily mastered by those who so treat her than by those who are more timid in their approaches."

What "awaits" The Black Community? It is a wide community: that fact sometimes seems negligible, since not all members flash their membership cards. The community is seen in its True Strength, however, when Union, obviously, is absolutely necessary, as it was when Harold Washington decided to run for the mayorship of Chicago. The Big Persons remembered that they, too, go to the bathroom every day, if health permits, and joined the workaday and the wee.

All together came the proud and the profane, the handsome, the homely, the spotty and the spangled, the galloping and the halt, the wheeled and the becrutched, the devilish and the demure. They grinned at each other. They hollered, "Here's Harold!" And they put their Prince in a City Chair.

Is there a Decision?—do Blacks need another Martin, Malcolm, Medgar, Ida, Fannie Lou? Let's go back to looking at those Littles. Their pictures overwhelm my Gallery. I reemphasize: perhaps what we need is not another individual to be roared up, royalized, routed—but lots of the Littles, understanding the strength of clean cooperation, responsibility. From Primer for Blacks: I go on believing that the Weak among us will, finally, perceive the impressiveness of our numbers, perceive the quality and legitimacy of our essence, and take sufficient, indicated steps toward definition, clarification, connection.

All Family Pictures looked at. With clean eyes.

There are no magics, no elves
no timely godmothers to guide us.

We are lost, must wizard a track
through our own screaming weed.
An emphasis is paroled.
The old decapitations are revised,
the dispossessions beakless.
THEN we sing.

Louis Farrakhan's Ministry of Misogyny and Homophobia

Irene Monroe

IRENE MONROE *is a doctoral candidate in religion, gender, and cultural studies at the Harvard Divinity School. She is a 1997 recipient of a Ford Foundation grant and a board member of the Women's Theological Center in Boston, MA. She is a former board member of Christian Lesbians Out Together.*

God don't like men coming to men with lust in their hearts like you should go to a female. If you think that the kingdom of God is going to be filled up with that kind of degenerate crap, you're out of your damn mind.

—Minister Louis Farrakhan
Kansas City, 1996

I happen to believe that being homosexual is submission to circumstances rather than anything genetic or innate in the human being. . . . I consider it a problem. Maybe they don't consider it a problem, but AIDS is manifesting that there is a problem somewhere in this kind of social behavior.

—Minister Louis Farrakhan
New York City, 1985

To demonize Minister Louis Farrakhan's stance on gays and lesbians would be unfair because it would allow other African-American religious leaders unjustly off the hook. His stance on gays and lesbians is emblematic of the long-standing beliefs in the Nation of Islam,

275

in the Black Church and, by extension, in most of our families and communities. What Farrakhan says is just a clear and pointed example of what basically underlies the theology and social actions of our African-American communities and churches. The fact that his homophobic statements are quoted more in the media than are statements by ordinary African-American Christian clerics speaks more about the white public's obsessive fear about Farrakhan than about the media's advocacy of life, liberty, and the pursuit of happiness for gay, lesbian, bisexual, and transgendered African-American people. This is not to say, however, that Minister Farrakhan's vitriolic statements about gays, lesbians, bisexuals, and transgendered people in the African-American community should go unopposed. A particular look at the theme of the "endangered black male" in Farrakhan's public comments and social ministry will give us some insight into how misogyny and homophobia are critical elements of his model of leadership. It will allow us to see how his Afrocentric theology and social action are predicated on the devaluation of women, gays, lesbians, bisexuals, and transgendered people. It also reveals how his views are deleterious for an inclusive and effective African-American leadership at the dawn of the new millennium.

On January 24, 1994, at an armory in Harlem, and on March 10, 1994, at the Strand Theater in Boston, Minister Louis Farrakhan called for "men only" meetings entitled "Stop the Killing" to discuss the endangered state of African-American men in America. In his opening words at the Strand Theater Farrakhan purported

to do something I don't believe has ever been done before in the history of our sojourn in America and that is a black man would call together black men to discuss the future of us as a people. This call is not meant to discriminate against women for without women none of us would be present. Our beloved mothers, living or dead, have anguished in their lives over the suffering of their children, particularly the suffering of the black male. To the women who are outside who are very very disturbed because they want to see their brothers too, we say to you that until and unless we strengthen the black man and make the black man what God intended for him to be there will be no family. There will be no real progress for us as a people. . . . Black men represent power to make change, and to make it real.[1]

Actions to stop the oppression of African-American men have historically been our preoccupation, at the expense of the rest of the community. The belief that African-American males are the only endangered members of our community predominates in the African-American psyche. For example, in the introduction of Jawanza Kunjufu's book *Countering the Conspiracy to Destroy Black Boys,* we read: "Although the reader may question [Kunjufu's] emphasis on African-American boys over African-American girls, one cannot easily dismiss the fact that European-Americans have done nearly everything imaginable to malign and subjugate African-American males."[2] Louis Farrakhan stated at a rally in Kansas City in 1996 that "the aim of this world is to destroy the black man."[3]

In the 1990s this phenomenon has been apparent in the African-American community. When Rodney King was flogged by the Los Angeles Police, there was a national outrage expressed in African-American communities. In contrast, when King battered his wife, and subsequently she fled to a shelter for protection, there was barely a whimper in the African-American community. In the Anita Hill–Clarence Thomas hearings, Hill was perceived by many to be the culprit in Thomas's "high-tech lynching." Rumors of her being a lesbian floated about because only a man hater, and "race traitor," would try to bring a "good black brother" down. Many African-American women along with African-American men blamed Hill for bringing charges of sexual harassment against Thomas, given his precarious status in society as an African-American man and the importance of the position he was seeking, whether or not he deserved it. As African-American feminist cultural critic bell hooks states, "Thomas' 'pain' at being the object of what he strategically implied was the continuation of white male rape and castration of black males was seen as far more brutal than any pain Hill could possibly have suffered."[4] Similarly, in the O.J. Simpson trial, the knowledge of Simpson being a batterer and possible murderer took a back seat in much of the African-American reaction because of the historical and everyday injustices African-American men incur in a racist society. Consequently, only the suffering and victimization of African-American men were on trial. The belief that only African-American men are endangered keeps African-American women and children subject to continual violence and abuse by both white and African-American men.

Another long-standing myth, which complements that of "the endangered black male," is that of "the black matriarch." This myth, most notoriously articulated in Daniel Patrick Moynihan's 1965 report, "The Negro Family: The Case for National Action," proposes that African-American women are complicit with white patriarchal society in the emasculation of African-American men by becoming heads of households and primary job holders. The myth's assumptions that African-American men have been feminized and African-American women have been masculinized have only served to contribute to black male physical and psychological violence against women. Belief in the myth of the black matriarchy is reflected both in the Nation of Islam and in the Black Church, and it has heightened the belief that African-American men are the only endangered members of our community. Farrakhan states, "The traditional nuclear family is an endangered species. . . . Women are working more than men, so the women are providing for their children and even for the men, bringing home the money. Black men sittin' at home, lookin' at soap operas, [and] she's talking with the man's voice. God's order has been turned around. Whenever the natural order of God is violated, there are serious consequences."[5] The myth of the black matriarch has caused many African-American men and women to rally in panic around this gender-biased belief, and consequently it has reinforced imbalanced gender relations between us. It has taught African-American women to protect African-American men at their own expense, fearing that the alternative is to be left alone and unprotected in the world. Farrakhan states, "And if there is no man, sister; if you gotta be like Hagar, running in the wilderness by yourself with your child; if you gotta be like Mary, with your baby running from Palestine under death threats from those who are planning against you into Egypt where you can be safe—then the burden will be upon you to start the process of building a new man and a new woman to create a new reality."[6] Some men have spoken out against this gender-biased perception without reprisal. On the other hand, some women who have spoken out have been castigated as race traitors or lesbians, both of which are seen as antithetical to the collective consensus for liberation.

The belief in the "endangered black male" is also kept in place by homophobia, which places blame on African-American gay men and lesbians for not upholding their prescribed gender roles. With the shortage of African-American "heterosexual" men due to street violence and imprisonment, African-American gay men are perceived as race traitors for not upholding their racial responsibility to be "real black men" just as lesbians are seen as race traitors for not upholding their responsibility to produce such men. Moreover, within homophobia, there is gender discrimination. As Audre Lorde, the African-Caribbean lesbian poet and activist, observes: "If the recent hysterical rejection of lesbians in the black community is based solely upon an aversion to the idea of sexual contact between members of the same sex—why then is the idea of sexual contact between black men so much more easily accepted, or unremarked?"[7] Much of the form of homophobia that Audre Lorde depicts is connected to phallocentrism and misogyny. Since the belief is that only the phallus legitimates a sexual act, then all "real" sexual acts must have the presence of a male. Lesbians, by inference, do not engage in "real sex" because there is no penis. If they engaged in real sex, the belief is that they would never be with a woman again.

Farrakhan's statement to lesbians was, "But when you meet a real man, Sister, you don't want no play thing when the real things come along, you understand. And there is something in the man, the real man, that God put in that no woman can give you—ain't that sweet?"[8]

One of the beliefs behind the notion of "real sex" is that penile-vaginal intercourse is the ultimate sexual satisfaction. However, according to a growing body of research, "Women report that masturbation produces stronger orgasms than penile-vaginal intercourse, and lesbian women report higher rates of orgasm than heterosexual women."[9] Since "real sex," from a conservative point of view, is about procreation, then lesbians enter a male domain of sexual expression: pleasure. Sexual pleasure as a male domain maintains relations of domination and submission and eroticizes female submission. In nonreciprocal sexual acts between males and females, females are relegated to being givers but not receivers of pleasure. According to Farrakhan, a male receiving pleasure from a woman is all part of her being his helpmate. Farrakhan exclaimed, "How could a man need a woman to help him do nothing? And then want her to give him pleasure? For what? You ain't worthy of no pleasure. Pleasure comes after work!"[10]

Because it is perceived that the needs, the survival, and the sexual pleasures of African-American men are first and foremost for the continuation of our race, African-American women's essential purpose for Farrakhan followers is reproduction. If we are not making babies, especially little black boys, we endanger ourselves because we become subject to patriarchal violence and social alienation. If we have no children and no community, then who and what are we? What value do we have to the cause of liberation? According to Farrakhan, "The woman when true to her feminine nature is really advanced over the man. Not because of her beauty, not because of her accomplishments . . . but because she possesses the womb."[11] Therefore, as Ntozake Shange states, "to take pleasure in ourselves is subversive."[12]

As a male domain, sexual pleasure is sought by African-American gay and heterosexual men. The issue for Louis Farrakhan and other African-American leaders is not so much how and with whom gay men seek sexual pleasure, but whether they identify themselves as gay. A gay identity threatens the construct of a monolithic racial identity. Historically, African-American nationalism constructs a heterosexual and male racial identity in the African-American community, despite the fact that the community is composed of both genders and a variety of sexual orientations. Therefore, since identity in the African-American community is predicated on who we say we are as a race of people, and not what we do sexually, homosexuality is viewed as an aberrant behavioral trait whose etiology is caused by and found in white society. Farrakhan states that "homosexuality threatens the perfect order laid forth by the Nation and is as such abominable, a perverse product of a sick society. When white society denies the black man the possibilities of being a real man, he runs the risk of degrading into a homosexual."[13] Considered a defilement of human flesh according to the Book of Leviticus, and substantiated primarily with the Sodom and Gomorrah narrative in the Book of Genesis, homosexuality within the tradition of Black Church leaders falls under the rubric of pastoral care and is not considered a social justice issue. In the Black Church one too often hears from African-American ministers on the issue of homosexuality that "we are to love the sinner but hate the sin." With the same sentiment Farrakhan says, "The understanding minister attacks the cause rather than the symptom . . . and appeals to his followers not to cast stones against the manifestations of sin, as none is without sin . . . [but] change homosexual behavior and get rid of the circumstances that bring about it."[14]

The belief that homosexuality is a behavioral trait brought on by the economic and political castration of the African-American man allows Farrakhan to believe also that there is no such thing as an African-American gay man, only an "endangered black man." Although his mosques contain a larger former prison population of

HIV positive men than the Black Church does, Farrakhan explains their homosexual behavior as part and parcel of single-sex environments. These masculine "heterosexual" men engaged in homosexual activity without risking stigmatization or a loss of status in the Nation because they did not identify themselves as gay. Their joining the Nation, the bastion of black manhood, is testimony to their heterosexual orientation and to their desire to eradicate the economic and political emasculation they faced before and during their imprisonment. However, African-American gay-identified men *are also* in the Nation. As with gay men in the Black Church, they cloak their sexual identity. In so doing, they participate in and perpetuate heterosexism and homophobia. Since the sacred and secular spheres of the Black Church and the Nation of Islam are conflated in the African-American community, when gay men park their homosexuality at the threshold of these sanctuaries, they end up situated outside both domains.

Although there may not be a visible leadership position for the identifiable gay Muslim in the Nation of Islam, there is one such spot for the gay Christian in the Black Church: the choirmaster or the minister of music. Although it seems paradoxical for the Black Church to have an acknowledged "gay-friendly" occupational role, the choirmaster is a nonthreatening position within its ecclesiastical structures. The choirmaster, or "choirmistress," as gay men choir leaders are sometimes referred to, is a nongendered position that may also be filled by a woman. Although a leadership position within the church, it is not within the church's governing and administrative hierarchy and, therefore, does not endanger the sexual integrity of the church. Only heterosexual men hold positions of authority and power. Although the choirmaster position is a visible entry point into the fold of the church, gay men assume that role at a tremendous cost to their personhood. As African-American cultural critic Michael Dyson notes, "The notorious homophobia of the black church just doesn't square with the numerous same-sex unions taking place, from pulpit to the pew. One of the most painful scenarios of black church life is repeated Sunday after Sunday with little notice or collective outrage. A black minister will preach a sermon railing against sexual ills, especially homosexuality. At the close of the sermon, a soloist, who everybody knows is gay, will rise to perform a moving number, as the preacher extends an invitation to visitors to join the church. The soloist is, in effect, being asked to sing, and to sign his theological death sentence."[15]

The stereotype of gay men as effeminate is another example of misogyny, because it is based on an antifemale sentiment rather than an antihomosexual one. Any man, heterosexual or gay, who does not conform to the dominant paradigm of manhood is seen as an effeminate male and, thus, a lesser human being. Like women, effeminate men are viewed as "other," and as other their inferior status among heterosexual men confirms heterosexual men in their superiority and manhood. Because effeminate gay men are seen as women, they are often sexually harassed, abused, and even raped by "real" men. According to Farrakhan, this type of man is "a woman trapped in a man's body, tryin' to get out."[16]

The effeminate gay man is feared, because he cannot be counted or accepted in the fold as a man. Considered a lost resource for the cause of liberation, he lives as a resident alien in the African-American community. He is a resident by virtue of skin color and culture, but he is an alien because of his feminine demeanor and assumed passive sexual behavior. Because he has broken away from the monolithic racial identity, should he continue to live in the African-American community, he will become a stranger among his people.

Paradoxically, the black macho male persona of the Nation of Islam and language of Farrakhan endangers the entire community. In Farrakhan's attempt to create solidarity and community, he ordains himself as the "resident prophet." He lives in the community speaking for, and policing the behavior of, his residents (in Farrakhan's case all African-American people) with intimidation and violence. His potential use of violence, although seldom physical, given the presence of his "divine" army, the Fruit of Islam, always creates a foreboding feeling. Farrakhan states, "While they should not be soft, they should hide their power and look on themselves as an army of saviors."[17] To dispel any doubts about his prophetic calling, Farrakhan legislates with righteous indignation. In so doing, he instills and inspires fear in members of his community with his fiery rhetoric on racial purity. If one is not an adherent to his brand of Afrocentricity, one is deemed an Afro-Saxon. As Henry Louis Gates, Jr., writes:

> A subject that receives far less attention is the fear that Farrakhan inspires in blacks. The truth is that blacks—across the economic and ideological spectrum—often feel astonishingly vulnerable to charges of inauthenticity, of disloyalty to the race. I know that I do, despite my vigorous efforts to deconstruct that vocabulary of reproach. Farrakhan's sway over blacks—the answering chord his rhetoric finds—attests to the enduring strength of our own feelings of guilt, our own anxieties of having been false to our people, of having sinned against our innermost identity. He denounces the fallen in our midst, invokes the wrath of heaven against us: and his outlandish vitriol occasions both terror and curious exhilaration.[18]

An important antecedent that gives rise to the belief that the African-American male is an endangered member of his community and must be saved in order to liberate his entire people is the gender bias in African-American Muslim and Christian appropriation of the exodus motif. As a central paradigm for liberation and leadership, the Exodus narrative has shaped African-American Christian and Muslim theologies and has called both groups to social protest and action. Casting himself as our modern-day Moses, Farrakhan uses the language of the exodus motif to urge African-American Muslims to establish a separate nation-state:

Black people, it's time to make an exodus. We got to come out, come out. Come out of what? And if we come out where do we go? We must come out of Egypt. Egypt only means a land of bondage. America has been and is a land of bondage to black people. We must come out of the mind, the spirit, the way, the values, the norms, the folkways, the mores, the culture of our former slavemasters and their children. You must come out of their mind of dependency. You must come out of this mind of inferiority. You must come out of this bondage of sin and ignorance, and we must develop an autonomy of mind and spirit.[19]

African-Americans, both in the Nation of Islam and in the Black Church, appropriate the Exodus story to narrate our experience in slavery. The trials and tribulations of the Jews under the totalitarian regime of Pharaoh and his army in Egypt are analogous to the trials and tribulations of African-Americans under slavery in the United States' South. The early biblical references about an oppressed male's life being endangered derive from this text.

The narrative opens with Moses precariously floating on water, because of Pharaoh's edict in Exodus 1:22 to "Take every newborn Hebrew boy and throw him into the Nile, but let all the girls live." It is the subversive acts of the midwives, Pharaoh's daughter, and Moses' mother and sister, all working in concert, that save Moses' life and defy the Pharaoh's infanticidal decree on Hebrew males. Unarguably, Israel's liberation from Egyptian bondage had its beginning with those women. However, a female-centered narrative abruptly moves to and remains fixed as a male-centered narrative, consequently focusing solely on the oppression of the Israelites and the election of Moses as their divine leader. Uncritical use of the same interpretation and images over and over again keeps the narrative in patriarchal captivity. Therefore, what we miss in the Exodus narrative is the fact that women make possible the survival and growth of Moses; that they refuse to cooperate with the Egyptian Pharaoh's decree because their obedience to God takes precedence; and that there is strength in females bonding against patriarchal oppression. However, what we derive from the fixed interpretation of the narrative is an account of imbalanced gender relations between men and women—women who act independently against male authority are ignored, and women are excluded from leadership positions. Nevertheless, when interpreted within the patriarchal constraints of the African-American experience, the Exodus narrative tells African-American women that only their men's lives are endangered. As women, we are to nurture, save, and protect our men for the survival of the race. As men, they have the ordained right to lead our liberation movements, and we are to organize and follow them. As Michael Dyson states, "Reducing black suffering to its lowest common male denominator not only presumes a hierarchy of pain that removes priority from black female struggle, but also trivializes the analysis and actions of black women in the quest for liberation."[20]

Although the African-American appropriation of the Exodus narrative is no different from that of most white Christian churches nationwide, our enactment of it has spearheaded social and political movements such as the Abolitionist Movement, the Garvey Movement, the Civil Rights Movement, and the Black Theology Movement. These movements have all showcased male leadership. Our Moses figures in history have been male, from Nat Turner to Martin Luther King, with the exception of one: Harriet Tubman, conductor on the Underground Railroad. Although Tubman was an exception to the rule, she neither negates nor disrupts the androcentric thought and base of African-American leadership from slavery to the present day. Some African-American men have argued that it doesn't matter that Tubman was female because they are "gender blind" when it comes to her leadership role in the emancipation of African-American people during slavery. Others have argued that they see her as female but ostensibly in a male role. Her husband, a free black man during slavery, saw her as a disobedient wife. He attempted to dissuade her from fleeing for her freedom, but Harriet Tubman, nonetheless, went north. When she returned home months later to get him, she discovered that he had taken up with another woman. As one who had transgressed the prescribed gender role for African-American leadership, Tubman paid a heavy price: her marriage.

In the Nation of Islam, the Exodus narrative is one of the central motifs in its theology and its social protest and action. It is buttressed by both a selective interpretation of scripture and an Afrocentric creation myth of the Original Man. In the Original Man story, African men were the original inhabitants of the earth. As descendants from the tribes of Shabazz, these thirteen tribes constituted an African nation united by black skin color, the Islamic religion, and reverence for Allah, a supreme black man among black men. The creation of the white race was an experiment in human hybridization by a brilliant but demonic African scientist named Dr. Yakub. Derived from the Original Man, there sprang forth a race of "blue-eyed devils" known as the Caucasian race who were genetically programmed to promulgate evil in the world. The Original Man story is basic to the Nation of Islam's fundamental premise of reclaiming for all men of African descent their central place in the creation and leadership of the universe. Former minister of the Nation of Islam, the Honorable Elijah Muhammad stated, "When the world knows who the Original Man is—and only then—wars will cease. For everything depends on knowing who is the rightful owner of the earth."[21]

The creator of the Original Man story was Wallace D. Fard, a mysterious but charismatic door-to-door salesman in an African-American neighborhood in Detroit, who told his followers in the 1930s, "I come from the Holy City of Mecca. More about myself I will not tell you yet, for the time has not yet come. I am your brother. You have not yet seen me in my royal robes."[22] Fard's purpose as the self-proclaimed Supreme Ruler of the Universe and the incarnation of Allah was "to bring freedom, justice and equality to the black men in the wilderness of North America,"[23] and "to reconnect with his lost-found nation [to] raise from among them a messenger."[24] Thus began the Islamization of the "endangered black man" theme through appropriation of the Exodus story.

To explain the upcoming demise of white world supremacy, the Nation of Islam's theology of the Original Man inscribes the Exodus motif into the New Testament apocalyptic narrative, the Book of Revelation. Fard argued that because white domination throughout the world "became too morbid and bestial . . . Allah himself was touched by the suffering and decided to send a mulatto prophet Moses in 2000 B.C.E. to assist in reforming the white race and free it from the clutches of barbarism."[25] Re-ascendancy of the Original Man will begin with a global conflagration of the Caucasian race and the death of Christianity and Judaism in the year 2000. Keeping consistent with the theme of the "endangered black man," the end of the black man's plight begins with the second advent of Fard. Before being forced out of town because of police harassment, Fard promised to return in order to deliver his "lost-found" African brothers in the wilderness of North America from the yoke of white oppression. His parting words to his crying followers outside of the Temple of Islam that he founded were, "I am with you; I will be back to you in the near future to lead you out of this hell."[26]

Whereas Fard was the creator of the Original Man myth, the Honorable Elijah Muhammad, who headed the Nation of Islam from 1934 until his death in 1975, was its messenger. Farrakhan, on the other hand, is now the sustainer of the Original Man theme. Mattias Gardell states that "Moses is Elijah Muhammad, who prepared to go and meet with God [Fard] and assigned Farrakhan to be his Aaron, leaving the Nation and his legacy in his charge."[27] On October 16, 1995, Farrakhan summoned almost one million of his "lost-found" African brothers for a "men only" meeting to converge on the nation's capital for a "Holy Day of Atonement, Reconciliation, and Responsibility." The objective of the march, according to the official position statement, was "to repent and atone.

Men are urged to come as a way of taking 'our place' at the 'head of families' and 'maintainers' of women and children. Women are urged not to attend, but to 'stay at home' while remaining 'by our side' and are thanked for their patience in 'waiting for us to take up our responsibility.' The march will be a day of prayer and petition to the government that manufacturing jobs need not be ceded to Third World countries. The Black community . . . in a partnership with government can unite to form the salvation army of the world."[28]

The Million Man March was a re-articulation of Farrakhan's theme of the endangered black man by a ritualized production of African-American male uplift. The belief that an emasculated African-American male image is to be salvaged by re-institutionalizing black patriarchy with black puritan mores only affirms male domination and control over women and children. It creates a gender hierarchy that keeps women and children subordinates to men and subject to patriarchal violence should they step out of their prescribed gender roles. Women who acquiesce to staying at home and to walking behind their men internalize patriarchal thought as a viable way to eradicate racism. Lauded as "good black women," they are esteemed by Farrakhan and the men in their communities for their loyalty to the struggle, and they become exemplars for other women. Women who choose not to acquiesce to these masculine terms for liberation and leadership because they are feminists or lesbians, both of which fail Farrakhan's racial litmus test, are for the most part silenced and invisible.

Because religion is a central component in African-American culture, the theme and the language of atonement, reconciliation, and responsibility appeal to African-American religious sensibilities and the desire to ameliorate our collective lives. However, not recognizing that the theme and language are constructed in emancipatory male terms, or perhaps too frightened to speak out in opposition to those terms, African-American women perpetuate black patriarchy while at the same time participating in their own oppression. The tension between women who endorsed the march and those who did not thwarts any attempts for a unified sisterhood, which is also necessary for a collective African-American liberation. Healing African-American male wounds should not come at the price of devaluing women. bell hooks writes: "Most recently the national focus on black men as 'endangered species' has added strength to those claims that the plight of black males is much more tragic than that of black females and must be attended to. While it is an accurate assessment that black male lives are threatened daily by encounters with white supremacist, capitalist patriarchy, it is equally true that black families are daily threatened in different ways by both this system and by sexism that condones and promotes black male violence against black females. The assumption that black men suffer more or are more endangered is rooted in sexist thinking."[29]

Many out-of-the-closet gay men attended the Million Man March to make their presence visible and to stand in defiance against Farrakhan's homophobic pronouncements. The march's theme of articulating the racial problems of African-American men impelled many African-American gay men to go and to stand in gender solidarity with their heterosexual brothers, hoping the issues of sexual orientation and AIDS would be addressed. However, homophobia prevailed because last-minute decision changes due to "time constraints" and "priority factors" canceled the only openly gay speaker. Nonetheless, the clarion call for African-American men to save and to liberate the African-American community echoed across sexual orientations because it also spoke to some gay men's belief that they too are to lead in correcting the entire African-American community's problem. Keith Boykin, executive director of the National Black Gay and Lesbian Leadership Forum, asked, "And who is better suited to lead the long-overdue revolution against patriarchy and violence against women than black gay men?"[30] Of course, replacing heterosexual patriarchy with homosexual patriarchy replicates the male power dynamics that Farrakhan espouses. Boykin's statement shows how the foundation of African-American leadership is rooted in an Afrocentric messianic male tradition.

Because we are at the dawn of a new millennium, clearly the successes and failures of Farrakhan's model of leadership must be explored. Not all of us are included in Farrakhan's model of leadership, yet the number of African-American men and women in the Nation of Islam and its offshoots is beginning to threaten those in the Black Church. Despite his prescribed gender roles for women and his denunciation of gays and lesbians, the Honorable Minister Louis Farrakhan is still followed and extolled by many women, gays, and lesbians. Booted out by most of white society as a pariah, Farrakhan is acknowledged by many African-Americans as our modern-day messiah. No politically correct African-American will openly embrace him, but organizers of the African-American summit had to invite him because otherwise some African-American participants would have withdrawn. Even Henry Louis Gates has written, "We sat together at his big dining-room table, and it became clear that Farrakhan is a man of enormous intelligence, curiosity, and charm. He can also be deeply strange. It all depends on the moment and the subject. When he talks about the need for personal responsibility or of his fondness for Johnny Mathis and Frank Sinatra, he sounds as jovial and bourgeois as Bill Cosby; when he is warning of the wicked machinations of Jewish financiers, he seems as odd and obsessed as Pat Robertson."[31]

Known for his anti-Semitism and anti-Judaism, Farrakhan nonetheless spoke at the Parliament of World Religions in 1993. More Christian men than Muslim men were at the Million Man March. More working-class and middle-class professional men were at the march than poor and disenfranchised men, the group Farrakhan usually recruits. When a poll was taken at the Million Man March, 25 percent said they came to demonstrate solidarity, and 29 percent said they came to show support for the African-American family. A fact that was either absent from or distorted by the media was that 87 percent had a favorable impression of Farrakhan and that he ranked higher in their estimation than Jesse Jackson and Colin Powell.

As lesbian feminists, many of my friends and I constantly decry Farrakhan's misogyny and homophobia. Nonetheless, many of these same friends sent their male sons with their fathers or with male members of their families to the march while they and their daughters stayed at home. Although Farrakhan is known as a hatemonger, he is invited to speak at college campuses across the nation. Known around the world as America's black Satan, he nonetheless in 1996 went on a thirty-eight-day World Friendship Tour to Africa and the Middle East and was received in those areas as a dignitary from the United States. The media's attempt to isolate him from the public only gave him higher visibility and augmented his influence and popularity. Undoubtedly, Farrakhan mesmerizes as many African-Americans as he frightens. His charisma is a blend of messianic fervor, authoritarian charm, and oratorical eloquence. In spite of his blatant sexism and unchecked homophobia, his display of personal power, vocal opposition to white racism, political efforts to obtain reparations for slavery, and aggressive agenda for economic uplift devoid of government incentives, have many African-Americans, if not following him, at least wanting to hear from him. Clearly, African-Americans' ambivalent game of "go-away-closer" with Farrakhan speaks more about our belief in the need for a Farrakhan than about our doubts about him as a viable leader.

The success of Farrakhan's leadership has meant African-Americans' failure to recognize gender and sexual orientation as multiple sites of oppression. Because we participate in a social order that polarizes gender and sexual orientation from the racial equation of liberation and inclusive leadership, we oppress members in our own communities. With the role of leadership constructed and accepted in only emancipatory heterosexual male terms, female, gay, lesbian, bisexual, and transgendered African-Americans fall outside of the parameters of who deserves and who will obtain liberation from racial oppression. With black heterosexual patriarchy widely perceived as the most viable weapon against white supremacy, Farrakhan can ostensibly present the Nation of Islam as a refuge in a hostile white world.

In an interview with Henry Louis Gates, Jr., Farrakhan described his belief "that the Nation of Islam might be understood as a kind of Reformation movement in the black church—a church that had grown too accommodating to American racism."[32] As the new "nation within a nation,"[33] it has usurped the centrality of the Black Church and has replicated that church's discriminatory practices against women, gays, lesbians, bisexuals, and transgendered people in African-American communities. African-Americans' compliance with these discriminatory practices results from our conditioning to see racial liberation as dependent on the salvation of the endangered black male. In wanting to have some form of visible resistance in the face of racial oppression, the liberated endangered black male becomes our icon for freedom for the entire race. Many African-American women, gays, lesbians, bisexuals, and transgendered people also comply with these discriminatory practices because of the blatant racism we experience in both our feminist and our queer coalitions. Some of us retreat to the forms of compulsory heterosexism in the African-American community because we experience the pain of racism as much harder to bear outside of our homebase than the misogyny and homophobia in our homes and communities. Farrakhan's leadership wins over many female, gay, lesbian, bisexual, and transgendered African-Americans because "passing" as our gender roles dictate, and going into "the closet" as compulsory heterosexuality forces us to do, are perceived as a smaller price to pay than losing our roots in our African-American families and communities.

The Nation of Islam's success in recruiting and rehabilitating the African-American prison and addict populations has given them a stronghold in African-American communities and has pushed Farrakhan's model of leadership to center stage. Farrakhan's success has been his ability to impose his Afrocentric theological agenda for secular society on both males and females. His agenda calls for the re-institutionalization of black patriarchy in order to eradicate the temporal miseries of all African-Americans. With his self-improvement programs that promote self-discipline in diet and behavior, self-reliance, a strong work ethic, and reverence to Allah, he has transformed many former African-American prisoners and addicts into productive citizens, where the Black Church, African-American elected officials, and government programs have failed. With his Afrocentric educational programs, which emphasize the illustrious heritage of African men and the Original Man creation myth, Farrakhan replaces their criminal identity with a divine identity that Allah intended for them as his "chosen people." Announced as their "chosen leader" for the retribution against white supremacy, and supported by the successes in his outreach ministries, Farrakhan demands, as do his followers, an uncritical acceptance of his authoritarian theocracy. His ministry, therefore, is predicated on blind obedience as a mechanism of social control rather than on reasoned faith.

Farrakhan's finesse in bridging African-American religious, political, and gang divisions is an example of his unique and charismatic leadership. His efforts to bridge these divisions are part of his organizational genius and of his plan to simultaneously build a broad, united black front and build and expand the Nation of Islam as a worldwide religion. With his interest in saving the African-American male, he exploits the traditions of both religion and Black Nationalism to achieve his goal. Because religion is perceived to be a cohesive and liberating force for *all* African-Americans, and Black Nationalism has been fundamental to waging social struggles against white supremacy, Farrakhan combines the two, which are intrinsically misogynistic and homophobic, to articulate the erosion of the African-American male image and leadership. In placing himself in the center of these connected crises, Farrakhan exalts himself as the symbol and manifestation of the solution. By fashioning himself as a combination of Moses and Jesus, he exploits both the traditional icons of African–American leadership and the emancipatory potential of religion to liberate. Mattias Gardell states, "Though not as explicit as in the case of Silis the Saviour, to whom prayers can be addressed, Farrakhan is a divine liberator, ascending into messiahship. In the eyes of his followers, Farrakhan is an example of the divinity each black can aspire to realize."[34]

Although Farrakhan uses God language to promote hatred, violence, and disunity, his use of God language nonetheless seduces people into allegiance and adherence to his leadership. His proselytizing message is a marketing phenomenon. With his message distributed in Afrocentric bookstores and on urban street corners, and heard on radio, television, audio and video tapes, in lectures, broadcasts, and hip-hop music, Farrakhan is an omnipresent figure and voice in the lives of African-Americans. His successful crossover into the hip-hop culture is due to the misogynistic and homophobic sentiments heard in both rhetorics. Revered in hip-hop culture as a powerful icon of black manhood, he is praised in hip-hop lyrics. For example, Chuck D of Public Enemy, one of the big name groups of hip-hop culture, has favorably invoked Louis Farrakhan in his million-selling record, "Don't Believe the Hype."[35]

Attitudes of reverential homage and devotion to Farrakhan are due to his ability to articulate the truth about African-American suffering under white supremacy. However, he takes that truth and exploits it for his own self-aggrandizement. Many African-Americans thought the Million Man March was "cheap window dressing and the 'coronation' of a self-promoter."[36] Renowned African-American journalist Carl Rowan says that Farrakhan "establishes a truth and glues a . . . destructive lie to it."[37] Farrakhan's ascendancy to power is about a tradition of African-American leadership that is predicated on a messianic tradition that devalues women, gays, lesbians, bisexuals, and transgendered people.

In order for African-American leadership to be both effective and inclusive, we must implement an emancipatory model that encompasses a comprehensive analysis of race. Since racial oppression is the common reality that all African-American female, male, gay, lesbian, bisexual, and transgendered people confront every day of their lives, we clearly need a model of leadership that articulates simultaneously the multiple oppressions of race, class, gender, and sexual orientation. Because race links us across and between various identities, a racialized understanding of how class, gender, and sexual orientation imbricate us into the pernicious and intricate patterns of white supremacy would liberate us from the myopic view that only African-American males are the endangered members in our communities. In so doing, African-American leadership would have to shift from its traditional messianic paradigm, which is misogynistic and "homo-hating" in practice, to a collective and inclusive model of leadership.

The argument of whether African-American men are more endangered than African-American women is a fruitless debate and deleterious to the spiritual and emotional welfare of African-American men and women. Our fight should be a collective struggle to annihilate racism, classism, sexism, and heterosexism and not each other. However, internalized oppressions and self-hatred keep us fractured and keep our movements for liberation rolling in a Sisyphean pattern. As much as Farrakhan obsesses about the endangered black man, he has never stopped to examine how his ascendancy to power perpetuates and thrives on that concept. He may indeed pontificate about getting himself and African-Americans to the Promised Land, but let us remember two vital points: Moses never made it to the Promised Land, and he had a pillar of cloud by day and a pillar of fire by night to lead him through the wilderness. Farrakhan, having neither of them, invites us to a dubious destination. He would put us on a road without signposts and would take us on a journey without a road map.

Notes

The general usage of the term "the Black Church" refers to the pluralism of black Christian churches in the United States. This includes any black Christian who worships and is a member of a black congregation. The formal usage of the term "the Black Church" refers to those independent, historic, and totally black-controlled denominations that were founded after the Free African Society in 1787. They are the following: African Methodist Episcopal (A.M.E) Church, the African Methodist Episcopal Zion (A.M.E.Z) Church, the Christian Methodist Episcopal (C.M.E.) Church, the National Baptist Convention, U.S.A., Incorporated (NBC), the National Baptist Convention of America, Unincorporated (NBCA), the Progressive National Baptist Convention (PNBC), and the Church of God in Christ (COGIC).

1. Louis Farrakhan, "Stop the Killing," Strand Theater, Boston, Massachusetts, March 10, 1994.

2. Christopher Clark, "Farrakhan Targets Gay Men During KC Rally," *Bay-Windows* 14, no. 49 (November 29–December 4, 1996): 14.

3. Ibid.

4. bell hooks, *Black Looks: Race and Representation* (Boston: South End Press, 1992), 81.

5. Mattias Gardell, *In the Name of Elijah Muhammad: Louis Farrakhan and the Nation of Islam* (Durham, N.C.: Duke University Press, 1996), 331.

6. Ibid., 332.

7. Robert Staples, "Homosexuality and the Black Male" in *The Material Queer: A Lesbigay Cultural Studies Reader,* ed. Donald Morton (Boulder, Colo.: Westview Press, 1996), 233.

8. Gardell, *In the Name of Elijah Muhammad,* 336.

9. Christine E. Gudorf, *Body, Sex, and Pleasure: Reconstructing Christian Sexual Ethics* (Cleveland, Ohio: The Pilgrim, 1994), 31.

10. Gardell, *In the Name of Elijah Muhammad,* 331.

11. Ibid., 334.

12. Maggie Humm, *The Dictionary of Feminist Theory* (Columbus: Ohio State University Press, 1990), 166.

13. Gardell, *In the Name of Elijah Muhammad,* 336.

14. Ibid.

15. Michael Dyson, *Race Rules: Navigating the Color Line* (Reading, Mass.: Addison-Wesley, 1996), 104–5.

16. Gardell, *In the Name of Elijah Muhammad,* 336.

17. Ibid., 152.

18. Henry Louis Gates, Jr., "The Charmer," *The New Yorker* (April 29–May 6, 1991): 118.

19. William L. Van Deburg, ed. *Modern Black Nationalism: From Marcus Garvey to Louis Farrakhan* (New York: New York University Press, 1997), 319.

20. Michael Dyson, *Making Malcolm: The Myth and Meaning of Malcolm X* (New York: Oxford University Press, 1995), 98.

21. C. Eric Lincoln, *The Black Muslims in America,* 3rd ed. (Trenton, N.J.: Africa World Press, 1994), 71.

22. Ibid., 12.

23. Ibid., 13.

24. Gardell, *In the Name of Elijah Muhammad,* 59.

25. Claude Andrew Clegg, III, *An Original Man: The Life and Times of Elijah Muhammad* (New York: St. Martin's Press, 1997), 53.

26. Ibid., 34.

27. Gardell, *In the Name of Elijah Muhammad,* 127.

28. Patricia Williams, "Different Drummer Please, Marchers!" *The Nation* (October 30, 1995): 493.

29. bell hooks, "Confronting Sexism in Black Life: The Struggle Continues," *Z* magazine 6, no 10 (October 1993): 39.

30. Keith Boykin, "Gays and the Million Man March" in *Atonement: The Million Man March,* ed. Kim Martin Sadler (Cleveland, Ohio: Pilgrim Press, 1996), 17.

31. Gates, "The Charmer," 116.

32. Ibid., 119.

33. Evelyn Brooks Higginbotham, *Righteous Discontent: The Women's Movement in the Black Baptist Church, 1880–1920* (Cambridge: Harvard University Press, 1993), 11.

34. Gardell, *In the Name of Elijah Muhammad,* 340.

35. Michael Dyson, *Between God and Gangstra Rap: Bearing Witness to Black Culture* (New York: Oxford University Press, 1996), 166.

36. Zachary R. Dowdy, "Million Man March Stirs Enthusiasm and Debate," *Boston Globe* (October 13, 1995): 1.

37. Carl Rowan, "A Wake-up Call" in *The Coming Race War in America* (Boston: Little, Brown and Company, 1996), 73.

On Young Black Men, the Declaration of Independence, and New Definitions of Leadership: A Conversation with Joseph Marshall, Jr.

Amy Alexander

JOE MARSHALL, JR., *is executive director of the Omega Boys Club in San Francisco. A 1994 recipient of a MacArthur Foundation Fellowship, also known as the "genius" award, Marshall first became interested in rehabilitating troubled youth while teaching in public schools in San Francisco during the 1970s. Since 1987, the Omega Boys Club has provided college scholarships to dozens of young black men; Marshall has become host of the nationally syndicated radio talk show, "Street Soldiers," and published an autobiographical account of his work by the same name. We sat down to talk about Louis Farrakhan and black leadership in America on January 20, 1997, Martin Luther King, Jr., Day. Our discussion took place in the offices of the Omega Boys Club, located in a former schoolhouse at the foot of Potrero Hill in San Francisco. It is a tough neighborhood, one that you won't read about in San Francisco's tourism brochures, and that is home to many of Marshall's charges.*

I first met Marshall in the mid-1970s, when he was my math teacher at Aptos Junior High School in San Francisco. His "on the ground" contact with young black men makes his input vital to any productive dialogue about the future, indeed the very notion of, black American leadership.

AA: Here we are on Martin Luther King., Jr., Day. The walls in your offices are covered by posters of W.E.B. DuBois, Frederick Douglass, Mary McLeod Bethune. Where do you place Louis Farrakhan and the Nation of Islam within that group? You've said that you didn't go to the Million Man March . . .

JM: I didn't go to the march, but I agreed with the principle of self-determination that was behind it, and I sponsored several people who went there. I thought that being at the march was important but not as important as what happens on the day after the march, and the day after that, and the day after that . . . all these individuals, DuBois and Malcolm and Frederick Douglass, I'm not sure if I'd call them black leaders, no more than I'd call Farrakhan a leader, necessarily. First of all, I have a problem with the term "leader." I prefer the term "champion" because I think a champion is someone who looks around and does those things he feels need to be done, and who does it because it is the right thing to do. I don't think DuBois or Bethune or any of the others consciously saw themselves as leaders. The individuals you see on these posters, I think of them as participants in the larger struggle, what I call the long-distance, marathon relay.

They ran their part in the race, for however long, and then turned and handed the baton back to the next runner. And you'll notice that we do have a poster of Farrakhan, over on the other wall. . . .

AA: So you don't think young blacks should view anyone as a leader?

JM: I think we need realistic role models, or examples, because leadership is a funny thing . . . some people lead through fear. I know young brothers who can run a gang, keep their brothers in line and so forth, but what kind of leadership is that? That's what I call fearship. I think leadership, as most people understand it, implies too many things, namely that without this single individual at the front of the line, we can't accomplish anything . . . whereas, in the marathon, as I see it, someone will step up to grab that baton, even if it's dropped by the person in front. And because so many young people today are not connected—they do not read, they certainly do not understand the ebb and flow of their history—they can be misled. The best example of this, to me, is when Tupac Shakur died. These young people were calling the radio show, and they were really upset! They were saying that Tupac was the only one who spoke for their needs, the only one who "represented" for them. What does that say about our pool of so-called leaders? I think there's a dearth there, in terms of the whole issue.

AA: Well, many young black men give Farrakhan and the NOI respect, so aren't they candidates for positive role models?

JM: Yes, but to a point. I mean, I don't have problems understanding why Farrakhan is appealing to many of these young brothers. They see the Nation, and they appreciate what they see—these guys are clean, they're courteous, they don't do drugs, they're not into negative things—what's not to admire? The Million Man March was a watershed because of what you didn't see there—no guns, no drugs, no negativism, no fearship. All these brothers, from many different walks of life, who came together in search of betterment. Still, I'm sure a lot of black folks cringe at some of the things Farrakhan says. I cringe at some of the things he says. But I take a lesson from Malcolm X, who urged us to above all else learn to think for ourselves. I encourage the young men to look anywhere for positive messages that work for them, and if the Nation of Islam is beneficial in keeping them living a clean life, then I don't have a problem with that. If they want to read "Message to the Black Man" or "How to Eat to Live" [two NOI essays], then I want them to be improved by what they find there. I say the same thing to them whether they're reading "The Souls of Black Folk" or the *Final Call.*

AA: So as long as they arrive at the same point, it's cool.

JM: Yes, what we're really about here is developing your inner character to its fullest potential. And, see, the thing with this notion of "black leader," whether it's Minister Farrakhan or Jesse Jackson, is that they are viewed as leaders mostly because they are oft quoted. Everytime something happens dealing with race or with black people, you usually see in the media the same spokespeople, it doesn't matter *what* the story is really about. That's why, again, I think that Malcolm's advice about thinking for oneself is the best axiom we can give them. My job is to make sure that their spirit is healthy. My job is to urge brothers not to place their emphasis on the material values which surround them.

AA: But you didn't go to the march yourself . . .

JM: No, but not because of philosophical differences with Farrakhan or the NOI. I always believed something like the march could happen. My brother went and came away a better person because of it. Certainly, it was an open call, and I think this day happened because we asked it to be. But the goal should be to have more than just one day like that.

AA: Do you think anyone else could have pulled together such a march?

JM: I think that probably not anyone else could have pulled it off, or , I should say that if it *had* been anyone else, it wouldn't have had the same effect because, say what you want about Farrakhan, most brothers see him and the NOI as having the best interests of young black men at heart.

Plus, the NOI is very well organized when it comes to this sort of event, and this isn't often credited. I think what was also important about the march is that it allowed brothers to see one man running a large and effective organization. I don't think that's necessarily all about that one man himself, so much as about an example of organizing that they can visualize and see in action. Still, the Nation is a religious organization and as such is dogmatic, and you should expect a good amount of dogma in its methods.

AA: Black Americans can separate the message from the messenger, you mean.

JM: Yes, and more than that, I think the media should give us credit for being able to separate the wheat from the chaff. I think that Farrakhan says a lot of things you can agree with, and a lot of things that you do not agree with. It's not fair or accurate to say, "Uh oh, black people agree with Farrakhan because they supported the march." It's not right to say that's the barometer.

AA: Do you think Farrakhan's style is what draws so much media attention?

JM: Yes, and that makes me angry because what you see now is media shaping history as it happens. These newswriters, sportswriters, entertainment writers, whatever, they don't wait and just let things happen, let things play out. There is no distance or hindsight any longer. Everyone wants to put a spin on something while it's happening. I think black people get offended when they see white media intepreting Minister Farrakhan, tearing him apart. There's no objectivity. The trip about it is that the media is not able to separate, and black people are—we do it all the time! Maybe Farrakhan does have problems with the Jews, but most black folk, they don't see that as their problem.

AA: But you also say that too many young blacks seem to shape negative images of themselves based on what they see in the media. Are we not able to separate truth from fantasy where this is concerned?

303

JM: Well, I think that's true. They do tend to fall in behind this "leader" or that "leader," instead of looking for champions. I think we ought to spend our time and energy looking for a core of common values, and look toward those who are advancing the cause of the people. The Black Panthers, for example, the purity of their ideals was what people responded to. But we should expect some growing pains in this continuing quest for freedom and equality.

AA: You've been working with young black men for ten years now. Have things improved? Are you gaining ground?

JM: I think so. But there's still a long way to go. So many of these young people have adopted a certain mindset, a certain code of living that is destructive: guns, drugs, a twisted perception of what respect is. And all this code does is contribute to their problems. Added to that is the fact that they are bombarded with so many messages every day, messages that are nonfulfilling. They get it from TV, radio, the movies, billboards in their neighborhoods. Meanwhile, when they are searching for answers, they only go to each other, and all the negative messages are reinforced and becomes a whole mentality of, "Well, a brother's gotta do what a brother's gotta do." So much of their world is filled with hostile predators. It used to be that that sort of thing was outside and down the block, but now it's in their own house. A lot of them are born into situations that are far less than desirable. And unlike in days of old, when I was coming up in South Central Los Angeles, these brothers are armed to the teeth! The stakes are so much higher now, but too many of them will tell you they just don't care.

AA: How do you introduce them to what you've called the marathon? How do you show them the common core of values?

JM: Well, first you must come to them strictly out of love for them, in the hopes that that love can cut through the hard shell of hurt, pain, and mistrust that surrounds them. You have to have some answers for them but also be willing to admit that you don't know everything.

You would be surprised how disconnected and lonely many of these young brothers are, even in the midst of all their homeys. They rarely find genuine affection. "Ain't no love in the game," is how they say it. But you've got to find a way to pull them into the marathon, show them that they can be a part of something greater, do it in such a way that pulls them into this quest. I try to help them see their connectedness to the larger community and to the core of humanity that transcends individual people.

AA: So, in the ten years since you began the Omega Boys Club, you are seeing some progress in these areas?

JM: I've said this before: Young people want a way out, but they don't know how to find it. They don't want to go to jail, they don't want to die young, and they don't want to be destructive. They have definitely bought the hype and adopted a certain code of living that not only is destructive to others but is destructive to them. But even with all that, the big thing is that they are responsive. They are responsive and appreciate someone who tries to explain to them a way out of this malaise they're in. This is different than when I first started. Still the bombardment of negative messages is very strong, those messages telling them that material values are the most important values for them to hold. They are not grounded. They lack nurturing agents, mothers, fathers, extended families who will tell them differently. In many cases because of drugs they lack these nurturing agents. So, they go to each other, and like the blind leading the blind, they rely on each other and wind up with the wrong answers.

AA: So, in practical terms, how do you show people who are in that cycle a way out?

JM: I guess it helps being a teacher here. You know that they don't have the answers. If they had the answers, they wouldn't be killing themselves, killing each other, and going to prison. So you start with that premise. And, again, you do it strictly out of love for them, and for their development. You talk about the human struggle, and you essentially introduce them to themselves. That's what it is. You introduce them to themselves—themselves of twenty years ago, of fifty years ago, of a hundred years ago, themselves of two thousand years ago. It's not an intentional introduction, but as you give to them, for no other reason than to give to them, you're doing for them what those who came earlier have done. So, in this way, they are automatically introduced to the marathon. You are running it, and your running touches them and pulls them into the quest. I think, that historically, Africans see the world as the continuous orderly transition of the people. The only reason we're here, some-one once said, is to prepare for those who come after us. So, that is your charge: You learn and you pass it on, you learn and you pass it on. It doesn't mean you can't enjoy your life. It just means that there's something bigger than your life to consider.

AA: You mean you see it as a combination of self-awareness as well as awareness of your place in history—whether we're talking Farrakhan at the podium or MLK or Joe Marshall?

JM: Yes, it's not necessarily a black or white thing. It's a connected-ness, a sense of humanity. If you feel that way. A lot of people don't feel that way, a lot of people believe in power, dominance, and control of the people. A lot of the homeys pick this up, instead. I think that the schism or the dilemma of America is best demon-strated by the Declaration of Independence: "All men are created equal, endowed with certain inalienable rights . . . life, liberty, and the pursuit of happiness . . ." I think there's a huge schism between the words in that document and the actualization of that document. It's like, oh, that document? We really didn't mean that! Think about the times when the idea of blacks as "three-fifths human being" was acceptable; or the reality of the slave trade, the ownership of other human beings, and that fact that blacks and women were not able to vote were all things upheld at one time in the name of the Declaration of Independence and by the Constitution. That ain't exactly "all men are created equal." If you were to only follow that, then your definition of equality is really skewed. And so, I wonder how many Americans actually believe in that document, really and truly believe in it.

AA: How do you overcome that schism? By believing in a core of common values?

JM: That's a good question. That's why it's important for each of us to look within ourselves and see how we really feel about it. That's a self-examination question—not how do *we* overcome, but how do *I* overcome? You can facilitate things, make things happen that others can't, if you can answer those questions internally first. You can do a lot of good, but it has to be about how *I* can overcome this. We have to ask, "What is my commitment to this?"

AA: So, again, in the ten years you've been doing this, do you feel you're making gains?

JM: Let's put it like this: I have lots of anecdotal evidence of improvement in the lives of many young folks. Beyond that, I have a feeling of spirit that's different. When I see the turf scene in San Francisco change dramatically in ten years—not to say that it's perfect, but that is not the issue—the issue is, has there been progress? When we started the Omega Boys Club, it was like this: If you go from Hunter's Point to the Fillmore or vice versa, you were dead on sight. That has significantly changed. When I see gang members in Los Angeles stopping to a serious extent the pre-riot hostilities and ending the bloodletting that had gone on for so long down there, when I see them having dialogues about being different, I see enormous progress. There is now, much more than before, a spirit of live and let live. Much more so than there had been. There is definitely a spirit in the air, much like, I think, the Civil Rights Movement was accompanied by a spirit. I think the Million Man March is just another indicator of the spirit. When I meet men from all over the country who are working as hard as I am to do something about these issues, individuals who are working in a non-compromising, fully-committed way, I can feel that spirit.